Evangelization
and the
Catholic High School

James T. Mulligan, CSC

Evangelization
and the
Catholic High School

An Agenda for the 1990s

Foreword by Bishop John Sherlock, London, Ontario

NOVALIS

in association with the
Catholic Education Foundation of Ontario

Cover: Denis De Carufel

Design: Deval Studiolitho Inc., Montréal

©1990 Novalis, Saint Paul University, Ottawa

Novalis
P.O. Box 990
Outremont, P.Q. H2V 4S7

Catholic Education Foundation of Ontario
80 Sheppard Avenue East
Willowdale, Ontario M2N 6E8

ISBN: 2-89088-428-7

Printed in Canada

Canadian Cataloguing in Publication Data

Mulligan, James T. (James Terrence), 1942–
    Evangelization and the Catholic high school

    Includes bibliographical references.
    ISBN 2-89088-428-7

    1. Catholic high schools--Ontario. 2. Education
and state--Ontario. 3. Evangelistic work.
I. Catholic Education Foundation of Ontario
II. Title.

    LC504.2.05M84 1990   373.713   C90-090149-7

CONTENTS

DEDICATION

To three principals with innate understanding of the distinctive character of the Catholic high school and fierce commitment to preserving it :

Kenneth A. Burns, CSC — my principal in my senior years in high school ; a pioneer, a wise mentor. For 40 years he evangelized as a teacher and a principal. Now in retirement, having passed the torch to a team of committed lay leaders — ensuring hope for the future — he continues his evangelizing activity in Catholic education as a separate school trustee.

Rheal F. LeBlanc, CSC — my principal and co-evangelizer through the 1970s who stood fast during those years of greatest financial strain. He made every sacrifice that had to be made, walked every extra mile he could to keep tuition from becoming prohibitive. A tireless labourer in the vineyard of Catholic education who manifests in his life and work the sacrifice and dedication — the "cost" dimensions — required if we are to offer education with a difference.

John J. Belcastro — my present principal. With so much passion and conviction he carries on the tradition of Catholic education pioneered by a religious community. He leads in evangelizing today by enabling, empowering, and especially by promoting a gospel vision of what a Catholic high school education could be.

PREFACE

This book on evangelization in the Catholic high school is personal in that it is partly a kind of testament about my reasons for hope — and for concern — about the future of the Catholic high school. The fact that I have been able to write on the Catholic high school at all is, in truth, accidental! It was the impact of a decrepit Volkswagen Beetle against a Mack-truck-variety Peruvian vehicle in the black of night on the Titicaca highway 3800 metres up in the Andes that rendered me immobile for several months. In retrospect, while not meaning to suggest a similar accident as the pathway to a sabbatical, months of convalescence and immobility became for me an opportunity to reflect on two cherished themes : the Church's mission to evangelize and the future of the Catholic high school.

I returned first to Pope Paul VI's *On Evangelization in the Modern World*, an exhortation he wrote in 1975. Even 15 years later I find his humble but critical analysis of the Church and the ecclesial mission to evangelize most energizing. I am enriched and challenged by his prophetic theology of evangelization. I then delved into some recent documents from the Vatican Congregation for Catholic Education. It was not surprising to see this recent teaching on Catholic education very much imbued with Pope Paul VI's teaching on evangelization : the Catholic school is a place and instrument of evangelization. Certainly, this is a measure of the importance and influence of *On Evangelization in the Modern World*.

But there is another, equally important type of document that I tapped into this year — the document of life experience. I have had the deep and abiding conviction that a reflection on personal experience from the perspective of the gospel is a valid way to theologize. And when several concerned and committed followers of Jesus periodically share their success and struggles, their questions and hopes about life and work, it becomes a very practical theology that enriches, enlightens, encourages and enables. For any evangelization project, pondering the life document of personal experience is every bit as necessary as a study of the documents of Church teaching. Hence, the methodology employed in this book — I call it "theological eavesdropping" — is an attentive listening to the theology of the teaching Church and to the theology of the lived experience of, in this case, some committed Catholic educators.

In these pages my primary intention is to present for theological eavesdropping selected quotes from this rich mix of documents : some very challenging texts of the teaching Church on Catholic education ; some profoundly insightful reflections by colleagues and co-evangelizers in the Catholic high school ; and the commentaries and questions of a very interesting group of adolescents, students in our Catholic high schools. The narrative, some of it my own theologizing as a Catholic educator, is intended primarily to provide coherence for this disparate group of voices which speak so compellingly to those of us privileged to be engaged in Catholic education.

As I think about the future of the Catholic high school, especially in the Province of Ontario in the wake of full funding, I am of mixed emotion. Full funding challenges us ; it puts us squarely between blessing and curse. The financial relief is the obvious blessing, but the possibility, or perhaps inevitability, of compromising the Catholic character of the high school is very much curse. There is an urgent need to look hard at what we are about in the Catholic high school. I feel that we are meeting the "bricks and mortar" dimension of the full-funding challenge. I fear, however, that we have been very slow to understand and react to the evangelization dimension of full funding.

Yet, even without the urgency imposed by full funding in Ontario, our very times call us to bolder, more imaginative activity on behalf of the gospel. This is especially true for the Catholic high school as an instrument of evangelization for the local Church. Speaking of our times, Pope John Paul II insists in his 1989 *Vocation and Mission of the Lay Faithful* : "The hour has come for a re-evangelization." My hope is that this book on evangelization in the Catholic high school is both a firm step forward in elaborating the evangelization dimension of the full-funding challenge, and a creative response to Pope John Paul II's call for the re-evangelization of Catholic education.

I do not intend this writing on evangelization as a comprehensive, academic treatise. It offers, I hope, an accurate portrayal of Catholic high school education in Ontario as we begin the 1990s. And while this portrayal is drawn from my experience and my perspective in southern Ontario, I hope that much of the evangelizing analysis, experience and agenda elaborated in these pages might be relevant and consequently of benefit for Catholic high school educators throughout Ontario, and even in other provinces — Alberta, Saskatchewan, Quebec and New-foundland — who also have fully-funded Catholic high schools and must meet the demands of the hour for re-evangelization!

I mean this book as an invitation to colleagues in the Catholic education community to take up together, in small groups wherever we are, the challenge, the privilege and responsibility that is ours to do what must be done to maintain the Catholic character of our schools ; to make our schools more effective instruments of evangelization. For this purpose I attach as an appendix a study guide that can be used for personal reflection and small-group sharing.

Since I am one given to the importance of tradition, I would not want to dispense with the tradition of a writer's expression of gratitude. I acknowledge, first and foremost, all of the teacher and student participants, who were exceptional in their co-operation, in their generosity with time, and in the candour of their personal reflections. The time spent with them in group reflections was privileged time, and the hours going over the taped proceedings of the group experiences became for me a lasting evangelizing experience.

I am especially indebted to my friend and colleague Eileen McCarthy, who typed and edited the manuscript, and whose encouragement was a constant source of inspiration. Her many suggestions for improving my wording and for elaborating ideas more precisely were indispensable. I extend a very special note of thanks to the Catholic Education Foundation of Ontario and to Ed Nelligan, Executive Secretary, for undertaking the publication of this book. At the Ontario English Catholic Teachers Association, Frank Reutz, CR, Brian McGowan and Paul Howard have my thanks for their moral support.

I feel blessed to have had the following readers for my manuscript : Dr. Mary Malone of St. Jerome's College, Waterloo ; Msgr. Dennis Murphy, Director of the Institute for Catholic Education, Toronto ; Rev. Wilfrid Murchland, CSC, President of Newman Theological College, Edmonton ; Lorne Howcroft, Principal, Notre Dame Secondary School, Brampton ; and Donna Lacavera, in the doctoral program at the Ontario Institute for Studies in Education. Their comments, suggestions, questions and encouragement were invaluable to me as I developed the text. I am most grateful. My thanks as well to co-evangelizers Therese Parent and Gary Bowron for their suggestions and ideas for the study guide, and to Mildred MacIsaac, CSM, and Dorothy Ravazzolo for proofreading. And since the immediate context for this writing was convalescence, I must extend my gratitude to my confreres at the Holy Cross House of Studies in Toronto who were most therapeutic for me in their hospitality, interest and fraternity.

Finally, I thank Bishop John Sherlock of London, whose presentation on evangelization to the Canadian Conference of Catholic Bishops rekindled my interest and fired my sense of purpose for this undertaking. He has been unstinting in his energy and support for this reflection on evangelization in the Catholic high school. I am most grateful that Bishop Sherlock has taken the time to read the manuscript and write the foreword.

James T. Mulligan, CSC
Toronto
January, 1990

FOREWORD

In April, 1988, on the occasion of the *ad limina* visit of the bishops of Ontario to Rome, Pope John Paul II addressed them. To their pleasant surprise he chose as his topic Catholic education in Ontario. His remarks revealed an intimate knowledge of the present state of Catholic secondary schools after full funding, and complete support for the efforts of the Church community to promote the Catholicity of the schools.

It was this very concern which prompted the bishops several years earlier to establish, in collaboration with the Catholic educational associations of the province, the Institute for Catholic Education. Encouraged by the Holy Father's remarks, they issued a pastoral letter on Catholic Education, *This Moment of Promise*, in 1989.

The moment of promise to which they refer is the historic event of full funding, with its consequent enormous increases in numbers of, and enrolments in, Catholic secondary schools. It is also a moment when, finally relieved of the exhausting task of fund raising for survival, the Catholic community can devote its energies to ensuring that fully-funded schools are truly different from other tax-supported institutions.

Father Mulligan's book, which I am privileged to introduce and recommend, is an inspired effort to analyse realistically the present situation of our secondary schools and to provide clear guidelines for promoting Catholicity in our schools.

The realism is revealed in his understanding of the cultural context in which Catholic education must occur. Individualism, consumerism and materialism dominate the cultural scene, providing models of success far removed from Christ's injunction that " They who would lose their life for my sake and the sake of the gospel will find it. " These cultural influences impinge on family stability and family life so that large numbers of our students come from single-parent homes. The same influences minimize the sense of community and create alienation and self-centredness. They reduce the awareness of transcendent reality in the minds of students and the importance of prayer and participation in Mass and the sacraments. They encourage part-time work so that students may participate in the " good life " as the culture defines it.

Father Mulligan recognizes the widespread pessimism about education with a " difference " in this cultural climate, but his research forbids him to share it. Extensive consultations with teachers in many disciplines, with principals, vice-principals and senior students have revealed two things. First, their experience leads them to believe that there already exist important differences in Catholic schools. Second, they are convinced that it is possible to maintain and strengthen the Catholic character of their schools.

The process which Father Mulligan used was to bring small groups of teachers and students together to reflect, in the light of their experience, on papal and episcopal documents about Catholic education, evangelization, the role of the laity in the mission of the Church and justice in the world. The conclusions drawn from this process provide the guidelines which he proposes for evangelization in the 1990s.

Teachers are the key to Catholic education. Already there exist core groups of informed, devoted and apostolic teachers who powerfully influence their students because, in the words of Pope Paul VI, " They are witnesses. " These teachers recognize that it is not religion classes alone, however excellent and important, which make a Catholic school, but the integration of Christ's own vision into every aspect of life and every academic discipline. They and the students also recognize the need of creating in the school the sense of a caring community where the intrinsic dignity of each person is affirmed in deed as well as word. In the light of these challenges, Catholic teachers who see their work as a true vocation and their role as a participation in the church mission to evangelize are the great need of this moment of promise. The mutual support which such dedicated teachers provide to one another and to beginning teachers is vital to sustain their dedication, especially as schools and staffs rapidly grow.

Father Mulligan responds in detail to the expressed need of teachers for formation — spiritual, doctrinal and vocational. He also spells out the necessity for our schools to be courageous in teaching the gospel which is " counter-cultural " and which challenges the common assumptions of our society. That challenge must be addressed not only to students and to teachers but to trustees and administrators whose processes of leadership and decision-making need to be examined in the light of the gospel.

The pastoral letter of the bishops was a plea to Ontario's Catholics : " Please help us to promote the Catholicity of our schools. " This book is Father Mulligan's reply.

His answer is : " It can be done. Here is how it can be done by all the ' partners in Catholic education. ' " I hope every bishop, priest, parent, trustee, director, administrator, principal and teacher will read it and apply it. As a bishop I thank him for providing me much assistance in my responsibility as a teacher of the Catholic faith.

†John M. Sherlock, DD
Bishop of London
January, 1990

PART ONE

The Challenge
of Evangelization

CHAPTER 1
ARTICULATING THE CHALLENGE
FULL FUNDING : BLESSING OR CURSE?

"Will full funding — the long-awaited completion of the public-ly funded Catholic school system in Ontario — prove to be a blessing or a curse?"

This question has been asked often enough since June of 1984, when then Premier and former Minister of Education William Davis announced through Bill 30 that the Government of Ontario intended to allow Ontario's Catholic high schools to become fully public. The subsistence existence that had been eeked out through tuition, often paid at great price, would end. The injustice of a publicly funded, truncated Junior Kindergarten to Grade 10 system was finally recognized — and to be righted.

There is no question! Completion can be a blessing. Release from the burden of tuition is significant relief for many parents, students, dioceses and religious communities. The financial dimension of the blessing is even more acutely appreciated when we look at other Canadian provinces deprived of a publicly funded Catholic school system, and when we look at Catholic schools in the United States, completely private and totally dependent on the sacrifice of parents and parishes, now struggling to survive under the staggering costs of education.

We can see blessing, too, in the rapid increase in enrolment and the consequent proliferation of new Catholic high schools. Our schools now are fully accessible! More importantly, students want to be in them.

And teachers experience the blessing, especially the veterans of the private Catholic high schools who were asked to teach more classes and larger classes than their counterparts in the public high school, and who were called on to walk the many extra miles that had to be walked to keep the private schools viable and vibrant.

Yet, only five years later, I believe it is accurate to say that within the Catholic community — students, teachers, administrators, parents and parishes — the relief of the blessing of funding has become noticeably tempered by the potential of curse.

Recently I listened to some thoughtful senior students reflect on the meaning of a Catholic high school education. Some of them are skeptical about the future. Listen to the testimony of Michael, 19 :

> Will I send my kids to a Catholic high school twenty years from now? Yes, I will! I've loved it here. But my fear is full funding and what that might do to the system. I'm skeptical. We really do need to protect the difference. There is a real danger that the Catholicity will be watered down, that we will become impersonal, losing our spirit, the teachers becoming mechanical. When we were in Grade 9 the senior kids were paying tuition. There was sacrifice on the part of students and teachers. But now the school board rules over all. The community thing isn't nearly as strong now.[1]

Michael outlines here what could be the curse of full funding :

* the blurring and eventual disappearance of the vision of the Catholic high school with the watering down of " Catholicity " ;
* the total bureaucratization of Catholic education — impersonalization, loss of spirit, teachers and administrators doing a job mechanically, not living a vocation ;
* the absence of sacrifice so essential to live the gospel faithfully and to inject spirit, meaning and dynamism into a common Christian endeavour like Catholic education.

I believe that we enter the 1990s in the " in-between time " — a time between *blessing* or *curse*. And if this is the case, then we are indeed at a moment of great crisis and a moment of great challenge. Michael, 19, previously quoted, has correctly identified the crisis : " There is a real danger that the Catholicity will be watered down. " The pre-eminent challenge, then, must be to ensure the Catholic character of the high school.

I have also listened to some very sincere teachers who take seriously their vocation as Catholic educators. Listen to this testimony of a religion teacher who describes so well our present context — between blessing or curse — and the pressing challenge to ensure the Catholic character of the high school :

> I started teaching at a school run by a religious communi-

ty. There were some excellent priests on staff, updated... some great discussions. The religious did a lot to provide renewal for the staff, not in a pushy way, but it was there. It seemed, too, that there was lots more time then. I'm very grateful for that formation. Now it's different. A lot of the new teachers have not had that experience. There is more isolation. There isn't the leadership now that the religious provided.[2]

This reflection is most pertinent. The question of leadership is formulated, and it is first and foremost the question of faith leadership. The rich tradition bequeathed to separate school boards by many religious communities is acknowledged. The urgent need for faith formation for a new leadership to continue that Catholic tradition established by religious communities is underscored. Faith formation and faith leadership — both are essential to ensure the Catholic character of our schools. This is the challenge for the individual teacher, and for the school community, for the board or system. To ignore this challenge is to squander the blessing of full funding. To ignore this challenge is to realize the curse of full funding. Entering the 1990s, we are very much living out a moment of crisis and a moment of challenge because of full funding.

THE MOMENT OF CRISIS
AND THE CHALLENGE OF EVANGELIZATION

To ensure the Catholic character of the high school means that the central players in the drama of Catholic education must have a very clear understanding of the purpose of the Catholic high school. Increasingly in the Church today, the purpose of Catholic education is understood as *evangelization*. The 1988 document from the Congregation for Catholic Education, *The Religious Dimension of Education in a Catholic School*,[3] describes the Catholic school as a means of evangelization for the local Church :

The Catholic school finds its true justification in the mission of the Church ; it is based on an educational philosophy in which faith, culture and life are brought into harmony. *Through it, the local Church evangelizes*, educates, and contributes to the formation of a healthy and morally sound life-style among its members.

[#34, emphasis added.]

Through the Catholic high school, "the local Church

5

evangelizes!"

For most of us in Catholic education today, evangelization is a new concept. Yet it is really a very traditional and very much a gospel concept used to describe the mission of the community of believers in Jesus Christ, the Church. It was Pope Paul VI who proposed that we look at our role and mission in the Church as evangelization. In 1975, in his very powerful pastoral exhortation, *On Evangelization in the Modern World* [*Evangelii Nuntiandi*], profoundly aware of the speed with which we were approaching the year 2000, Pope Paul VI urged that the Church and local Churches embark upon :

> ... a program of pastoral action with *evangelization* as its basic feature, for these years which mark the eve of a new century, the eve also of the third millennium of Christianity.[4]
>
> [Emphasis added.]

And what exactly is evangelization ?

It is to bring the good news of Jesus Christ to people. In the Catholic high school, to evangelize is to facilitate a deeper encounter between our students and the person of Jesus ; it is to accompany our students as they explore in more and more detail the richness of our Catholic tradition and as they discover the personal and communal demands of following Jesus and living out his " good news. " Indeed, it is Pope Paul VI himself who best defines the purpose of evangelization as " the renewal of humanity " — a task most fitting for the Catholic school.

> For the Church, *evangelizing means bringing the Good News into all the strata of humanity*, and through its influence transforming humanity from within and making it new : " Now I am making the whole of creation new. " But there is no new humanity if there are not first of all new persons renewed by Baptism and by lives lived according to the Gospel. *The purpose of evangelization is therefore precisely this interior change*, and if it had to be expressed in one sentence the best way of stating it would be to say that *Church evangelizes when she seeks to convert*, solely through the divine power of the message she proclaims, *both the personal and collective consciences of people, the activities in which they engage*, and *the lives and concrete milieu which are theirs.*
>
> [*E.N.*, #18, emphasis added.]

I am convinced that a reflection on Catholic education as evangelization is most timely now in the in-between time of blessing or curse, and can be helpful in two fundamental respects : as local Church we can take an imaginative, faith-inspired step forward in implementing Pope Paul VI's "program of pastoral action" as we move towards the millennium ; and as Catholic educators, we can look anew at our evangelizing mission, which in itself can become an occasion for the evangelization of the evangelizer. What Pope Paul VI writes about the Church is equally true of the Catholic high school and the Catholic educator as "evangelizer." Consider this challenging text of Pope Paul VI, substituting "Catholic high school" for "the Church" :

> The Church is an evangelizer but she begins by being evangelized herself. She is the community of believers, the community of hope lived and communicated, the community of love ; and she needs to listen unceasingly to what she must believe, to her reasons for hoping, to the new commandment of love. She is the People of God immersed in the world, and often tempted by idols, and she always needs to hear the proclamation of the "mighty works of God" which converted her to the Lord ; she always needs to be called together afresh by Him and reunited. In brief, this means that she has a constant need of being evangelized, if she wishes to retain freshness, vigor and strength in order to proclaim the Gospel.
>
> [E.N., #15]

EVANGELIZATION IN THE CATHOLIC HIGH SCHOOL : CLARIFYING THE CONCEPT

But with the term evangelization there is sometimes the problem of language or understanding. Many Canadians and indeed many Catholic educators associate the term "evangelization" with the antics and style of the electronic evangelists : Jimmy Swaggart, Jim and Tammy Bakker, and even the more sincere but still entrepreneurial types such as Robert Schuller and some of the regional fundamentalist evangelical preachers. Talking about "the evangelization project" with people conditioned by the likes of Swaggart and Bakker yields nothing but disdain and mockery.

But evangelization as enunciated by Paul VI and described by the

Canadian bishops in their 1988 General Assembly has little in common with the popular notion of tele-evangelism.[5] The latter tends to be an individualist enterprise void of the communal and sacramental dimensions and social critique which are so essential to the gospel message. The constant pitch for money, the spectacular extra-curricular activities of a few TV preachers and the right-wing political agenda of a few others all serve to tarnish the electronic preaching of the gospel and result in making evangelization a questionable proposition in the eyes of many. But, as we shall see, a reflective reading of even the first few pages of *On Evangelization in the Modern World* will provide a more profoundly theological and challenging understanding of evangelization, an evangelization proper to the very vocation and mission of the Church :

> Evangelization is a task and mission which the vast and profound changes of present-day society make the more urgent. Evangelizing is in fact the grace and vocation proper to the Church, her deepest identity. She exists in order to evangelize, that is to say, in order to preach and teach, to be the channel of the gift of grace, to reconcile sinners with God, and to perpetuate Christ's sacrifice in the Mass, which is the memorial of His death and glorious resurrection.
>
> [*E.N.*, #14]

So, that is one obstacle to overcome — disassociating the meaning of evangelization from the television preachers. But even in authentic Catholic theology, language can still be problematic. Here we have to sort out the meaning of the vocabulary of evangelization : *evangelization, pre-evangelization, catechesis,* and *religious education*. When we talk about the evangelization project in the Catholic high school, for example, what is it we mean? Assorted comments about evangelization by three Catholic educators in Alberta help clarify the meaning we give to the evangelization project in the Catholic high school :

Evangelization — a new word!
Evangelization is a new word for most religious educators in Alberta. They need to do much reflecting on evangelization, pre-evangelization, evangelism, catechesis and religious education in and out of the classroom.

Evangelization and pre-evangelization.
The main point I wish to make is that we need to take evangelization in the broad sense and this would include pre-evangelization. Most of our students in Alberta Catholic schools are unchurched. Many are so unchurched that I would have to

admit that after 12 years in our schools they are only at the pre-evangelization stage, despite years of religious education. Unless our rhetoric about evangelization reflects this reality that teachers face, we should keep silence.

Evangelization — broad sense and narrow sense.
In the broad sense, evangelization might entail an exploration of how the Good News of the Kingdom is presently being proclaimed by everything that happens in the school: in math classes, phys. ed., discipline policies, band, cafeteria, etc. In the narrow sense, evangelization might be focused on conversion more directly, thus entailing an exploration of how the Good News of the Kingdom should be proclaimed in order to lead students toward a faith commitment.

The above comments are instructive. At the level of social context and local Church, Alberta and Ontario are not dissimilar. It is likely that the majority of students at Catholic high schools in Ontario are unchurched, lacking a solid faith background in the family. It is very difficult for faith in Jesus Christ as proposed and explained in religious education classes in Catholic schools to take deep roots if there is little faith at home or if the expression of faith in Jesus Christ or active membership in the Church are just not priorities.

It is helpful, too, to distinguish between the broad and restricted notions of evangelization. In the very strict sense, evangelization has to do with conversion, with interior change. Reflect again on Pope Paul VI's words:

> The purpose of evangelization is therefore precisely this interior change, and if it had to be expressed in one sentence the best way of stating it would be to say that the Church evangelizes when she seeks to convert, solely through the divine power of the message she proclaims, both the personal and collective consciences of people, the activities in which they engage, and the lives and concrete milieu which are theirs.
>
> [E.N., #18]

The interior change means to accept Jesus Christ, the Son of God; to proclaim Jesus Christ as Lord:

> There is no true evangelization if the name, the teaching, the life, the promises, the Kingdom and the mystery of Jesus of Nazareth, the Son of God, are not proclaimed.
>
> [E.N., #22]

9

In the very strict sense, evangelization as conversion or interior change certainly does take place in the Catholic high school, but not on that wide a scale. The reason, it seems to me, has to do with the nature of the act of faith and the religious receptivity of the adolescent. The interior change demanded by evangelization in the strict sense is a very adult thing. The norm for conversion, for the deepening of faith and the welcoming of new believers, is the R.C.I.A. — Rite of Christian Initiation for Adults. But more than a few young people in our schools are already there — open and ready to grow deeper in their faith commitment.

As a priest-educator, I have been around young people and Catholic high schools for 20 years. For me, some of the most moving and rewarding moments of this ministry come every Advent and Lent during penitential celebrations. There are " churched " young people in our schools who know and love Jesus in a deeply personal way, and there are " unchurched " kids who catch a glimpse of the merciful and compassionate Jesus in the sacrament of reconciliation. To see young people grow in their commitment to Jesus and to listen in the sacrament of penance to young people — some of whom you get to know quite well over five years — talk about their efforts to pray, to live, to make sense out of life, to find Jesus in everyday life, is to experience the deep effects of evangelization in the very strict sense.

Official Church documents and religious educators often distinguish between catechesis and religious education.[6] One could say that, looked at in the light of evangelization, catechesis would be evangelization in the strict sense.

> The distinction comes from the fact that, unlike religious instruction, catechesis presupposes that the hearer is receiving the Christian message as a salvific reality. Moreover, catechesis takes place within a community living out its faith at a level of space and time not available to a school : a whole lifetime.[7]

> The aim of catechesis, or handing on the Catholic message, is maturity : spiritual, liturgical, sacramental and apostolic ; this happens most especially in a local Church community. The aim of the school [religious education], however, is knowledge. While it uses the same elements of the Gospel message, it tries to convey a sense of the nature of Christianity, and of how Christians are trying to live their lives.[8]

> In most high school religion classes it is rare that the religious edu-

cator pinpoints the specific moment that "the hearer is receiving the Christian message as a salvific reality." This does not mean that there are not catechetical moments in the classroom when the young person meets Jesus in an intellectual as well as an affective way, moments which lead to a deepening of faith and prayer.

But we run the risk of getting bogged down. The real value in distinguishing evangelization in the broad sense and in the strict sense, and religious education and catechesis, is that it serves to remind us of the centrality of Jesus in the entire evangelization project. In our efforts, be they at the level of school community, classroom teaching, teacher-student relationships or one-on-one counselling, the key is to grow in our knowledge of and love of the Lord Jesus. The call for interior change and spiritual and liturgical maturity challenges us to keep Jesus Christ and his gospel central to all that we do.

Given the faith reality and context in which we now find ourselves in Catholic education, it is appropriate to understand that what goes on at the Catholic high school in terms of the *traditio fidei* — the handing down of the faith — is *evangelization in the broad sense.* Looking at our situation in Ontario, where we enjoy a complete Catholic school system, we have to consider ourselves extremely fortunate. Our schools, especially our Catholic high schools, can be important instruments for evangelization if Catholic educators take seriously their mandate to evangelize. Listen again to the Vatican document, *The Religious Dimension of Education in a Catholic School*, describe the school as a place of evangelization :

> At least since the time of the Council therefore, *the Catholic school has had a clear identity, not only as a presence of the Church in society, but also as a genuine and proper instrument of the Church. It is a place of evangelization, of authentic apostolate and of pastoral action* — not through complementary or parallel or extra-curricular activity, but of its very nature : its work of educating the Christian person.
> [#33, emphasis added.]

THE CATHOLIC HIGH SCHOOL AS PLACE OF EVANGELIZATION : AN ASSESSMENT

At the level of Church teaching and at the level of lived experience, we tend to set some very high ideals for ourselves as Catholic educators. Listen to this testimony about the centrality of Christ in the doing of Catholic education, first from the 1977 Vatican document, *The*

Catholic School :

> Christ is the foundation of the whole educational enterprise
> in a Catholic school. This revelation gives new meaning to
> life and helps us direct thought, action and will according to
> the Gospel, making the beatitudes our norm of life. The fact
> that in their own individual ways all members of the school
> community share this Christian vision makes the school
> " Catholic " ; principles of the Gospel in this manner be-
> come the educational norms since the school then has
> them as its internal motivation and final goal.
>
> [#34]

And now consider this comment by a principal of a Catholic high
school :

> I have heard the word " ministry " used a lot, and I equate
> evangelization and ministry. It's a sharing of yourself and
> your faith with the people we work with and the kids in the
> Catholic high school. Every chance we get we should draw
> parallels between what's happening in the school and what
> is in the gospel. Evangelization really is to see Christ as the
> model for our own lives and the lives of the kids... the
> students.

These ideals are lofty indeed! And they are critically important.
But ideals are one thing. Reality, alas, is quite another. Too often, unfortunately, our ideals fail to enflesh and direct our everyday life. Any
reflective teacher can look over the last four or five days in school and
list counter-gospel experiences : three or four teachers who are friends
isolating a colleague out of jealousy ; kids in a class gradually destroy-
ing the confidence and reputation of a classmate by sarcasm and in-
nuendo ; the board administrator whose main concern is efficiency, but
an efficiency devoid of sensitivity and blind to the vision of what an
evangelizing Catholic education could be. And yet, in spite of all of this,
there is the imperative to evangelize, and an authentic evangelization
always means a readiness and a willingness to struggle, in the institutional context of the Catholic high school, to bring our ideals to bear on
every aspect of school life.

Consequently, as we play out the blessing or curse scenario that
full funding imposes, it is important that we assess the struggle — what
it is we are about in the Catholic high school in light of the Church's invitation for the school to become a place of evangelization. And it is important that we critique ourselves thoroughly and critique ourselves
often!

We have already encountered two such critical assessments. The student, Michael, is skeptical. He fears that Catholicity will be watered down ; that we are becoming impersonal ; that teachers will become mechanical. And the religion teacher sees a vacuum in faith leadership in our schools : who is forming the teachers, who is evangelizing the evangelizers? Both of these critiques are invaluable, as they represent a critique from within. But at the same time, it is imperative that we hear a critique from without, an external assessment of how effective our Catholic high schools are in being what they claim to be — places of evangelization.

A significant external critique or challenge to the Catholic high school as a place of evangelization is that of Martin Royackers, SJ, whose " Catholic Schools Must Be Alternative Schools " was featured in the October 1988 issue of *Compass*.[9] In this cogent theological analysis of the Ontario Catholic high school in the new era of full funding, Royackers profiles what many would see as the ideal Catholic school product :

> The typical, or perhaps ideal, Catholic school product is a person who in secular life is a successful business person or civil servant or professional, scrupulously honest in business dealings, moderately prosperous with a home in the suburbs, voting for the Liberals but joining the occasional Conservative tides, likely with a stable family life, a good spouse and parent. On the religious side, this person is a good Catholic, going to church every Sunday, giving generously to the parish, the alma mater, and other worldly causes, possibly actively involved in parish groups and activities, critical of the rigid and unfriendly pastor the parish may be saddled with but also critical of loose and radical ideas masking as Catholicism, sending the children to Catholic schools and going to school reunions.[10]

Now, Royackers' straw person could be an individual or a composite of individuals ; it doesn't matter since all have the same flaw. This " ideal Catholic school graduate " has the tendency to compartmentalize faith. Religious faith is a private affair : there is faith and family life on the one hand and work and public life on the other. To support his thesis on the separation of faith and public life, Royackers cites a 1979 series of interviews with 35 senior civil servants who had been to Catholic schools. The study demonstrated that " their personal faith plays no explicit part in the respondents' view of their work. "[11]

Royackers contends that the recent struggles of Ontario Catholic educators to secure full funding might well have been a reflexive exercise, void of the necessary concomitant theological analysis. He sees the problem as a contextual one : our notion of the world, society or culture. He suggests that in many instances the working principle of the Catholic school is to prepare the student to fit into the culture, to be prepared for the world, not to have faith critique the culture :

> For example, economics class in a Catholic school is less liable to relativize our economic system in light of the radical demands of Christian faith than to relativize these demands in the light of the exigencies of the system. After all, our schools do have a responsibility to our students to equip them for living in the real world. [12]

Unless Catholic high schools are seriously intent on presenting the Christ who transforms culture, and on producing agents of social change, we run the risk, Royackers argues, simply of doing the same humanizing and socializing work of the public, non-denominational system. [13]

A second equally significant critique of the evangelization or lack of evangelization that takes place in the Catholic high school is that of Kenneth Westhues, a professor of sociology at the University of Waterloo. Westhues has written extensively on education in Canada and has given more than a little attention to the status and functioning of separate school education in Ontario.

The principal thesis of his penetrating sociological essay, "Catholic Separate Schools : An Ambiguous Legacy, " published in the March 1985 *Grail*, [14] is that given the realities of contemporary Canadian life, the continued existence of a Catholic system of schools is an anomaly. If we were starting from scratch today, putting together a Canadian constitution and fashioning a charter of rights, there is no way that the Province of Ontario would have two public systems of education : one Catholic and one non-Catholic. What we have today in our publicly-financed Catholic school system is "a curious inheritance."

In elaborating on the social, political, economic and cultural trends that make the legal enshrinement of the rights to Catholic schools obsolete, Westhues underscores the dominant social and cultural forces that also militate against an effective evangelization. Two of these trends, secularization and cultural homogenization, or the standardization of cultural values, are relevant to our discussion. Indeed both give further credence to Martin Royackers' observations and his interpretation of the imperative of an education that produces agents for social change.

14

In contemporary Ontario, according to Westhues, religion has dramatically diminished as a cultural priority. Westhues argues that as religion loses its importance in our culture, the maintenance of a religious or a Catholic school system becomes unnecessary. The corollary of this observation for evangelization is that even though we may have an institutional structure in which to teach the faith, it is still an enormously difficult task " to hand down the faith " in such a religiously indifferent cultural climate. As well, cultural values have become more and more the same across Canada. The religious, regional and cultural pluralism that used to characterize the province of Ontario is breaking down. (The case of language for Francophone Ontario is the exception.)

> The result is that schools increasingly resemble one another. It is hard for any school to go its own way given the standardized culture the mass media instill in Canadian youth, and given constraint by a common set of provincial regulations and teachers' demands. [15]

Westhues reinforces the statement of Martin Royackers that there may be little or no difference in the moral spheres found in public and Catholic schools :

> Research shows scant differences in moral values or achievement between graduates of tax-supported Catholic schools in Canada and graduates of public schools. [16]

As for predicting the future, based on a sociological analysis of the present trends, Westhues is not optimistic that Catholic schools will become more Catholic or religiously differentiated over and against public schools. He foresees that schooling for Canadian youth will become increasingly homogeneous, irrespective of religious affiliation. The unifying and centralizing forces of mass culture and the economy are too powerful :

> This is to say that life outside the school is becoming steadily more of one piece, stretching all across this continent and beyond. As pluralism declines in the economic and cultural spheres at large, it must perforce also decline in formal education. However organized, schooling cannot be more diverse in substance than the society it serves. [17]

Westhues sees Catholic schools eventually assuming an increasingly secular character. He bases this prediction on the fact that more and more Canadian Catholics are really no different from Canadian non-Catholics :

Whether the characteristic is income or occupational prestige, unemployment rate or retirement age, church attendance or contraceptive use, attitudes on capital punishment or fear of nuclear war, Canadian Catholics do not differ much any more from non-Catholic Canadians. Why then should a mainstream Catholic school system differ much from a mainstream non-Catholic one? It shouldn't. Increasingly, it won't.[18]

Certainly Ken Westhues' sociological appreciation of contemporary Canadian culture does not seem very heartening for those of us who want to take seriously the mandate to evangelize through the Catholic school. If the bottom line reads that both the Catholic and public systems have become similar and, because of culture, are likely to become more so, then why carry on? Isn't it all a charade? And aren't we really cheating the taxpayer with an expensive duplication of infrastructure and resources?

Westhues' bottom line is not, however, a bottom line etched in stone. "The probable future is not a necessary one," he contends. Individuality and autonomy are powerful human qualities in their own right. He joins Martin Royackers in seeing an activist role for Catholic education based on the social teaching of the Church. Schools would serve as conduits for Catholic social thought. This would be a new raison d'être for Catholic education and would certainly diminish the ambiguity that blurs our present self-understanding. And in keeping with the spirit of Catholic social thought, Westhues suggests that Catholic education associations and institutions pioneer new ways of organizing themselves founded on the co-operative ethic of the gospel rather than the adversarial and management models of the capitalist economy.

While a first reading of Westhues' critique might give the impression that it is a devastating attack on the usefulness and continued existence of the Catholic high school, closer scrutiny shows his study to be a solid, significant, much-needed contribution to the effort to make our Catholic high schools become what they are intended to be : relevant Catholic high schools in the 1990s that have a very important role in the evangelizing mission of the Church and the reformulation of the common social project in the Province of Ontario.[19] Westhues raises the hard questions, the contextual questions. Through his analysis of the social, economic and cultural forces that provide the context for evangelization, we can gain more insights into **the what** and **the how** of evangelization. Throughout our reflection on evangelization in the Catholic high school, it will be useful to return often to the external critiques of both Kenneth Westhues and Martin Royackers.

THE CATHOLIC HIGH SCHOOL AS PLACE OF EVANGELIZATION : THE POTENTIAL

Critique from within and from without are necessary to deepen our self-understanding as evangelizers, as Catholic educators. Such critique is essential, too, to clarify our common project and to elaborate a shared evangelizing vision for the Catholic high school. Yet critique does have a grace dimension. There is presently blessing in abundance surrounding Catholic education in Ontario as we begin the 1990s. How many countries, indeed, how many Canadian provinces have the luxury of a tax-supported Catholic school system? Monsignor Dennis Murphy of the Institute for Catholic Education puts it in this perspective : " 30,000 people are preaching the gospel in Ontario to 500,000 young people on a budget of two billion dollars a year. "[20]

So the structure and the resources are there for the Catholic high school to be a place of, and an instrument of, evangelization. In the broad sense, evangelization is much more than the religion class or school Mass or visit of the parish priest. It has very much to do with personal relationships and attitudes and the ways the adult faith community (staff) provides a learning environment characterized by love and respect. For many young people, their years at the Catholic high school might not be much more than pre-evangelization : an introduction to Catholic symbols and maybe memories of some very committed women and men for whom Jesus and the beatitudes were extremely important. For some young people evangelization might be the development of basic gospel attitudes and the desire to direct their own lives towards changing the unjust and sinful structures of our world and helping their less fortunate brothers and sisters. For some, Catholic education will be an introduction into the more complex ethical questions of our time and a familiarity with the gospel responses and Church teaching.

Undoubtedly, more than a few will go through the Catholic high school untouched by the gospel and completely indifferent to what the school and many committed teachers intend. (Hopefully, it will not be from lack of trying on the part of the Catholic high school.) And for a few, years in the Catholic high school might provide pastoral assistance, understanding and support as they weather difficult personal or family crises. And I think it is safe to say that for the vast majority of young people in our Catholic high schools, the evangelization process that happens will not become terribly meaningful until they themselves,

17

years after, having matured in their own faith as the followers of Jesus, insist on having their own kids at the Catholic high school, because of the values and environment it provides and because of the quality and faith commitment of the adult members who make up the staff.

TOWARDS AN AGENDA FOR THE 1990s

Our schools now are places of, and instruments of, evangelization. I say that unabashedly because there are too many committed Catholic high school teachers in Ontario for it to be otherwise. But then there is also the down side to consider. Why isn't there more of a difference between public high schools and most Catholic high schools? How come our graduates are not significantly different, in the Royackers-Westhues sense? And if we are spending two billion dollars a year with 30,000 teachers (evangelizers!), surely the school environment should be more loving and the bureaucracy less dehumanizing and the approaches to negotiating and administering more co-operative and the teaching more evangelically challenging! This is our predicament : the confrontation of two authentic but conflicting bits of reality. Here it is important to go back to the words of Pope Paul VI describing the Church as evangelizer, but a Church in need of evangelization :

> The Church is the People of God immersed in the world, and often tempted by idols, and she always needs to hear the proclamation of the " mighty works of God" which converted her to the Lord ; she always needs to be called together afresh by Him and reunited. In brief, this means that she has a constant need of being evangelized if she wishes to retain freshness, vigor and strength in order to proclaim the Gospel.
>
> [E.N., #15]

Like the Church, our Catholic high schools and Catholic educators have a constant need to be evangelized if we are to confront our own idols in any serious fashion and embrace whole-heartedly the evangelizing mission that is ours as an extension of the local Church. And an excellent place to look for some evangelizing freshness and vigour is in Pope Paul VI's own meditation, *On Evangelization in the Modern World.*

The bishops of Ontario, in their 1989 pastoral letter on Catholic education, *This Moment of Promise*, speak of *"the awesome privilege and responsibility"* of those involved in Catholic education — the privilege and responsibility to maintain and deepen the Catholic character of our schools.[21] Yet, I have often been struck by the seeming lack of resources we have in the Catholic high school to help us execute "this privilege and responsibility." There is not now any place one can go to learn to be a Catholic school administrator, or even for that matter, to be a Catholic school teacher. The professional qualifications required are the same bachelor of education programs, principals' courses and supervisory officers examinations which inform, form and qualify our public school counterparts. And while religion courses are necessary and beneficial for personal renewal and faith formation, there is a paucity of common experiences and written resources to help educators in the Catholic high school appreciate and live their unique vocation as evangelizers.

I would like this book to be such a resource. Our moment of crisis — between blessing or curse — is at the same time a moment of promise, a moment of challenge. I am convinced that a more profound understanding of Catholic high school education as evangelization is the efficacious and necessary response to the challenge, enabling us to enjoy and increase the blessing and escape the curse! Catholic high schools, however, must have an agenda for the education they propose for the 1990s. By listening to and recording the reflections of the teaching Church and dedicated Catholic educators :

- on evangelization ;
- on our social and cultural context ;
- and on the struggles and hopes of adolescents, our students, it is my hope to contribute to the elaboration of such an agenda for evangelization in the 1990s.

And in my experience, the most excellent place to begin is with Pope Paul VI's own meditation, *On Evangelization in the Modern World*.

NOTES
Chapter 1

1 In March, 1989, I listened to 40 senior students from five Ontario Catholic high schools reflect on their experience in, and impressions of, Catholic high school education. Refer to Chapter 9, " Listening to Youth — Reflections on the Catholic High School. "

2 The testimonies of colleagues constitute an essential element of this reflection. These reflections, of approximately 30 Catholic high school teachers in Ontario, were shared in four reflection groups that met for three-hour periods three times between December, 1988 and April, 1989.

3 The following Vatican documents will be referred to frequently throughout this reflection on evangelization in the Catholic high school : a) *The Catholic School*, Congregation for Catholic Education, March 19, 1977 ; b) *Lay Catholics in Schools : Witnesses to Faith*, Congregation for Catholic Education, October 15, 1982 ; c) *The Religious Dimension of Education in a Catholic School*, Congregation for Catholic Education, April 7, 1988.

4 Pope Paul VI, *On Evangelization in the Modern World [Evangelii Nuntiandi]*, Rome, December 8, 1974, #81. Subsequent quotes from *Evangelii Nuntiandi* will be documented at the conclusion of the quote with *E.N.*, and the paragraph number.

5 Evangelization was the major theme for the Canadian bishops at their annual general assembly in October, 1988. Paul VI's *On Evangelization in the Modern World* was the principal source and point of departure for Bishop John Sherlock's [London] major presentation at the assembly. As well, a number of dioceses across the country have initiated offices, committees or study groups to look at evangelization as essential to the mission of the Church.

6 Graham Rossiter, " The Need for a ' Creative Divorce ' Between Catechesis and Religious Education in Catholic Schools, " *Religious Education*, January-February, 1982, pp. 21-40.

7 Congregation for Catholic Education, *The Religious Dimension of Education in a Catholic School*, #68.

8 *Ibid.*, #69.

9 Martin Royackers, SJ, "New Identity in the Making — Catholic Schools Must be Alternative Schools," *Compass*, October, 1988, p. 23. The special focus of this issue of *Compass* is education.

10 *Ibid.*, p. 24.

11 *Ibid.* Reference to E. Colin Campbell, SJ, *From the Ghetto to Ottawa : The Experience of the Catholic as Mandarin* (Regina : Campion College, 1979), p. 10.

12 *Ibid.*, p. 25.

13 *Ibid.*, p. 26.

14 Kenneth Westhues, "Catholic Separate Schools : An Ambiguous Legacy," *Grail*, I, 1 (March 1985) : 51.

15 *Ibid.*, p. 57.

16 *Ibid.*

17 *Ibid.*, p. 59.

18 *Ibid.*, p. 60.

19 Kenneth Westhues, presentation at the symposium "Partners in Catholic Education," Institute for Catholic Education, May, 1984.

20 *Catholic New Times*, March 22, 1987.

21 Ontario Conference of Catholic Bishops, *This Moment of Promise*. A Pastoral Letter on Catholic Education in Ontario (Toronto, 1989), p. 16.

CHAPTER 2
A MEDITATION
ON EVANGELIZATION

This invitation to the Catholic high school community to accept the challenge to become a more authentic alternative to public high school education can be facilitated by a dynamic I call "theological eavesdropping." Incorporated into this book are selected texts from Church documents which I believe provide theological insight, guidance and inspiration to help us deepen our understanding of the vocation of the Catholic educator and the unique mandate of the Catholic high school to become an integral instrument of evangelization in the Pope Paul VI sense of that word. A reflective reading of — and a reflective "listening to" — the content taken from documents proposed by the teaching Church, I call "top-down" theological eavesdropping. The thoughtful listening to colleagues or students as they share experiences of — and reflections about — Catholic high school concerns such as are raised in this book, I call "bottom-up" theological eavesdropping. This dynamic was chosen deliberately because both of these resources are readily available — and indispensable — for any group of Catholic educators who want to work together at this most important challenge of authenticity.

I am convinced that Pope Paul VI's apostolic exhortation, *On Evangelization in the Modern World* [*Evangelii Nuntiandi*], is foundational for the learning we need to do and the understanding we need to acquire about the intrinsic responsibility of the Church — and, therefore, of all members of the Church — to evangelize. Pope Paul VI sees the Catholic school as a privileged instrument and rich resource for the Church to carry out the mission to evangelize. Through his apostolic exhortation, *On Evangelization in the Modern World*, he invites "the Faithful of the entire world" to deepen our appreciation of the sacredness of our call as followers of Jesus and to make ourselves ever more ready for the collaborative task of evangelizing in our unique time and place. I believe his reflections have special meaning for Catholic educators as educators of faith.

On Evangelization in the Modern World is an excellent instrument of education because it both informs and inspires. One of its endearing qualities is its graceful, meditative style. Now, anyone who has had experience with official Church statements knows that this is not always the case. Paul VI's style is reflective and biblical; it is not dense; there is not a lot of jargon or abstraction to wrestle with. At the same time, his thought is clear and orderly, easy to follow. I have chosen six passages, themes from *Evangelization in the Modern World* that I believe constitute the foundation for our evangelizing efforts in Catholic education. They are also passages that invite top-down theological eavesdropping. I would like to share my reflections on them with you.

1. EVANGELIZATION: EVANGELIZING AND BEING EVANGELIZED MUST COST!

As an evangelizer, Christ first of all proclaims the Kingdom of God. As the kernel and centre of his Good News, Christ proclaims salvation, which is liberation from sin and liberation from everything that oppresses us.

> This Kingdom and this salvation, which are the key words of Jesus Christ's evangelization, are available to every human being as grace and mercy, and yet at the same time each individual must gain them by force — they belong to the violent, says the Lord, through toil and suffering, through a life lived according to the Gospel, through abnegation and the cross, through the spirit of the beatitudes. But above all each individual gains them through a total interior renewal which the Gospel calls "metanoia"; it is a radical conversion, a profound change of mind and heart.
>
> [*E.N.*, #15]

As a Catholic educator for whom teaching is more than just a job, I consider my own faith journey. For some reason that I am not able to comprehend, I have experienced often and in a rich variety of ways the grace and mercy of God. This fact must always be my starting point in whatever thinking or evaluating I may do about my role as an evangelizer. I am first and foremost loved by God. I am gifted with grace and mercy. I am awed and humbled by this fact. I actually experience Jesus'

23

Kingdom and his salvation in my life.

But at the same time, my experience tells me that believing and hoping and loving are also struggle. There is pain and hurt and suffering, some of which I can explain, some of which I can't. I know deep down that life ultimately is to work at living the gospel, the beatitudes, the cross. I hope somehow that these convictions about grace and mercy, the beatitudes and the cross will be real: in my relations with my peers and my students, in my attitudes, in the hundred different little things that constitute my everyday life. Sometimes it is so hard: the institution, the bureaucracy. Sometimes it is discouraging realizing what could be and what is! I guess that is part of the toil and suffering. But what always must be there on my part is the personal need to change, to work more creatively at realizing the ideal, and to put more quality into what I am about as an evangelizer. I can't really evangelize unless I am constantly being evangelized myself, and being evangelized is tending to the call to change.

* * * * * * * *

2. EVANGELIZATION: CATHOLIC EDUCATION IS TO PARTICIPATE IN THE EVANGELIZING MISSION OF THE CHURCH

The Church is born of the evangelizing activity of Jesus and the Twelve.

Having been born consequently out of being sent, the Church in her turn is sent by Jesus. The Church remains in the world when the Lord of glory returns to the Father... And it is, above all, Jesus' mission and His condition of being an evangelizer that the Church is called upon to continue. For the Christian community is never closed in upon itself. The intimate life of this community — the life of listening to the Word and the apostles' teaching, charity lived in a fraternal way, the sharing of bread — this intimate life only acquires its full meaning when it becomes a witness, when it evokes admiration and conversion, and when it becomes the preaching and proclamation of the Good News. Thus it is the whole Church that receives the mission to evangelize, and the work of each individual member is important for the whole.

The Church is an evangelizer, but she begins by being evangelized herself. She is the community of believers, the community of hope lived and communicated, the community of mutual love; and she needs to listen unceasingly to what she must believe, to her reasons for hoping, to the new commandment of love. She is the People of God immersed in the world, and often tempted by idols, and she always needs to hear the proclamation of the "mighty works of God" which converted her to the Lord; she always needs to be called afresh by Him and reunited. In brief, this means that she has a constant need of being evangelized, if she wishes to retain freshness, vigor and strength in order to proclaim the Gospel.... The Church must be evangelized by constant conversion and renewal, in order to evangelize the world with credibility.

The Church is the depositary of the Good News to be proclaimed.... It is the content of the Gospel, and therefore of evangelization, that she preserves as a precious living heritage, not in order to keep it hidden but to communicate it.

Having been sent and evangelized, the Church herself sends out evangelizers. She puts on their lips the saving Word, she explains to them the message of which she herself is the depositary, she gives them the mandate which she herself has received and she sends them out to preach. To preach not their own selves or their personal ideals, but a Gospel of which neither she nor they are the absolute masters and owners, to dispose of it as they wish, but a Gospel of which they are the ministers, in order to pass it on with complete fidelity.

[E.N., #15]

For the Catholic educator, this paragraph may be the single most important passage in Paul VI's entire meditation on evangelization, for it is here that we find the purpose and the source of energy and motivation for our role as evangelizers. Everything I understand as the purpose or rationale of Catholic education — school mission-statements, philosophies or theologies at the board level, professional development days devoted to Catholicity or the Christian dimension of the school, pep talks and homilies and exhortations on the school as Christian community — everything touching on *the what* and *the why* of

Catholic education is linked to the evangelizing mission of the Church.

Note the double emphasis underscoring evangelization as the responsibility of each individual member of the Church: *"the whole Church receives the mission to evangelize, and the work of each individual member is important for the whole"* and *"the Church herself sends out evangelizers with a mandate to preach the gospel and pass it on with complete fidelity."* Why do we have Catholic schools except to pass on the gospel with complete fidelity!

And the gospel we pass on is not a lifeless record of do's and don'ts or a literary tale of the life of Jesus. The content of the gospel is the content of evangelization. This is what the Church preserves as a precious living heritage. It is first and foremost the Church's experience of the Jesus of history, the Jesus living today, and the Jesus who is to come. And it is, in a personal way, your experience of Jesus and my experience of Jesus. The *traditio fidei* — the passing on the faith — is essentially sharing with others our experience of Jesus, sharing this by our actions and our words. The Catholic school is very much a privileged place in which to share that experience.

Through the words of Paul VI we experience a humble Church, a Church constantly needing to be evangelized, to be renewed, to be converted. It is important for us to appreciate this dimension of the Church. At times, it is easy to be frustrated by the insensitivity, annoyance and triumphalism we encounter in the Church. But through the powerful words of Paul VI we meet a Church with needs: "the need to listen unceasingly to what she must believe, to her reasons for hoping, to the new commandment of love." Reflecting on this fragile face of the Church, a Church in need of evangelization, can be therapeutic in the way we handle some of our anger and frustration emanating from the weaknesses and flaws of an institutional Church immersed in the world and tempted by idols. At times, too, such reflection can serve to deflate some of our own pretensions and self-righteousness! There is something graceful about sin; that is, the recognition of weakness and shortcomings at both the personal and communal level. The grace is that it can become a moment of "metanoia," of turning again to the Lord.

In this meditation, it becomes very clear that the Church is not simply something over there — in Rome or Toronto or Ottawa. The Church is here. It is us. It is listening to the Word and the sharing of bread at Sunday Eucharist or at a school liturgy. It is being attentive to the apostles' teaching, to the teaching and preaching of the Bishop of Rome and the bishop of the local Church. It is accepting our own responsibility as members of the Church to participate in the evangelizing mission of the Church.

And then there is the Catholic high school. It certainly can be and should be an instrument of evangelization, a time and a place to assist in the evangelizing mission of the Church.

* * * * * * * * *

3. EVANGELIZATION: THE GOAL OF EVANGELIZATION IS THE TRANSFORMATION OF HUMANITY

For the Church, evangelizing means bringing the Good News into all the strata of humanity, and through its influence transforming humanity from within and making it new: "Now I am making the whole of creation new." But there is no new humanity if there are not first of all new persons renewed by Baptism and by lives lived according to the Gospel. The purpose of evangelization is therefore precisely this interior change, and if it had to be expressed in one sentence the best way of stating it would be to say that the Church evangelizes when she seeks to convert, solely through the divine power of the message she proclaims, both the personal and collective consciences of people, the activities in which they engage, and the lives and concrete milieu which are theirs.

[E.N., #18]

The underlying conviction here is that the world is good: "Now I am making the whole of creation new." This optimistic approach to the world, to history and society and the different human projects that engage us, is very much in the spirit of the *Church in the Modern World* document of Vatican II. As Catholic educators we try to evangelize in order to continue the redemptive, transforming mission of Jesus. Baptism makes us co-workers in "the bringing of the Good News into all the strata of humanity." To do evangelization in the Catholic high school means that I have to be in touch with the demands of my own baptism. To work at transforming humanity means that I must go about my life and work in the spirit of the beatitudes. (And that spirit is not a private, individualistic quality that characterizes the "born again" converts of the television world.) I am in for the long haul! There will be ups and

27

downs, gains and losses. The key is to go back often to the meaning of baptism in my own life, to my vocation as a Christian in the world, to my baptismal responsibility as a Catholic educator to bring the Good News to that little part of the world and history that is my turf to tend.

Unfortunately, many of us really haven't mined the depths of our baptismal vocation as Christians. To be sure we are familiar with baptism and acquainted somewhat with the role of the laity, but it is all too easy to confuse familiarity with understanding and acquaintance with assimilation of the meaning. The theology emanating from Rome on Catholic education finds its starting point here in the transforming exigency of baptism and the responsibility of the Catholic educator to promote this transformation.[1] The present shortage of ordained ministers in the Church makes it all the more urgent that the laity and, in our reflection, Catholic educators, assume with new seriousness and vigour their vocation as transformers of humanity.

And what does it all mean? What does it mean "to convert... both the personal and collective consciences of people, the activities in which they engage, and the lives and concrete milieu which are theirs"? This is an enormous question that will be looked at gradually as we proceed with our reflection on evangelization in the Catholic high school. But for sure it demands personal conversion (which is more authentically a daily experience than a born-again event) and an ongoing communal reflection on what it is that we are about, the 15 or 50 or 80 of us who make up the staff of any Catholic high school. Imagination and creativity are called for as well in the critiques we level and the strategies we adopt.

There are also the students, the young believers in our care. How much of our Catholic education, our religious education, our guidance and chaplaincy care is directed at challenging the students to become more aware of their baptismal responsibilities? We guide them in career choices, in the selection of courses; we pastor them in moments of crisis and pain; but how well do we help them discover the meaning of their baptism — that they are co-workers in the things of the gospel and have to have a heavy stake in the transformation of humanity and making it new?

* * * * * * * * *

28

4. EVANGELIZATION : THE POTENTIAL OF CATHOLIC EDUCATION — TO OFFER AN UPSETTING EVANGELIZATION

> Strata of humanity which are transformed : for the Church it is a question not only of preaching the Gospel in ever wider geographic areas or to ever greater numbers of people, but also of affecting and as it were upsetting, through the power of the Gospel, humankind's criteria of judgement, determining values, points of interest, lines of thought, sources of inspiration and models of life, which are in contrast with the Word of God and the plan of salvation.
>
> [*E.N.*, #19]

I don't think we do this very well. That is, for the most part our Catholic education is not at all that disturbing and upsetting. And this is exactly the point that Martin Royackers and Ken Westhues underscore in their critiques of Catholic education : our failure to challenge the taken-for-granted assumptions of our culture by the power of the Word of God. But to be sure, the very same critique can be made of the Sunday homilies in our parishes. How many of Ontario's "churched" Catholics have any understanding of *Sollicitudo Rei Socialis*, Pope John Paul II's 1988 encyclical on the *Concern for the Social Order*, an encyclical that is a very powerful example of a disturbing and upsetting evangelization? As the saying goes, the best kept secret in the Church is the Church's social teaching.

This and the preceding passage on the transformation of humanity make it abundantly clear that Paul VI envisages evangelization as something much broader than the education of the soul. He talks about the "collective consciences of people, the activities... lives and concrete milieu which are theirs." He continues with his notion of "an upsetting evangelization" : through the power of the Gospel to critique our criteria of judgement, our values, our lifestyles, our sources of inspiration. What is the model of education that we propose to our students? What definition of success do we set before them? Our teachers come from universities across the country. In their formation and preparation to be teachers in Catholic high schools, what place is given to this upsetting power of the Gospel as a critique of our social, economic and cultural priorities? I rather doubt that John Paul II's gospel critique of capitalism is accorded importance or discussed at length in leading business schools or in other programs offered in our predominantly secular universities.

This "upsetting notion" of evangelization should be most pertinent to the men and women who exercise the ultimate responsibility for Catholic education : the trustees and administrators of separate school boards and the leadership teams of OECTA. Yet, one wonders how far away we are from their collaborative implementation of this model of education when their own interaction tends to display few signs of movement towards strategies founded on the co-operative ethic of the gospel and away from an adversarial management-labor model. The dynamic of salary negotiations can be one measuring rod, but it is time for us to look from a gospel perspective at the entire content of collective agreements for priorities and emphasis, for tone and spirit. And we need to look at the dynamic of decision-making about matters which involve or affect the direction and quality of Catholic education or the well-being of school administrators, teachers and students. Are consultation, collaboration, collective visioning and shared decision-making occasional public relations devices, or are they intrinsic to an educational management model steeped in gospel values and spirit? An autocratic, top-down, hierarchical, authoritarian model of management needs as much scrutiny from a gospel perspective as a bullish union mentality that makes self-interest the highest priority. Wherever we find ourselves situated between these extremes we can no doubt identify areas for improvement. A too-pervasive secular model of management-employee relations — and an unattractive and most often counter-productive secular model at that — is both disturbing and discouraging from the point of view of evangelization. Again, it is opportune here to return to Kenneth Westhues' critique in the first chapter. It is incumbent upon Catholic education to pioneer new, collaborative ways of organizing ourselves if we really are to justify our existence as an alternative system of education. It is especially incumbent upon the leaders in Catholic education to understand that authentic evangelization must be systemic. It has to touch and influence our very structures, our decision-making, our organizational foundation. It cannot be regarded simply as "the faith activities for students" in a board's annual report. In a word, evangelization must be upsetting.

Paragraph 19's "upsetting notion of evangelization" [*E.N.*] is the critical challenge for all of us in Catholic education. It articulates the potential for and, indeed, the responsibility of Catholic education to make a transforming difference in our society. And if we understand our first meditation, then we know well that to evangelize in an upsetting way is bound to cost us. There will be conflict from within and from without. There has to be conflict when the Word of God confronts some of the values, models of life, points of interest and sources of inspiration which are in contrast with it. Yet, that is precisely what we must be about: to offer a Catholic education that unmasks, questions, critiques and challenges the non-gospel values of our culture and society. So the challenge for Catholic educators is twofold: to work at understanding and living out this "upsetting" dimension of our own baptism, and to help our students in the process of both discovering and taking more and more ownership of their own faith and the upsetting and challenging dimensions of that faith.

* * * * * * * *

5. EVANGELIZATION: THE PRIMARY IMPORTANCE OF WITNESS OF LIFE

Above all the Gospel must be proclaimed by witness. Take a Christian or a handful of Christians who, in the midst of their own community, show their capacity for understanding and acceptance, their sharing of life and destiny with other people, their solidarity with the efforts of all for whatever is noble and good. Let us suppose that, in addition, they radiate in an altogether simple and unaffected way their faith in values that go beyond current values, and their hope in something that is not seen and that one would not dare to imagine.

Through this wordless witness these Christians stir up irresistible questions in the hearts of those who see how they live: Why are they like this? Why do they live in this way? What or who is it that inspires them? Why are they in our midst?

Such a witness is already a silent proclamation of the Good News and a very powerful and effective one. Here we have an initial act of evangelization. The above questions will ask, whether they are people to whom Christ has been proclaimed, or baptized people who do not practice, or people who live as nominal Christians but according to principles that are in no way Christian, or people who are seeking, and not without suffering, something or someone whom they sense but cannot name.

Other questions will arise, deeper and more demanding ones, questions evoked by this witness which involves

31

presence, sharing, solidarity, and which is an essential element, and generally the first one, in evangelization.

[E.N., #21]

Generally speaking, young people despise hypocrisy, even though they have no monopoly on this sentiment, and even though they themselves can fall victim time and again to obvious contradictions between what they do and what they say. They are especially critical of hypocrisy in the adults who serve as their mentors or teachers. Young people today tend to be on the skeptical side in matters of religion, especially those that have to do with believing and living out the gospel. Paul VI is aware of this skepticism when later on in his meditation on evangelization he notes that people today listen more willingly to witnesses than to teachers, and if they do listen to teachers, it is because they are witnesses.[2] This is an absolutely essential insight for the teacher in the Catholic high school. Ten years from now our Grade Twelve physics students are not apt to recall too much about what we covered in the second part of Unit 3! But they might remember us. What is the wordless witness that we project? How clear is it that teaching is more than just a job? And as educators in a Catholic high school, how evident is the living out of our baptismal vocation?

And that is the whole point! Adult ownership of faith and the living out of my faith in Jesus Christ and my membership in the community of believers should not be a source of embarrassment or an added burden to carry because I teach in a separate Catholic high school. Rather, this occasion to evangelize through witness must be looked at as gift and seen in light of the evangelizing mission of the Church. It is at the level of presence or of witness, as Paul VI writes, that we will often do our most effective evangelization.

The pivotal question to ask: my style of teaching, my rapport with students, the ways I reveal my values and life priorities — what does all of this "wordless witness" say to kids about me? Does my wordless witness go very far in helping students discover a little more about the meaning of life and the important questions that should be addressed on their own pilgrimage through life? There are some very powerful gospel lessons preached in wordless ways. Very few of us are academic theologians or professional catechists or religious educators, but most of us have been initiated into the community of believers through baptism. We are theologians and religious educators by baptism. Catholic education is a marvellous opportunity for us to share our experience of Jesus through the ways we do education and the way we live the gospel. If the students are to take us seriously as Catholic educators, it will be because of the authenticity of our witness. It is not too much to ask, and yet, it is everything to ask.

There is something very fragile about the witness dimension of teaching in a Catholic high school. While the real attempt to own my faith and to live the gospel in an adult way can be effective evangelization, indifference or anti-gospel witness can be critically damaging to the overall evangelization project in the school. Witnessing to gospel values is never neutral. My lifestyle says something about what I feel to be important and worthwhile in life, whether I am aware of it or not and whether I like it or not. Ultimately, my life makes a statement either for the gospel or against the gospel. Adolescents can be very quick in understanding the statements we communicate in wordless sorts of ways. And that is the fragility of it all. In a way, there is a burden to being a Catholic educator: the burden of sincerely and genuinely tending to the gospel values and principles we profess as the followers of Jesus. Doing this conscientiously is the adult Christian thing to do. It is also a most effective way to evangelize as Paul VI explains.

* * * * * * * * *

6. EVANGELIZATION: THE NEED TO PROCLAIM; THE DUTY TO EVANGELIZE OTHERS

The Good News proclaimed by the witness of life sooner or later has to be proclaimed by the word of life. There is no true evangelization if the name, the teaching, the life, the promises, the Kingdom and the mystery of Jesus of Nazareth, the Son of God, are not proclaimed. The history of the Church, from the discourse of Peter on the morning of Pentecost onwards, has been intermingled and identified with the history of this proclamation. At every new phase of human history, the Church, constantly gripped by the desire to evangelize, has but one preoccupation: whom to send to proclaim the mystery of Jesus? In what way is this mystery to be proclaimed? How can one ensure that it will resound and reach all those who should hear it?

[E.N., #22]

Finally, the person who has been evangelized goes on to evangelize others. Here lies the test of truth, the touchstone of evangelization: it is unthinkable that a person should accept the Word and give himself or herself to the Kingdom without becoming a person who bears witness to it and proclaims it in turn.

[*E.N.*, #24]

In this final reflection on six themes from *On Evangelization in the Modern World* which I propose as a foundation for the evangelization project in the Catholic high school, Paul VI helps us once more to get a perspective on just what it is we are all about in Catholic education. It is the very nature of the Church to be concerned about proclaiming the mystery of Jesus Christ to every generation in every possible circumstance. In Canada, in the local churches of the dioceses of Ontario, bishops and laity have co-operated for more than a century in building up a publicly financed school system for Catholic families. In retrospect, how evangelically fortunate we are to have such a privileged instrument for talking about Jesus and the gospel, for evangelization.

The question for us, the preoccupation for the Church in Ontario, is not so much how to create new ways and means of evangelizing adolescents, but to look seriously at how much quality there is now in our Catholic school system. Of course, outside evaluation and assessment is important in education. But even more urgent is the need for Catholic education to measure itself against the imperatives of the gospel. "Quality control" is the management argot we need to implement, but a quality control steeped in the content and spirit of evangelization. There is a very great danger that, with full funding, Catholic school boards will engage in an expansion frenzy, establishing new Catholic high schools here and there and everywhere without asking the "gospel quality control" questions. Many of those schools will be built on sand, not on a firm gospel foundation. To proclaim the mystery of Jesus Christ, to present his promises and his Kingdom, demands committed leadership, men and women serious about living out their baptism with an adult faith. That is the "touchstone" Paul IV speaks about, the test of whether we are serious about evangelizing through our Catholic high schools: when we have Catholic educators so in touch with their own baptism and with the many different ways that they have been evangelized themselves, that evangelization, sharing their experience of Jesus, is part and parcel of what it is to teach in a Catholic high school. Anything less than that should be unthinkable.

The happy reality is that the presence of such teachers does in fact grace our schools. You will be introduced to some of them in the next chapter. Their reflections on these passages from Paul VI's *On Evangelization in the Modern World* clearly illustrate for evangelizers in the Catholic high school the critical importance of communal sharing.

34

I believe, too, that their reflections, based on the day-to-day experience of doing Catholic education in the high school, can be a great help, pointing out possibilities, identifying obstacles and proposing strategies.

NOTES
Chapter 2

[1] *Lay Catholics in Schools : Witnesses to Faith*
October 15, 1982, #3, #26, #34.

[2] *On Evangelization in the Modern World* [*Evangelii Nuntiandi*], Rome, December 8, 1974, #41.

CHAPTER 3

A REFLECTION ON EXPERIENCE — THE PRACTICE OF EVANGELIZATION

I remarked earlier that most of us are neither theologians of the academic variety nor professional religious educators. But we are theologians! Every believer in Jesus Christ, serious about living out his or her baptism, is capable of doing theology.[1]

In his *Theology of Liberation*, the renowned Peruvian theologian, Gustavo Gutierrez, writes: "There is present in all believers a rough outline of theology. There is present an effort to understand the faith. Theology is a critical reflection of 'praxis' — such a theology is based on a true analysis of the signs of the times and the demands with which they challenge the Christian community." The eminent French catechist and religious educator, Pierre André Liégé, OP, cites his Dominican confrere, Edward Schillebeeckx: "Without pretending to define theology, we consider it as a reflection by which Christians look at their Christian experience — in a determined place, culture and time."[2]

The point of departure for this type of theological reflection is the experience of the Christian, especially that experience which concerns proclaiming the gospel and passing on the faith. It is this reflection on the experience of evangelization in the Catholic high school that I would now like to consider.

It goes without saying that as Catholic educators we must listen frequently and keenly to the teaching voice of the Church, the top-down theological eavesdropping I introduced in Chapter 2. Such teaching is based on centuries of human wisdom and good gospel sense. I believe, too, that Paul VI's meditation on evangelization is an excellent example of such a teaching and is a bold, prophetic challenge to all Catholic educators everywhere.

36

At the same time, each of us in a very personal way must be open in prayer to the Word of God. Such openness in listening and readiness to discern God's will makes one's life journey and one's faith pilgrimage a much richer, more integral experience. Personal prayer as well certainly gives more meaning and focus to one's work and ministry as an educator in a Catholic high school.

But there is another dimension: the need to listen to one another. The Lord speaks through the convictions, enthusiasm, experiences, successes, and even the failures of the men and women with whom we find ourselves collaborating on the evangelization project in our schools. Such a "word" can be supportive, challenging and consoling; such a "word," too, based on the witness and proclamation of our co-workers, can go a long way in interpreting for us just what it is we are trying to do in the Catholic high school and in pointing out imaginative responses and even possible strategies to initiate.

Paul VI's *On Evangelization in the Modern World* and Congregation for Catholic Education documents are examples of a top-down theology of evangelization. Our peers' reflections about their own faith and the ways they try to live out their baptism and evangelize in the Catholic high school can be a bottom-up theology of evangelization — a necessary complement to the official teaching voice of the Church. This is theology in the practical sense, and it is a critically important type of theology if we are to exploit the real potential for evangelization our Catholic high schools present. And it is *listening* to such reflections of peers — and of students, as we shall experience further on — that I call bottom-up theological eavesdropping.

John Paul II doesn't know much about squeezing religion credits out of OS:IS. The Vatican Congregation for Catholic Education can't really appreciate the concrete circumstances and the psychology of the kids of ethnic parents in Toronto who are in school all day and then must work six hours every evening for the family to make ends meet. And even professional theologians on the Canadian scene have few answers as to how to evangelize kids who can pay out three or four hundred dollars for a winter formal or a spring prom! This is the theological turf of the educator in the Catholic high school: our "determined place, culture and time." And it is our experience in evangelizing that deserves articulation. Such articulation can add understanding and focus to what we do in Catholic education as well as become a source of encouragement for other Catholic educators.

To assist me with this reflection on evangelization in the Catholic high school, I invited 30 colleagues who work in a number of different

Catholic high schools to reflect on their experience as evangelizers in the high school. Four different groups met a total of three times; each meeting was three hours in duration. They shared and questioned and sometimes debated their views of evangelization. They contributed their own thoughts on the type of society and culture that constitutes our context for evangelization in the Catholic high school. They spoke in practical and ideal terms on the difference — the alternative vision — that should be ours in the Catholic high school. And they elaborated on the challenge of leadership in Catholic education today, particularly in the Catholic high school. I had no specific criteria in inviting these 30 educators other than their faith commitment and unbounded enthusiasm for evangelizing in the Catholic high school. My intention was to tap their experience — their ideas and ideals — to listen to and learn from their experience.[3] It is that experience that I now begin to share with you. Such bottom-up theological eavesdropping is, like top-down theology, a constitutive part of this entire reflection.

A REFLECTION ON EXPERIENCE — THE TEACHER AS EVANGELIZER

Question: Talk about your notion of evangelization in the Catholic high school.

This was the point of departure for close to 40 hours of communal discernment on the why, the what, and the how of Catholic education at the secondary level. Many perceptive insights were shared as each person reflected on his or her own experience and approach to teaching in the Catholic high school. Much of the theology emanating from the discussions complements and indeed makes more relevant and down-to-earth the principles of evangelization of Paul VI we have just considered. What is especially pertinent is that it is a theology lived — tried and tested and experienced in the trenches!

On Precising the Evangelizing Difference

In response to the invitation to talk about evangelization, almost immediately the question was raised as to the difference evangelization makes, could make, or should make!

Guidance teacher:

Okay... so we feel that ultimately what we are really concerned about is to hand down our faith to our students. I have some good friends who teach in public schools....

38

We talk about respect... justice... the dignity of the person.... even seeing Christ in our students.... These people in public schools do that. I think that is incumbent on *every* teacher! If they don't feel that those are values, why are they in teaching? I think we have to be more explicit.... Our Catholic high school has to be different than the public high school. Our mission is more than just the education thing.... There is "the Christian thing to do." Our job is to make it explicit. If people think that the separate school is just the place where you are nice to one another, that implies that in other schools they are not! Our mission... our evangelization is deeper. It has to be explicit. We are about something more!

Business and economics teacher:

The one thing we should have in the Catholic high school is a community of faith, an atmosphere. ... This is really an added dimension that enriches us that the gospel-committed teacher in the public school doesn't have.

English teacher:

In English I often say... "as a Christian" or "as a Roman Catholic" in class... in discussions and debate. I can certainly broach gospel questions and values. I feel comfortable doing that. I think I have an impact on kids doing this. This is more than just acting nice to each other. In a public school I don't think I could be that explicit.

Chairperson of English department:

We can't just go in a class and do dogma. I don't think Christ went in anywhere and said this is what you must believe. It was very much an empowering kind of a thing. But if we look at the two systems and they are identical, even though we have the opportunities to pass on the faith, then we are blowing it!... In the last few years, I have become more conscious about what I teach in literature and, where I have a choice, I no longer look at it only in terms of literary value, but also faith issues enter in. These are conscious choices I think we must make in a Catholic high school.

* * * * * * * * *

Witness: The Personal Investment Demanded by Evangelization

The system, the institution, the structure and organizational mechanics were often more hindrance than help, as we shall see. But where there was total agreement was on the commitment of the individual teacher.

English teacher:

> For me it's trying to live out as best I can what it is to be a Christian and to try to create in my classroom an atmosphere of security and respect... no fear or ridicule! And to explore literature from all aspects including the faith point of view.

Business and economics teacher:

> In teaching we have to build self-esteem, and I think we should take every opportunity to make a student feel good about himself or herself. And by the same token, that means I have to feel good about myself.... Students have to see that I am content, that I am not dragging myself through classes, that I'm not there just for the money, it's not just a job! Hell, what if they were to say: "This is a Christian who can't stand his job and finds this place a pain in the ass! Why do I want to be a Christian?" I have a responsibility to have fun and to live the joy side of the gospel. Kids will see that and see something important and deep about the gospel.

English teacher:

> Really, in talking about evangelization in the Catholic high school, we are not talking so much about teaching something as we're talking about being something.

* * * * * * * * *

The Centrality of Jesus in the Evangelization Project

And "being something" has to do with putting on Christ Jesus. It was encouraging, indeed humbling, to see the importance of imaging Christ and seeing Christ in others for these colleagues of mine in the Catholic high school. Proclaiming Christ through "wordless witness" or proclamation is the very heart of evangelization.

40

Vice-principal:

> Christ among us is part and parcel of each of us. I remember a homily, and I don't remember too many homilies. The priest referred to the women who went to the tomb at Easter and were looking down, and the messenger, the angel, said: "Why are you looking down! He is not here!" And at ascension, they were all gathered looking at the sky, and the angel said: "Why are you looking up? He is not there." The whole point is: if he is not down or up, then he is right here among us. We have to find Christ in one another... and be Christ for one another.

Another vice-principal:

> The other day my second youngest was scolded by my wife, and she said: "Mommy, I don't like you, but I love you." I thought: that is pretty profound! And I can see that a lot of times with kids in my office! I think that! I don't say that to them, but I think that! When they are in my office and leave the office... I try to see Christ in that person... then I have gone a long way. My hope always is that they leave the office with a little more dignity than what they came in with. That is a first step.... I'm not sure I do it all the time, but often when I am driving home I replay the day... and look at my plus-minus stats. That's what it is all about: I don't like what you're doing, but I'll try to see Christ in you. I mean, that's our mandate.

Priest-teacher — English and religion:

> My notion of evangelization means my notion of me as an evangelizer. I begin from the point that... I believe... all people are fundamentally good. Christianity doesn't have a monopoly on goodness. I believe that there are good people in all schools. What makes the Christian for me is that a person has a relationship to Christ. That is the central thing for me. So that when I see myself as an evangelizer... it means nothing more than I try to be Christ for everyone I come into contact with, not just inadvertently but overtly and deliberately, so that when I deal with staff, for example, I try to deal with them the way Christ would; that is, welcoming and forgiving and sometimes challenging. The same I think would be true of the students with whom I deal, so that when they come to me they might find someone who is going to listen to them. Maybe in coming

to know me... those kids will come to know Jesus. The Catholic high school to me, then, is the place where we can all share that notion. I would hope that the people I work with all have that notion. Everything flows from that. If Christ isn't central... it might be good, but it's not Christian.

* * * * * * * * *

Realistic Considerations in Evangelizing

Such theologizing was fascinating and always helpful. Some could articulate more easily what others felt and lived. To be sure, there are many ideals proposed. But the happy thing about these people was the way they managed in their own approaches not to let the sometimes oppressive clouds of reality darken and dampen their enthusiasm or their ideals. Time and time again realism worked at tempering their idealism.

English and drama teacher:

> You talk about how easy it is now to share faith with other staff members! That has not been my experience. It may be the ideal, but.... I look back to a PD day last year: men on one side and women on the other side for a staff Mass. Can you believe it? The most uncomfortable experience in my years as a teacher in a Catholic school. I really haven't shared much of my faith in my three years teaching in a Catholic high school.

Priest-principal:

> One of the problems we experience in high school... either in or outside of the classroom, is the fact that what we do in high school is somewhat in isolation to home and parish. For example, our school liturgies... These are good experiences, but I suspect for many of the kids this is the only experience they have of liturgy. Our group is homogeneous; the parish isn't. It is easier for us. And at home, what is going on? And then, there is the group mentality. Kids are so influenced by others. [It's] hard to detect how much personal commitment there is.

Principal:

> The teaching of religion in the Catholic high school is more an intellectual thing now... in a professional educational

context. Kids never really perceive it as personal. I have begun to think you can perhaps do more evangelizing teaching literature than teaching religion. There is a built-in resistance. But if kids meet people who do it — not just because it is their job but because they have a commitment to it — then they have a credible witness. More and more our kids see us with our own lifestyle which is the North American dream — which is part of the problem! The real work of evangelization doesn't take place in that setting. It is the peripheral stuff that goes on when people are credible witnesses.

* * * * * * * * *

Religious Education as Evangelization and the Need for a Critical Transforming Education

There was universal agreement that evangelization meant much more than teaching religion. While there was a critique as to the effectiveness of the teaching of religion, there was also a spirited defence as to what goes on and what could be possible in religious education.

Principal:

Evangelization is preaching the Good News, and where we have done it well is with our religion program . . . for example. Kids are not complaining about our courses the way they did years ago. The program does mean something to them. But my worry is the practice of it: many kids don't seem to practise their faith.

Chairperson, religion department:

But you can't really fault the religion department. It is the whole school community. There is a place for intellectual consideration of our faith. In religion class we try to articulate the kids' lived experience. That's important. Now, the pastoral side of the school has to be everyone's responsibility.

Instructor of theology course, faculty of education:

For me, one of the key features is the transformation of values on a personal and societal level. This really is the reason for evangelization. I think in the elementary school there is an emphasis on the affective life that evangelization brings about.... Whereas, in the high school, the concentration is more on content and the reasonableness of our faith. This is a key task of evangelization in the high school. That has to be there for the adolescent mind which is starting to cope with all sorts of ideas: psychological development, sexuality, knowledge of science. Kids have to see that our faith also can stand as a reasonable thought system. Here, too, ... see the importance of other curriculum areas to reinforce faith.

Physical education teacher:

Somehow we have to see that what we are doing has to do with our society and culture. My understanding of theology today is to see the Church as trying to change what is evil in our culture. In our Catholic high school we have to get at this: if Christ is the transforming presence in the world, that's us, that's the Christian, the follower of Jesus. And that is what we should teach our students to be. I think we do this by first of all affirming the kids, and then by teaching them to be critical thinkers.

Religion teacher:

I am a convert to Catholicism. I taught in the public school. I think they do a very good job. But in Catholic education — elementary, where I taught for many years, and now secondary — I see evangelization is really to get the students to be critical, to look at the things in society that oppress and stifle. The question and challenge for us: how do we get the kids and ourselves to recognize the evil and problems in culture and society and to work on it?

* * * * * * * * *

Evangelization: An Experience of Relationship

Many eloquent and sensitive observations were shared as to the personal face of the evangelization experience: counselling situations in guidance and chaplaincy offices; conversations in corridors or after class; the dynamics of relationships amongst staff and with staff and students; the relativization of content and curriculum and the consequent primacy of the person.

Chaplain:

Part of the evangelization project is the dynamics involved

with people. It is not just courses and knowledge. It is how we do that with students . . . the community spirit . . . ! How do we treat students? Respect, justice, compassion — this is the positive gospel that must be in sync with our courses. . . . The negative gospel is the opposite of this, and the kids pick up on it quickly. Forgiveness is so important. If kids feel it and experience it, they are going to believe it. If we give up on them — and we have a lot of tough kids — that is not proclaiming the Good News! The dynamics: staff and students and staff and staff at all levels are all parts of evangelization. The heart of community is forgeveness, and the flip side of this is conversion, and that is the whole point of evangelization.

Physical education teacher:

We always have to remember that we are teaching people, not teaching subjects. Too often, I feel, a lot of the time, the focus is on curriculum and information and not on the fact that we are trying to help young individuals develop through a variety of experiences. Evangelization covers the halls and cafeteria and extra-curricular experiences as well as the classroom. . . . It is a process that doesn't end . . . and it is what we are there for. We need to remind one another of this often and in different ways.

Religion teacher:

I think an important part of the evangelization process in the high school is the fact that it doesn't just take place in the religion class. Some of the key themes and issues can come up in other curriculum and courses. We are a Catholic high school! We don't have to defend our value stance based on the gospel in economic and political and social questions. To ignore this possibility should cause us to ask why we exist as a Catholic high school! I feel that it is very important that this common, this community sense be developed, and that evangelization be seen as something that just doesn't happen in religion class.

* * * * * * * * *

DIFFICULTIES IN EVANGELIZING IN THE CATHOLIC HIGH SCHOOL

Question: What are some of the concrete problems the Catholic educator faces in trying to proclaim the Good News and witness to Jesus Christ in the Catholic high school?

This was the next level of questioning, and in many ways it was a useful device to explore more deeply the practical implications of evangelizing. Here the theory, the ideal, the theology meets head on the practice, the real, the field of experience that often frustrates, stumps, infuriates and disappoints. These discussions, though focusing on obstacles — or the negative — were surprising for a number of reasons. My colleagues demonstrated a heightened sense of self-knowledge and an elaborate understanding and analysis of the more global, institutional problems. While sometimes frustrated and disappointed, they remained tenacious in their own personal investment in the system — in the Catholic high school project — and were intent on the struggle to evangelize, to make our system a viable alternative. They could admit to their own limitations and inadequacy, and they recognized the ongoing need for the evangelizer to be evangilized : "We have met the obstacle, and it is us!", as one participant aptly phrased it.

There was a consistent acknowledgement that the teacher often got in the way of evangelization. "Sometimes we just don't recognize our limitations. We are afraid to admit a mistake or to say 'I don't know.' We try to do it ourselves instead of empowering." Several times the incomprehension of the adolescent context and culture surfaced.

Religion teacher :

> We don't really address the experience of students.... There are so many forces influencing them. We tend to come at them on a theoretical level and not really address them where they are at. The culture we are in really fragments the kids as far as identity is concerned. I'm not sure we really address these questions, and until we do, what we talk about will not really be internalized. It will stay foreign to them.

In Part Two, we will explore in greater detail the more global, cultural and social factors creating the context for our teaching and evangelizing in the Catholic high school. Here I just summarize briefly several observations made by the teachers in their reflections vis-a-vis aspects of the student and the student's context that make evangelization a difficult proposition.

• Students have a skeptical regard for evangelism and in some instances religion. In the *Rattle and Hum* concert version of "Bullit the Blue Sky," Bono of U2 related to roaring applause: " ... or a

46

preacher of the old-time gospel hour stealing money from the sick and the old. Well, the God I believe in isn't short of cash, mister."

- Many students are very mark-oriented and are taking courses like business or science because they perceive these to be the routes, after university study, to the most lucrative jobs.

- Because, in more than a few instances, the family environment is so fragmented or violent, many kids lack a healthy concept of self and personhood. And then there are the more modern, trendy parents: "Some of our parents with strange yuppie values can really impede a student's human development and faith development." Peers then become even more important for them, which is great if the friend is solid. As a vice-principal puts it: "In my office, if I can't get a kid to do something, I go to his friend who will get it across to him." But if the friend is a negative influence?

- There is an all-pervading "relativism" and a diminished sense of truth and the "absolute." "That's my opinion! How can you criticize me for that? I deserve marks."

- The lack of participation in the parish was a genuinely perplexing question for everyone. It was remarked that it is an enormous challenge for the Catholic high school to speak the gospel and present the priorities of a lived faith. And we are presumed specialists! We are supposed to have an insight into how young people tick! It is even a bolder challenge for the parish. We are not doing this very well, but not certainly for a lack of effort!

* * * * * * * * *

Much disillusionment finds its source in the lack of support and commitment of other members of the staff.

Chaplain:

My experience as a chaplain makes me zero in on counter-witness. The attitudes of some of the staff at school liturgies were striking. They would stand at the back or not be there at all. And the kids saw this!

Voices from other schools:

We all have them!

Now, counter-witness is counter-witness! But we can distinguish a passive counter-witness from an active counter-witness. It is the latter type that is most demoralizing and vexing.

English and drama teacher:

> Sometimes I feel lessened by other staff. I teach kids how to
> sell tickets; another teacher teaches them how to scam. It
> is so blatantly counter-gospel.

Chaplain:

> My problem is with the teacher teaching economics who re-
> fuses to use the Church documents — [Remember, we are
> a Catholic school!] — on economic and political critique,
> saying: "This is not the place to teach religion. This is
> where we teach business or economics." The ignorance of
> such a person irks me to no end. The kids are being
> deprived of a whole other view of economics because of his
> closed-mindedness, not allowing a critique of our present
> system.

*   *   *   *   *   *   *   *   *

The most analytical critique of obstacles to the evangelization
project in the Catholic high school, however, was systemic in nature:
the system, the board, the bureaucracy, OECTA. Here the experience
was very negative. My own feeling is that it was a negativity not so
much based on the increased paperwork or inefficiency, or even the impersonal nature of a large organization — all part of the bureaucratic
package — but a negativity resulting from missed opportunities to
evangelize.

Monsignor Dennis Murphy of the Institute for Catholic Education
makes this case for Christianizing the institution:

> In our day and age, in the highly complex world of educa-
> tion, much of this caring must be mediated through institu-
> tions. As Christian and Catholic educators, we are coming
> to realize that the caring, the healing, and the reconciling
> must in large part be accomplished not only through in-
> dividual efforts but through institutions. For Catholic edu-
> cators this development means institutions which are
> Christianized. It means that Catholic educators adopt a dy-
> namic and creative attitude rather than simply a caretaking
> attitude towards that institution which is the Separate
> School System.[4]

But "Christianizing the institution" is a formidable challenge, even for the most committed. The collective experience is that we have a long way to go, and administrators and those who have the responsibility must move beyond the lip-service plateau.

Question: Is evangelization really a priority?

Religion teacher:

> ...the failure, much of it is deep within the system. For example, the question of teaching religion in the classroom from an academic or a pastoral-contextual perspective.... A discussion of this nature usually happens between two people who care, who are converted if you will... who already see evangelization as the real purpose of the school! But, I don't think this represents the majority opinion. Read minutes of a board meeting, or a heads of department meeting... we don't hear the term evangelization. It is not a priority. I find this a real disappointment. We are in big trouble because I believe that this question of evangelization is a non-question for the majority of Catholic educators.

Question: Is completion a blessing or a curse?

Principal:

> The failures are systemic, particularly since the completion of the system.... It has been so hard! Look at the incredible, almost unbelievable proliferation of bureaucracy everywhere! What has come with that is a kind of perpetuation of bureaucratic values everywhere. The institution is paramount.... Self-perpetuation becomes the principle of operation: an alienation of the people who are in the front lines doing the teaching. A real distancing! I also see an incredible pursuit of upward mobility on the part of increasing numbers of Catholic teachers. So many people are ambitious in what I see as a non-gospel sort of way. I am not a pessimist, nor am I a cynic. I fought for completion for 25 years. I thought eventually we would see some of this happen, but the bureaucracy of it all has hit us like a tidal wave! We seem to accept the secular demands of leadership as normal and natural.... There is so little time and interest in the religious dimension... except to logically legitimate "Catholic education."

Question : Can bureaucracy be evangelized?

Chairperson, religion department:

> Another thing that affects us now in the Catholic high
> school... the growing power that technology and
> bureaucracy have. We see the bureaucracy thing in the
> school. The board and the ministry... are the new sacred
> thing! Too many of our colleagues are into the politics and
> promotion thing to get ahead. They have no sensitivity, no
> feel for the gospel vision for our students and education.
> Bureaucracy is a real subtle attack on evangelization, be-
> cause bureaucracy always seems so reasonable and logical
> and sane. Bureaucracy has its own type of "theology":
> religion is equated with externals, God is male and distant,
> sin is strictly a personal matter between me and God, the
> sacraments are channels of grace, etc. Now we have the cri-
> sis of leadership in our schools. They are run by
> bureaucrats. And there is no room for conversion and
> transformation — what evangelization is all about — in
> bureaucracy! What gives evangelization its direction should
> be the notion of the Kingdom of God.

Such are some of the difficulties in evangelizing in the Catholic
high school. A second reading of this experience of obstacles — this critique from within — will show a strong resonance with the critique
presented in the first chapter — the external critique. Certainly, serious
consideration of these obstacles demonstrates the urgency of Pope Paul
VI's insistence that "evangelizers be evangelized." Like the Church,
Catholic educators and the institutions and system we create easily fall
victim to idols.

* * * * * * * * *

SUCCESSES IN EVANGELIZING
IN THE CATHOLIC HIGH SCHOOL

And yet, the gospel is being preached! Jesus and his healing power is
being experienced! The neighbours — brothers and sisters — are being cared for. And "the personal and collective consciences of people"
are being informed and challenged. A principal pretty well summed up
the grace side of evangelization in our high schools in these words:

50

I see the successes as not tied into the system ... or structure ... not institutional ... although the school itself — staff and kids — can be effective. The successes I have seen and experienced have really been individual: a person committed to a vision of the gospel and reflecting it in his / her life. Here is the credible witness of Catholic education.

Certainly the high school atmosphere and community is a very effective instrument for evangelization.

Our school liturgies have really developed over the years. Kids enjoy them; they help organize them. I think they even pray. These experiences they remember.

The possibilities to promote life, to enhance life — we present a thorough catechesis on life in religious education, and other subject areas reinforce it. It is not only the question of abortion, although that certainly is the centrepiece of our catechesis, but the life-threatening and life-depriving evils of the arms race, capital punishment, insensitivity towards the sick and elderly. Just to have this chance is worth the cost of the system.

I can't get over the impact peer tutoring has at our place. I mean, the TRs and severely developmentally handicapped are a great blessing for us. Their presence makes us more human. We get much more out of it — staff and kids — than we can give.

Finally, it would be a serious mistake to gloss over the potential for evangelization the Catholic high school represents even for many of our students who are "unchurched." The testimony of a young chemistry teacher, a graduate of a Catholic high school, eloquently speaks to this potential:

Personnally, my parents are pretty indifferent to faith. The Church is really not a part of their life. I didn't have any home faith environment, but they did send me to the Catholic schools, and it is from the Catholic school that I developed in faith. Even if there is no home faith life ... my experience is that something can develop in the Catholic school. What we have to present is the positive in life, in humanity — that there is more good than evil in the world — and share this perspective with the kids. In our atmosphere and religion courses we really do hammer away at "other-centredness," responsibility for neighbour, charity and justice activities. This is all so important. I really believe that my faith was nurtured there.

* * * * * * * * * *

There is, too, the prayer factor. It is something hard to measure, but the experience is that it is definitely real:

Retreats, COR, SEARCH — these are all part of the program or connected to the school. All of this adds the affective dimension to the cognitive dimension of religion class. I'm quite amazed by the depth of perception of some of these kids at the experiential level. A mark of the impact here is the number of university kids who come back to animate a retreat. That is impressive.

I believe a real success is the new openness to kids about confession or the sacrament of reconciliation. Kids will go now, face to face with the priest. There used to be such a fear, but today it is so open. Advent and Lent reconciliation days are one of the highlights of the year for us.

To me the school must be a place where these kids can have peace — a community and people who care — because some of their family situations are so destructive. It is a real sign of hope. And I know some of the same care goes on in the public school. But for me, and I think for others, the gospel and Jesus — that's the motivation! And prayer: some of these kids ask for a prayer. They ask for prayer for others. Prayer is really a factor.

And there is the peer ministry factor:

Last June, in dealing with the cancer death of a very popular Grade 12 student, there was an awful lot of shaken faith of young kids, but handled so terribly gently! And it is still being dealt with now. The way the pastoral team helped kids deal with grief and anger! They hit the question of God's mercy: how can a poor young person be mutilated — cancer operations and amputations — how can God allow this? The chaplain and some kids and some teachers continue to work on these questions with the kids. The mother of the child still comes to the school to find support! Other kids visit the mother, ministering to her needs. The school community is still ministering.

* * * * * * * * *

Frequently, people spoke of the significant personal difference stemming from one-on-one relationships and teacher-student friendships. Indeed, much evangelization is realized in brokenness:

> Another thing, working with kids individually, I hear some of the horror stories about their life.... We are trying to evangelize kids who are living in really broken situations. I think to myself: if I had to live in some of that garbage, would I still be here! Some kids live in just awful home situations, yet they are able to survive.

> One thing I see in terms of relationship with kids: when you work with them and don't give up on them, they begin to see the sacredness of their life. You see some of them over a period of time. You begin to see that they are worth something, and that says plenty about how we treat them! You spend time, you even go out on a limb; you don't give up! You say to the student: "You are important as a person. Your life is important!" And when the kids start believing that, their behaviour changes!

* * * * * * * * *

There are many hopeful signs and potentially wonderful opportunities for evangelization in today's context: a yearning on the part of kids for meaning; the creative use of media; the witness and supportive collaboration of other members of the staff.

> I think today I sense a yearning on the part of kids... for meaning! In class discussions, doom and gloom scenarios can lead to a sense of hopelessness or to a new co-operation.... This is an impressive insight: the enthusiasm and freshness of youth. We need to tap into it. Many kids are open to it.

> ...Our students are much more informed. As bad as the media are, there are a lot of pluses with them — **if** used intelligently. A lot of programs with some good analysis; for example, three hours on the politics of food, four to five hours dealing with the cold war. There are opportunities to help them become more critical. Our classroom clientele,

some of them are very informed. Also, some are opinionated; a real challenge for us to deal with is how they form opinion.

I think one of the positive things: in spite of much of the gloom and doom analysis, there are still people who hope, who believe it is not a lost cause! And in personal and individual ways as parents and teachers... we try to make a difference. The commitment of many is really very encouraging.

The single most strength... the most positive aspect that we have in the Catholic high schools is ourselves: teachers who care, are concerned, support one another, witness! This has to be a great example to students: the way teachers relate to one another. This is a great resource for evangelization: our sense of team and community spirit!

* * * * * * * * *

And finally, there is the classroom. Certainly Jesus is proclaimed! Kids can and do grow in their understanding and love for Jesus, and not just the advanced academic kids. Listen to testimony of three religion teachers:

One year we had two kids who could not get into community college. They would not pass basic level work, but they were not trainable retarded. Now these two kids were the only two students who defended all the way the prodigal son story! All the more advanced kids in class took the older brother's position or took another side and said what the father should do! You see, it was the university-bound who could not grasp what that story was about! We really have to be welcoming and sensitive to everyone! It is so easy to shut out "the little ones."

In the Grade 12 religion course, the last chapter of the book we use is called "Parting" — how to deal with anger, including the anger you feel toward God! Difficult because we are not supposed to be angry toward God! There has always been something positive about this: for kids to experience a liberating experience of faith and God.

An example. We begin class with a prayer. Every class: five to fifteen minutes with silent prayer. I brought the principal

54

in to tell the kids they can no longer do this: they are falling behing other classes; they won't be prepared for the exam! And they fought him every inch of the way! Now, to set up this prayer experience demands skills: the how you do it is crucial! It can be done. I try to take my 70 minutes and say: let's look at Jesus and how he taught. Why was he successful? In religion, I wonder how many teachers consider this before they start. So I give the kids the prayer, a desert experience every day — quiet! I try to have every kid speak in every class. I try to touch each student by name and invitation at least once. Whatever points I want to make about content, scripture, I save till the end of class. Usually kids will discover it. I think it is key for us to find out how Jesus taught.

* * * * * * * * *

Indeed, there are successes. As one teacher said, taking the last word and summing up this reflection on the positive, on our successes in evangelizing in the Catholic high school: "There are successes all over the place. God doesn't stint on his grace, even when we might."

Whether it be a total school endeavour such as a food drive or an Ash Wednesday liturgy; a conversation in the corridor or in a counselling situation; in the classroom or in a small-group retreat experience — because of the innate goodness of so many of our students and the solid faith commitment of some Catholic educators, evangelization happens.

All of this brings us to the next challenge: the context. For anyone serious about evangelizing in the Catholic high school environment, the ongoing task is to work at understanding as much as we can about "the context" — the culture and society in which we find ourselves evangelizing. "The context" is the challenge we explore and analyse in Part Two.

NOTES

Chapter 3

1 The following discussion on practical theology is taken from: James T. Mulligan, CSC, *The Theology of the Separate School Trustee* (Toronto: OSSTA, 1976), Chapter One, "Theology: Content and Expression."

2 *Le Point Théologique*, 1, 1971.

3 Each of the following sections of this reflection will include a reflection on experience — the teacher as evangelizer. Here I present the first such reflection, focusing on what it is to evangelize in the Catholic high school. This particular discussion touches on several dimensions of evangelization. I have taken the utmost care to transcribe faithfully the taped recording of discussions. I am also very sensitive to the possibility of manipulating quotes or texts. I have tried very hard to avoid that. My intention is simply to present a "practical theology of evangelization" in a coherent and ordered way. I hope to achieve that through the format: the categories or topics I propose as headings. I am personally convinced that, as in the case of Paul VI's meditation on evangelization, we have much to learn here in listening to our co-workers in the Catholic high school reflect on their own evangelizing experience.

4 *The Catholic Register*, November 15, 1986, p. 7.

PART TWO

The Context for Evangelization in the Catholic High School

CHAPTER 4
THE GOSPEL AND CULTURE

Listen again to a religion teacher commenting on one of the fundamental obstacles we face in evangelizing in the Catholic high school:

> We don't really address the experience of students. There are so many forces influencing them. We tend to come at them on a theoretical level and not really address them where they are at. The culture we are in really fragments the kids as far as identity is concerned. I'm not sure we really address these questions, and until we do, what we talk about will not really be internalized. It will stay foreign to them.

The preoccupation here is *the context*. It is the correct preoccupation, a prerequisite to the reflection on youth as the beneficiaries of evangelization in the Catholic high school in the next section. The challenge is for the Catholic high school educator to be ever more aware of the many different cultural and social factors constituting the environment for evangelization in the Catholic high school.

To describe the context for doing Catholic secondary education in Ontario today is an enormous task, involving, among other things, an analysis of the different ideologies giving shape to our North American society and culture; an analysis of the social effects of domestic economic control and political power; a study of youth culture and the adolescent world (a full-time, ongoing vocation in itself!); a sensitivity to the impact of the wide variations of students' home environment and family life; and an awareness of the more global economic and political movements at play and impacting on our society.

And then there is the *ecclesial context*! As Catholic educators, we not only prepare young people for post-secondary study, employment and adult life, but we intend to hand on our faith: to pass on our experience of Jesus; to share with them the richness of our understanding of what it is to be Roman Catholic. To do this effectively, we need to appreciate the Catholic tradition and the situation of the Church now — in our time and place.

There is an interesting paragraph concluding The Congregation for Catholic Education document, *The Religious Dimension of Education in a Catholic School*, that underscores the importance of studying the context :

> The Congregation would like to suggest that further study, research, and experimentation be done in all areas that affect the religious dimension of education in Catholic schools. Much has been done, but many people are asking for even more.... Local experience must be the determining factor.
>
> [#115]

Local experience of the culture and a *local analysis* of the social and cultural factors shaping the context are the best analysis. The evangelization project in any Catholic high school can only be enhanced when a group of Catholic high school educators look seriously both at the obstacles to proclaiming the gospel inherent in our culture and at the signs of hope prevalent in our time and place and which can add meaning and depth to our evangelization.

In the following pages my intention is to propose some of the elements that should be looked at when we consider the context. Since our purpose is to provide an education with the gospel difference, then we should reflect on the challenge of doing this in our particular circumstances and situation. And then, what about " our circumstances and our situations "? It will be helpful to consider briefly some of the social and cultural factors that make evangelization a difficult task, as well as some of the " grace " moments and occasions present today that should be exploited in our evangelization. Particular consideration of the Church " circumstances and situation " is pertinent, mindful that the Catholic high school as an instrument of evangelization is an extension of the local Church. And to complete each of these analytical sketches with some first-hand intuition into our culture rooted in the lived experience of the Catholic high school, we will listen to evangelizers : how do some very concerned and committed Catholic educators describe their context? What are their insights? This reflection in Part Two is essential, yet it is but a point of departure for the real challenge, which is situated at the local level and must be accomplished in each individual Catholic high school.

1. LISTENING TO THE CHURCH — THE CHALLENGE OF THE CONTEXT

In the last 25 years, a fundamental shift has taken place in our understanding of the role of the Church in society and in our understanding of the relationship between gospel and culture. Some of the tension existing in the Church today certainly finds its source in the fact that more than a few Catholics have not made the transition to a Vatican II understanding of Church and world, gospel and culture. This failure can be attributed to any number of things : poor pedagogical strategies on the part of the teaching Church ; the overwhelming force of secularization that has, for many Catholics, put the Church on the margins of relevance as far as life priorities are concerned ; for some, the reluctance to break out of certain categories common in the pre-Vatican II Church — a private faith and a Sunday, other-wordly Catholicism based on a dichotomy between the religious and the secular ; and for others, a resistance to the post-Vatican II emphasis that the social dimensions of faith and the gospel and the critical, prophetic voice of the Church actually do challenge a person's social, economic and political practice.

2. THE GOSPEL AND CULTURE

Paul VI frames the gospel-culture challenge beautifully in *On Evangelization in the Modern World* :

> The split between the Gospel and culture is without a doubt the drama of our time, just as it was of other times. Therefore every effort must be made to ensure a full evangelization of culture, or more correctly of cultures. They have to be regenerated by an encounter with the Gospel. But this encounter will not take place if the Gospel is not proclaimed.
>
> [E.N., #20]

The gospel has to encounter culture! Perhaps one of my own experiences with trying to come to grips with the Vatican II interpretation of the relationship between gospel and culture illustrates this process. I began to teach in the early '70s. At the time, I was pretty confident that I was working out of a renewed theology, a Vatican II understanding of liturgy, scripture and ecclesiology. I was imbued with the spirit of *Gaudium et Spes* — Vatican II's *Constitution on the Church in the Modern World*. I was very taken with Pope Paul VI's encyclical in 1967, *On the*

61

Development of People. As a religious educator in touch with youth, I was aware of the unbounded enthusiasm and generosity adolescents could generate for "causes." Third World, developing nations, the gap between the rich world and the poor world : these were issues that could capture the good will of the students. And so, much of my effort in religious education centred on the Third World. My approach was theological : it was a question of Christian charity, a question of solidarity — the rich and the poor sharing the same world ; we are our brothers' (and sisters') keepers ; the strong must care for the weak.

It was a colleague on staff, a very good friend who taught business and economics, who stretched my understanding of how the gospel must encounter culture. Over a number of months of animated conversation and argument in the staff room and over pizza and beer, he kept hammering away at the point that my theology alone was not sufficient to understand the problem of the Third World ; nor was it adequate to lead the students to a sense of responsibility and solidarity with others (in this instance, the poor of the Third World) based only on charity. "Your theology, your gospel approach to the Third World needs my economics to effectively understand the Third World and do something about it," he was wont to say. He was right! And gradually we both came to realize the centrality of justice. It was not enough just to give assistance. It was necessary to ask why assistance for the poor is needed. We found that the gospel was illuminated and given even more force by research into history, economics and politics. The line of demarcation between the religious and the secular gradually disappeared. The gospel had a prophetic function : to critique economics and politics. The effectiveness of evangelization increased considerably when the gospel could use the insights of the social sciences.

During the 1970s and 1980s, the Church developed a challenging body of social teaching :

- 1970s — Labour Day Statements of the Canadian bishops
- 1971 — Synod document : *Justice in the World*
- 1975 — Pope Paul VI : *On Evangelization in the Modern World*
- 1982 — Pope John Paul II : *On Human Work*
- 1983 — Canadian bishops : *Ethical Reflections on the Economic Crisis*
- 1987 — Congregation for the Doctrine of the Faith : *Instruction on Respect for Human Life in Its Origin and on the Dignity of Procreation*
- 1988 — Pope John Paul II : *On the Dignity and Vocation of Women*

62

This prophetic social teaching has helped erase the notion that a Christian's relationship with God has only a vertical dimension, that faith is only something private, that the Church has no right or expertise to comment on political and economic questions. Indeed, today, perhaps like never before, we are very much involved in the drama of bringing the gospel to bear on the taken-for-grantedness of our culture. Bishop Remi DeRoo outlines this project for the Canadian Church :

> My vision is of a dynamic, healthy and hope-filled Canadian culture which, because it respects the impoverished, the helpless and the weak, is certain to respect every human person. A culture open to perspectives other than those of the powerful and wealthy ; recognizing the common links in diverse struggles ; transcending narrow self-interests and creating a genuine community. Such a culture demands a religious presence — the commitment of hearts, the conviction of dedicated action, the awareness of the human person as sacred. Privatized, passive, reactionary religion is insufficient for this cultural challenge. [1]

3. THE CULTURAL CONTEXT AND EVANGELIZATION IN THE CATHOLIC HIGH SCHOOL

The primary, universal, most fundamental principle in teaching is " to meet the students where they are at " ! It is counter-productive to begin at the third level of abstraction — even though the course outline and curriculum guideline say so — if the students have no notion at all of levels one and two. This principle applies as well to evangelization in the Catholic high school : meet the students where they are at ! Begin from there ! Don't pretend they are other than where they are ! Now the trick is to analyse and understand " where they are at. " The starting point for our evangelization, then, has to be a thorough, intensive, objective cultural, psychological, sociological and economic analysis of " the circumstances and situation " of our students. This point is sharply underscored by the 1982 Congregation for Catholic Education document, *Lay Catholics in Schools : Witnesses to Faith* :

A teacher must also be constantly attentive to the socio-cultural, economic, and political environment of the school: in the immediate area that the school is located in, and also in the region and the nation. Given today's means of communication, the national scene exerts a great influence on the local situation. Only close attention to the global reality — the local, national, and international — will provide the data needed to give the kind of formation that students need now, and to prepare them for the future that can now be predicted.

[#35]

Here again we are back to the critical importance of local experience and local analysis:

- What are the social pressures on our kids (students)?
- Generally speaking, what is the family situation of the kids in our school: traditional, latch-key, single parents, yuppie parents, abusive, rural, inner-city, suburbia?
- What are the problems in our area: drugs, crime, gangs, unemployment, industrial pollution, high percentage of welfare, exaggerated consumerism?
- Who and what are the cultural influences on the students?
- What are the obstacles that make it very difficult to evangelize, to talk about Jesus?
- What are the possibilities for the gospel — areas where the gospel can make the difference: brokenness, issues of justice and peace, charity?
- What are the attitudes that are gradually being formed by our students in this cultural environment?

The great Protestant theologian Karl Barth contended that the Christian should face each day with the Bible, the Word of God, in one hand and the newspaper, the record of the cultural, economic and political events of the day, in the other. I have always liked that bit of Barth's theology, not only because it might justify my own penchant for newspapers, but because of the power and dynamism he attributes to the gospel and the imperative he assigns to the Church and the Christian to bring that challenging and critical Word of God to bear on the unjust, non-gospel values of society. I feel that if this is part of the vocation of the Christian, it is especially an essential part of what it is to be an evangelizer in the Catholic high school. The Church, too, through the document *Lay Catholics in Schools: Witnesses to Faith*, insists on the need for Catholic educators to understand their social context so that they may better evangelize that context :

> The vocation of every Catholic educator includes the work of ongoing social development : to form men and women who will be ready to take their place in society, preparing them in such a way that they will make the kind of social commitment which will enable them to work for the improvement of social structures, making these structures more conformed to the principles of the Gospel. Thus, they will form human beings who will make human society more peaceful, fraternal, and communitarian. Today's world has tremendous problems : hunger, illiteracy and human exploitation ; sharp contrasts in the standard of living of individuals and of countries ; aggression and violence, a growing drug problem, legalization of abortion, along with many other examples of the degradation of human life. All of this demands that Catholic educators develop in themselves, and cultivate in their students, a keen social awareness and a profound sense of civic and political responsibility. The Catholic educator, in other words, must be committed to the task of forming men and women who will make the "civilization of love" a reality.
>
> [#19]

It is clear, then, that the Church has developed a very rich theology of the gospel and culture. It is also evident that the task of Catholic education is to privilege everything in our culture which is compatible with the gospel and which we can use to evangelize more effectively and to critique the elements of our culture which are obstacles to evangelization, the non-gospel values and attitudes that take hold of people making conversion impossible ; and to critique, too, the non-gospel structures that prevent the transformation of society — "the conversion of the collective consciences of people and the activities and concrete milieu which are theirs."2

There can be wonderful opportunities for evangelization for teachers in the Catholic high school who reflect together on the relationship between the gospel and culture. These are the same opportunities suggested by Martin Royackers and Ken Westhues cited in Chapter 1. Our education with a difference in the Catholic high school is to discover and present the Christ who transforms humanity, who transforms society. This can be done best by taking seriously the marvellous body of social teaching elaborated over the last two decades and making of our schools "conduits of Catholic social teaching."

We have listened to the challenge the Church presents to us : our circumstances and situation indeed must be studied and our context must be analysed if we hope to evangelize effectively. We cannot be blind and deaf to the social realities. Now, let us look briefly at some of the contextual elements of Canadian society in the 1990s. After all, this is our determined culture, place and time!

NOTES

Chapter 4

1 Bishop Remi DeRoo, *Cries of Victims — Voice of God* (Ottawa : Novalis, 1986), p. 152.

2 Pope Paul VI, *On Evangelization in the Modern World* [*Evangelii Nuntiandi*], Rome, December 8, 1974, #18.

CHAPTER 5
SOCIETY:
SOME CONSIDERATIONS
CONTEMPORARY BARRIERS TO GRACE:
OBSTACLES TO EVANGELIZATION

What happens then when the gospel encounters culture? If Christians or the evangelizers in the Catholic high school should greet each day with the Bible in one hand and the newspaper in the other, what are they likely to find? What sort of a cultural environment is it that engulfs our students and ourselves, fashioning our attitudes and tastes, influencing our behaviour and decisions in non-gospel ways? What are some of the obstacles to evangelization inherent in our social context? Page One of the January 30, 1989 *Globe and Mail* provides a typical example:

> ... Yet Mr. [Fred] Mathews [a psychologist and counsellor with Central Toronto Youth Services], who has studied the growth of gangs in Toronto and other cities, said he is not surprised that they have resorted to stealing clothes. "Adolescent culture is very expensive," he said. Roots, a chain of stores that has been a victim of gang-style thefts, sells leather jackets for between $565 and $2000 — lofty sums for most teenagers.

> In a wealthy city such as Toronto, youthful have-nots face a lot of social pressure. "Money is the root of normalcy in our society," Mr. Mathews said, adding that many teenagers feel the need to wear the latest and most expensive clothes to fit in.

> "If they don't have the money to participate in popular youth culture, they will find an alternative," he said. That alternative can sometimes be a gang, which Mr. Mathews

sardonically describes as "community economic development using unsanctioned means."

About this account of some of the trends in our society, the point should be made that these cultural values are not simply characteristics of youth culture. Youth culture reflects mainstream culture; youth culture is an offshoot of mainstream culture with adult-run corporations making millions of dollars manipulating and dictating adolescent tastes in fashion and music. In Canada today there is increasing peer pressure and social pressure; incidents of stealing and violent assaults are on the rise; money does seem to determine our ideas of status or normalcy! Check out the style and fashion on non-uniform days at school; ask about March break trips; see how easy it is for youth to come up with $40 or $50 for a concert ticket! Adolescent culture is very expensive, and consequently fraught with pressure and anxiety for the kids who can't afford it.

In some background reading on evangelization in the American Church, I recently found another description of society. While the writer, Louis J. Luzbetak, focuses on the American, middle-class, Catholic "circumstances and situation," I believe there are substantial parallels in the Canadian scene in the 1990s:

> It is sometimes said that very few Catholics leave their Church for theological reasons, a claim I personally would question. We Americans are actually swimming in heresy. I mean the heresy of secularism, materialism, hedonism, sexism, extreme personalism (i.e., nobody and nothing counts except me), scientism (i.e., an idolatrous worship of science and technology), satisfaction with a purely civil religion that neutralizes most of the Gospel, and a greedy rather than a just economic system, allowing profit to decide what should or should not be done. This is the air we breathe day in and day out in America.[1]

This desciption of the cultural context hits upon just about every "-ism" there is to hit. Yet, it is a useful description because it lists the influences, trends and ideologies that continually work on us and shape us — "the air we breathe day in and day out." The really insidious thing is that we absorb almost by osmosis much of the destructive spirit of these "-isms," even though we don't want to.

I am writing this on Ash Wednesday. The noon news on the radio just reported from the Vatican that Pope John Paul II, in his Ash Wednesday homily, exhorts all Christians to be aware of the trends and ideologies today that are dehumanizing and so exploitative and manipulative of others. I can't help but feel that this is a particularly apt Lenten exercise for evangelizers in the Catholic high school. I believe that there are four ideologies in particular that shape our North American society, our context in a decisive way, and contribute significantly to the manner in which we relate to one another, establish our system of values, and make our choices. The brief summary of each which follows is intended to stimulate some realistic personal and group reflection on our social context. There is a wealth of other material that can be enormously beneficial and instructive for such personal and communal social analysis.[2] As *The Religious Dimension of Education in a Catholic School* points out, however, ultimately "local experience must be the determining factor."

1. THE IDEOLOGY OF LIBERAL CAPITALISM

In his encyclical, *Concern for the Social Order*, Pope John Paul II contends that so much of the instability and lack of development in the world is due to the existence and the global influence of two opposing blocs governed by two opposing ideologies: the East, inspired by Marxist collectivism, and the West, inspired by liberal capitalism. It is liberal capitalism and its consequences that is our concern here. In the same encyclical and elsewhere,[3] Pope John Paul extensively analyses the limitations and abuses inherent in liberal capitalist ideology:

- an ideology which gives priority
  — to profit over people,
  — to capital over labour,
  — to the wants of the rich over the needs of the poor;
- an ideology based on the principle of survival of the fittest, consequently leaving the weak, the marginalized, the victims, by the wayside.

It is imperative for us evangelizers in the Catholic high school to be aware of the dominant ideology of our society because, like it or not, it works on us, molds us and conditions us. To be sure, it is not easy for us to be aware. First of all, most of us are doing quite well, thank you. Why rock the boat? Secondly, as a people, we haven't really developed "a critical sense." We simply take for granted that "this is the way it is," and "it is not so bad! It sure beats the other system: you sure wouldn't want to live in Russia, would you?"

But maybe it is worse than we think! It is not necessary to go into an elaborate analysis of capitalism and free enterprise and individual initiative. Let's just consider briefly some of the consequences of liberal capitalism, the dominant ideology of our society.

a) CONSUMERISM

Consider two commentaries on consumerism as it is perceived by two markedly different sources.

*From the *Toronto Star*, January 27, 1989 (p. 19):

> [headline] **Baby boomers' kids "enthusiastic consumers" pollster says**
>
> [Emphasis added.] Today's 15- to 24-year-olds, already "enthusiastic consumers," will become even bigger spenders in the 1990s, Environics Research Group Inc. said in a statement yesterday.
>
> The pollster says *youths are driven by pleasure-seeking desire to explore and try new things.* At the same time they are struggling to assert themselves while they search for an identity.
>
> They are *buying things "almost compulsively,"* sometimes just for the pleasure that it gives, rather than to satisfy a real product need. "In this regard, *young people are on the cutting edge of a trend that is pushing all of society towards materialism.*"
>
> Environics said young people will be *buying things that "make a personal statement about themselves,"* in an effort to project *the right image to their friends.* As a result, many of the things they buy might be *expensive and trendy*, but *not rational.*

*Pope John Paul II:

> [Emphasis added.] There is a form of *superdevelopment*, which consists in an excessive availability of every kind of material goods for the benefit of certain social groups; this superdevelopment easily makes people *slaves of "possession,"* and of *immediate gratification....* This is the so-called civilization of "consumption" or *"consumerism"*, which involves so much "throwing away" and *"waste"....* All of us experience firsthand the sad effects of this *blind submission* to pure consumerism: in the first place *a crass materialism*, and at the same time a *radical dissatisfaction*, because one quickly learns — unless one is shielded from

the flood of publicity and the ceaseless and tempting offers of products — that *the more one possesses the more one wants*, while deeper aspirations remain unsatisfied and perhaps even stifled.[4]

So much valuable critique is contained in pope John Paul II's idea of superdevelopment. It is an important passage to reflect on personally; to use as a mirror for one's own teaching; to present to our students. "We are what we possess" — "immediate gratification" — an advertising industry based on the creation of artificial needs, making people into things and things into people!

* * * * * * * * *

b) GREED

Greed reigns now as the engine for our economic system, as the working principle for living in our society. Evaluate the different understandings of greed illustrated in the following texts.

*From the *Toronto Star*, June 25, 1986 (p. 1):

[headline] **Learn to be greedy, minister urges natives**

[Emphasis added.] Native Canadians should try to be economically self-sufficient — *even greedy* — if they want to govern themselves, says Barbara McDougall, minister of state for finance.

"There's one underlying motive in business shared by all — it's greed, " McDougall said at the Native Business Summit in Toronto yesterday. *"There's nothing wrong with that. We support it* wherever it happens, " she added.

* *Webster's New World Dictionary*:

greed - n. excessive desire for acquiring or having; desire for more than one needs or deserves; greediness; avarice; cupidity.

*From the *Globe and Mail*, January 15, 1988 [p. 9]:

[headline] **Greed thriving on campus, study finds**

[Emphasis added.] New York — A record three-quarters of U.S. college freshmen feel that *being financially well off is an "essential" or "very important" goal*, a recent survey shows. At the same time, the *lowest proportion of freshmen in 20 years, 39 per cent, put great emphasis on developing a meaningful philosophy of life.* And the number of freshmen saying that a key reason for their decision to attend college was *"to make more money"* has reached a new high of 71 per cent.

"Despite *Newsweek's* announcement that greed is dead, our data show that it is alive and well," said Alexander Astin, director of the 22nd annual survey of entering freshmen.

"Students still tend *to see their life being dependent on affluence* and *are not inclined to be reflective,"* Mr. Astin said. "Our data confirm the *decline in interest in existential questions."*

Being well off financially was identified as a key goal by a record 76 per cent of freshmen, up from 73 per cent the previous year and nearly *double the level of 39 per cent in 1970.* Mr. Astin noted that it is unusual to see a trend continue unchanged, as this one has, for so long a period. *"Obviously,"* he said, "we are seeing something very profound in the society."

*From the Gospel according to Luke, 12:13-21 *(The New Jerusalem Bible)* :

On Hoarding Possessions

[Emphasis added.] A man in the crowd said to him, "Master, tell my brother to give me a share of our inheritance!" He said to him, "My friend, who appointed me your judge, or the arbitrator of your claims?" Then he said to them, "Watch and be on your *guard against avarice of any kind, for life does not consist in possessions, even when people have more than they need."*

Then he told them a parable, "There was once a rich man who, having had a good harvest from his land, thought to himself, 'What am I to do? I have not enough room to store my crops.' Then he said, 'This is what I will do: I will pull down my barns and build bigger ones, and store all my grain and my goods in them, and I will say to my soul: My soul, you have plenty of good things laid by for many years to come; take things easy, eat, drink, have a good time.' But God said to him, *'Fool! This very night the demand will be made for your soul;* and this hoard of yours, whose will it be then?' *So it is when people store up treasure for themselves instead of becoming rich in the sight of God. "*

* * * * * * * * *

c) COMPETITION AND VIOLENCE

Competition is at the heart of the free enterprise system, but in our society today competition is running wild, and people are being exploited and dehumanized because of it. Merely consider the high school and the emphasis some of us place — and some of the students place — on grades. In fact, how much of the entire education system revolves around competition!

"Survival of the fittest" and "rugged individualism" — these notions are promoted by the liberal capitalist ideology and together give birth to the "best and brightest" and "we're Number One!" ideals which permeate the business, sports and social life of our country. But where does that leave the less gifted, the handicapped, the worker who makes minimum wage, or the unemployed? It becomes more and more obvious that ours is not a classless society!

It is only logical that a society whose economy depends so much on militarism (the arms and weapons industrial complex of the United States; Canada participating by way of branch plants and now more integrally through free trade) is bound to beget violence! And increasingly we see violence as a consequence of liberal capitalist ideology.

A recent poll in the United States, taken to ascertain the great concerns of American citizens, showed that "personal safety," not health or standard of living, was the first and fundamental concern.

A commercial for the U.S. Army on an American television channel promotes a three or four-year military hitch as the ideal formation to enter into the white collar world of business: assaulting walls, storming buildings with M16s and AK-47s and plotting trajectories of missiles are the skills and strategies that will make one a successful broker or entrepreneur!

And now our bankers and politicians have become sensitive to the international debt crisis and the possibility of default on the part of some Third World countries. Here especially we see the institutionalized violence of international capitalism: millions of the poor in our world suffer cutbacks in social spending while their governments try to service merely the interest on their foreign debt. Yet if one looks back to the early '70s, our Western bankers were queuing up to loan big sums of money to these countries because of greed — the "get rich quick" possibilities loans offered them, because of immediate gratification. But in the long term: millions suffer, the gap between rich and poor widens, and bankers are frightened as they begin to realize the fragility of the system they have been instrumental in creating.

What about the ecological or environmental violence our system has produced? The ecosystem is threatened by the systematic deforestation and industrialization of the Amazon rain forest (an operation supported by Brazil's government to generate wealth to pay their foreign debt!). And the violence to our air, and to lakes caused by acid rain? And the ultimate violence threatening us constantly in nuclear waste and the ever-increasing potential for a nuclear accident?

It would seem, from observing the statistical evidence over the years, that our Canadian system allows for a five to twenty percent unemployment margin. Alternative strategies based on zero percent unemployment could be adopted, but the understanding between the private sector and politicians continues to allow for a significant number of Canadians to experience the violence of unemployment, a violence manifested in: the loss of personal dignity, family violence and breakdown, enormous emotional stress and strain, increased reliance on alcohol, and at times the ulimate personal tragedy of suicide. But we as a society have institutionalized unemployment!

Bishop Remi DeRoo:

> So prevalent and integral are violence and competition to our culture that they characterize our educational system, our television entertainment and our sports. Only the fittest deserve to survive. We have to be Number One. Christians believe there is another way: that security is not a matter of grasping but of sharing; that courage consists not in killing but in dying for others; that power is not the ability to exploit but the love strong enough to overcome death.[5]

* * * * * * * * *

2. THE IDEOLOGY OF INDIVIDUALISM

In the first unit of the senior theology course that I have been teaching (on marriage-family-vocation — social critique from the gospel point of view), there is a point where I attempt to get the students to stand outside of their own experience, their own social and cultural world, and try to look at the foundations on which our entire social project rests. I say "attempt" because such an abstract exercise often proves to be too discombobulating an experience for these adolescent wizards, products of the computer age! By means of documentation, personal research, and some rather deft classroom teaching on the part of the teacher, Max Weber's idea of the relationship between Protestantism and capitalism is looked at; that is, the notion that a Calvinistic theology and value system were the stuff out of which capitalism could both function and continue to be justified. As a consequence, it was not unusual to end up with a basically religious value system (the Judeo-Christian tradition) undergirding, legitimizing and serving as the ethical framework for a basically capitalist society.

There were two points to this exercise: to demonstrate the key role ideas and ideals play as a foundation for a social system; and to demonstrate that insofar as people in a society continue to be conscious of and remain rooted in their foundational ideals, drawing energy, inspiration and meaning from them, the social project will work reasonably well. The desired outcome of these discussions was to discover that the social and cultural foundations we were examining — our own social world, once firmly rooted in Judeo-Christian values, now seemed to be crumbling; that religion and those Judeo-Christian values did not appear to be very relevant for most of the people in our society.

Yet, the taken-for-granted assumption on the part of our society seems to be that our core values and ideals still obtain. But secularization has done much to distance people in our society from the ideals that have given our society focus and meaning. Those ideals find their source in Judeo-Christian values, yet most of us don't understand the values well enough for them to be meaningful or for these values to draw us into any deep ethical commitment. There is no common vision any more, no common values that we share; hence an explanation for the social, cultural and moral crisis we now experience.

Indeed, ours is a society that is inexorably breaking away from the historical and moral moorings of the Judeo-Christian ethic. Quickly taking the place of these traditional religious values is the ideology of individualism. I believe that it would be quite irresponsible for anyone engaged in evangelization in Canada today to work away at it without at the same time becoming more and more conscious of the destructive potential of exaggerated individualism which so permeates our contemporary social and cultural life.

In *Habits of the Heart — Individualism and Commitment in*

American Life, the American sociologist Robert Bellah and a team of researchers describe the impact of individualism on the American "character" and present us with a fix on the social, cultural and moral health of American society.[6] This is a critically important study for any cultural analysis of English-speaking North American society today. Let us reflect for a moment on individualism as an ideology by briefly referring to some of Bellah's findings.

There is a healthy individualism and a destructive individualism. Bellah locates healthy individualism in the "biblical" and "republican" traditions which served as the matrix for American cultural life. Such individualism has a strong ethical component; there is individual freedom, but it is a freedom tempered by a genuine feeling for the common good and a strong sense of social responsibility. The more destructive individualism, on the contrary, which Bellah contends is growing like a cancer in our society, is in the process of corroding our moral standards and eroding our "meaning" system! Unhealthy individualism can be "utilitarian" or "expressive." Utilitarian individualism sees life as an effort to maximize self-interest, often competitively with others; it promotes ambition and self-improvement unreasonably; and it privileges a private accumulation of wealth and status over any responsibility towards one's community or society. Expressive individualism is another strain of negative individualism. Here the accent is purely on "the self" — personal fulfillment at any cost, self-realization, a selfishness seen as a good in itself, a natural thing, much as greed is now seen as normative in society.

It is, according to Bellah, utilitarian and expressive individualism that is all pervasive and influential in our context today. This pernicious individualism, completely at odds with the gospel and evangelization, is gradually chipping away at the moral foundations of society and breaking down any sense of shared vision and common purpose we may have. Community, or a sense of shared history and common meaning, are essential for a people to sustain social and cultural life. But Bellah contends that for those in the grips of ideological individualism, the "lifestyle" concept supplants the ideal of community. In "lifestyle," it is a person's private life that is important; the private goals of consumption and leisurely living are prioritized; the search for the separate self, self-reliance and personal happiness are the ideals that set the parameters of involvement and give focus to one's life. Community, on the other hand, has to do with sharing and interdependence; community demands the integration of the public and private spheres; community means social responsibility, a sense of commitment to and obligations for persons and reality beyond oneself.

76

Bellah traces the results of individualism on love and marriage. An expressive individualism tends to downplay all forms of obligation and commitment in relationships, replacing them with "self-realization" — "I look for a partner who will help me be me." Here we have the maximization of one's own interests; it is a "give to get" model of relating, where one cunningly and selfishly calculates the "cost and benefits."

Over and against this individualism are those who opt to live their lives out of the "community of memory" tradition: there will be personal costs, sacrifice, pain, hurt and loss inherent in the marriage relationship. Freedom is realized in and with the other; the self is actually discovered in community and completed in what one is able to constructively contribute to community; sharing life becomes sharing history — the past with its traditions, values and especially meaning; a future that will be created through the telling of the common story, thereby using the hopes and fears, sins and graces, vision and values as the building blocks for social and cultural development.

It is worthwhile to listen to Robert Bellah and his associates. They invite us to shake off the selfish individualism so characteristic of our contemporary social and cultural life and to repossess and indeed create anew values such as interdependence, solidarity and commitment as the new foundation for the social project we call North American culture. This is a vision that is profoundly steeped in the gospel vision and gospel values. This critique is invaluable for evangelizing today; this proposal can be the agenda for evangelizing today.

[Emphasis added.] Yet we still have the capacity to reconsider the course upon which we are embarked. *The morally concerned social movement, informed by republican and biblical sentiments, has stood us in good stead in the past and may still do so again.* But we have never before faced a situation that called our deepest assumptions so radically into question. *Our problems today are not just political. They are moral and have to do with the meaning of life. We have assumed that, as long as economic growth continued, we could leave all else to the private sphere. Now that economic growth is faltering and the moral ecology on which we have tacitly depended is in disarray, we are beginning to understand that our common life requires more than an exclusive concern for material accumulation.*

Perhaps life is not a race whose only goal is being foremost. Perhaps true felicity does not lie in continually outgoing the next before. Perhaps the truth lies in what most of the world outside the modern West has always believed, namely that there are practices of life, good in themselves, that are inherently fulfilling. Perhaps work that is intrinsically rewarding is better for human beings than work that is only extrinsically rewarded. Perhaps enduring commitment to those we love and civic friendship toward our fellow citizens are preferable to restless competition and anxious self-defence. *Perhaps common worship, in which we express our gratitude and wonder in the face of the mystery of being itself, is the most important thing of all.* If so, we will have to change our lives and begin to remember what we have been happier to forget.[7]

3. THE IDEOLOGY OF RELATIVISM

In his book, *The Closing of the American Mind*, Allan Bloom remarks: "There is one thing a professor can be absolutely certain of, almost every student entering university believes or says he believes that truth is relative."[8] I think Allan Bloom is right.

I was disturbed to hear a fairly recent class of OAC students react to my description of the honour system which was *de rigueur* in Catholic high schools and universities just three decades ago. The code was a rather simple one: the teacher or professor would distribute the exam, clarify some of the questions and leave the room, returning at the end of two hours to collect the exams. The students would write the exam. Cheating — crib notes, looking sideways or over shoulders, whispering answers — did occur, but it is my impression that it was not nearly so widespread. There was a common understanding that cheating was wrong. There was the added "spiritual" factor of sin and personal guilt and the social outcast factor of "being considered a cheater" that allowed the honour code to work. To this phenomenon my students were incredulous. "No way that would work today." "One person would cheat. Then the next person would have to cheat to compete," to get marks, to get into university, to get a job! The disturbing thing about the reaction of these students is the attitude: "Everybody does it! Nothing is the matter with it! The only thing wrong about it is getting caught!"

In this prevalent attitude, realities such as "the good," "truth," "values," are no longer determined by an objective good or by an agreed-upon code of ethics, but rather by personal decision. Honesty and truth are victimized by the ideology of relativism.

A thoughtful reading of the newspaper confirms how all-pervasive the "truth is relative," "cheat to compete" reflexes are in our society. Consider the following items gleaned from a week's reading.

- Judicial inquiry uncovers layer upon layer of cheating in sports — weight lifting, track and field.
- U.S. colleges under investigation for altering grades, paying athletes.
- MPs investigated for fraud, accepting payoffs, promising contracts. One MP jailed.
- Former premier under investigation for insider trading.
- Insider trading shakes stock exchanges in New York and Vancouver.
- Literary critic accused of plagiarism.
- Toronto term paper writing firm raided by police.
- One fourth of Canadians cheat Revenue Canada in income tax returns (more than $5 billion a year, enough to pay for a complete federal day-care program).

In all of this the values of honesty and truth give way to such personal goals as getting ahead, win at any cost, unfettered pursuit of wealth and status. And what is the rationale for these goals, for the relativization of truth? Most often heard are the following: the need for high marks to get into university; the need to win a gold medal for Canada (not to mention the personal wealth from commercial contracts that inevitably accompany a gold medal); "everyone is doing it!" There is so much social pressure to keep up with others (e.g., a teenager stealing an expensive leather jacket or an MBA graduate cheating a client to purchase a BMW), and so much personal pressure to compete and win, and the need to stay in business and advance in business since business is a rat race.

On close examination it is clear that much of the ideology of relativism finds its source in greed and expressive individualism. And all of this unfortunately is a significant dimension of the context in which we evangelize, the very context we are called to evangelize.

4. IDEOLOGICAL HOPELESSNESS AND HELPLESSNESS

Ideology can be defined as "the manner or content of thinking characteristic of an individual or class" *(Webster's New Collegiate Dictionary)*. Under this rubric, then, it is entirely appropriate to label the widespread sense of hopelessness and overwhelming feeling of helplessness characteristic of our time and place as ideological. One encounters this resignation to the way things are even among the young. For more than a few it is inevitable that humanity has a date with the nuclear meltdown!

It is too bad, really, that many students are so cynical so soon. It is even more sad that we as adults too often fail to use the developing years of adolescence to share ideals and a vision of the way things might be, and to foster attitudes of stewardship and commitment for our world and society. I guess it is because we, too, in the face of it all — the consumerism and greed, the competition and violence, the rampant individualism and the breakdown of honesty — tend to throw up our hands and utter collectively: "What's the use? It's all so futile anyways!" In other words, we have bought into the ideology of hopelessness and helplessness.

Yet the object of this bit of critical social analysis is certainly not to measure how thoroughly depressed we all can become in the face of so much of the evil structured into our social and cultural context. The object, rather, is to understand society so that in the Catholic high school we can become better instruments of evangelization. It is important to remember our first reflection on evangelization in Chapter 2: evangelizing and being evangelized must cost! Bringing the gospel to bear on society is going to mean obstacles and setbacks, being misunderstood and rejected, failing and having to start over again. There is some excellent theology in a paragraph from *Lay Catholics in Schools: Witnesses to Faith* that illuminates in a realistic way the struggle that is part and parcel of evangelizing in our contemporary society:

> The identity of the lay Catholic educator is, of necessity, an ideal: innumerable obstacles stand in the way of its accomplishment. Some are the result of one's own personal situation; others are due to deficiencies in the school and in society; all of them have their strongest effect on children and young people. Identity crisis, loss of trust in social structures, the resulting insecurity and loss of any personal convictions, the contagion of a progressive secularization of society, loss of the proper concept of authority and lack of a proper use of freedom — these are only a few of the multitude of difficulties which, in varying degrees, according to the diverse cultures and the different countries, the adolescents and young people of today bring to the Catholic

educator. Moreover, the lay state in which the teacher lives is itself seriously threatened by crises in the family and in the world of labour.

[#26]

This is very much a realistic assessment of the struggle that is ours as evangelizers in the Catholic high school. It is consistent with the analysis we have been engaged in throughout this chapter. But realism here does not end in hopelessness or helplessness. Rather, it beckons us to deeper hope. It invites us to accept the fact that evangelizing must cost, because sharing in the mystery of the cross is the very heart of evangelization:

> These present difficulties should be realistically recognized. But they should, at the same time, be viewed and confronted with a healthy optimism, and with the forceful courage that Christian hope and a sharing in the mystery of the cross demand of all believers.

[#26]

This is a gentle reminder that to profess Jesus as Lord and to follow Jesus as evangelizers do not allow for hopelessness and helplessness! A more stern critique of the fruits of hopelessness — despair, pessimism, inertia — comes from Pope John Paul II in his encyclical *Concern for the Social Order*. Throughout the encyclical, Pope John Paul analyses the global context, the ever-widening gap between the rich and the poor, the underdevelopment of the poor and the super-development of the rich. He attacks head-on the paralysis that can grip us, rendering us useless because of fear and indecision. Not mincing any words, he calls this paralysis of fear "cowardice." John Paul II's diagnosis has it that global health is in serious, approaching critical, condition. Echoing Pope Paul VI, he urges us to creatively and energetically use the last decade of the second millennium to work at justice and peace. And speaking in a particular way to the women and men of our place and time, the affluent North, he underscores the responsibility that "rests on those who have more and can do more":

> [Emphasis added.] There is no justification then for *despair* or *pessimism* or *inertia*. Though it be with sorrow, it must be said that just as one may sin through selfishness and the desire for excessive profit and power, *one may also be found wanting* with regard to the urgent needs of multitudes of human beings submerged in conditions of underdevelopment, *through fear, indecision* and basically through *cowardice*. We are all called, indeed *obliged*, to

81

face the tremendous challenge of the last decade of the
second Millennium, also because the present dangers
threaten everyone: a world economic crisis, a war without
frontiers, without winners or losers. In the face of such a
threat, the distinction between rich individuals and countries and poor individuals and countries will have little value
except that *a greater responsibility rests on those who have
more and can do more.*

[#47]

CONTEMPORARY INVITATIONS TO GRACE: SIGNS OF HOPE FOR EVANGELIZATION

But the evil structured into so many of our contemporary systems
and patterns of relating is more than balanced by grace, by very tangible signs of God's presence in the world. And if, as Christians and evangelizers, we have a duty to critique the evil, the non-gospel structures
and activities of our time and place, by the same token we have the
duty to affirm: to say "yes" to what God is saying "yes" to in our
world; to use these gracious moments and movements when the
gospel encounters these grace-full elements of our culture! What are we
likely to find — that surprises us and affirms us — greeting each day
with the Bible in one hand and the newspaper in the other?

*From the *Toronto Star*, February 10, 1989:

[headline] **Empire Club hears outspoken teenagers**

Four high school students had the attention of Conrad
Black, John Craig Eaton and heads of schools and banks
yesterday....

It was the first time the 86-year-old Empire Club of Canada had been addressed by young people. "We haven't
heard these insights before at the Empire Club," the director Angus Scott said.

The two young men and two young women, all top students with backgrounds in debating, said they are worried
about the Brazilian rainforest, pollution, street gangs in
Toronto, poverty, guns and not having any real heroes.

"Here in this room we have some of the most powerful
movers and shakers of our nation," said Jane Park, 17, of

Martingrove Collegiate.

"We hope that you are concerned about the kind of world you are leaving us.... Presently we might very well be on the verge of a moral, social, environmental, economic and political world crisis. Everything is interconnected," she said, "like Brazil's rainforests and debt."

"Street kids and violent gangs are new and mainly a product of our generation," said 18-year-old Cynthia Godsoe. "Why is this happening to us? Why are so many young people, 14,000 to 18,000 in Metro Toronto alone, on the streets in a society that is richer than ever?"

And what, pray tell, is the good news, the sign of hope in this otherwise dreary picture of the world? There are really several very positive aspects connected to this event.

1. The quality of insight and the significant depth of their analysis. There are students in our schools capable of making this same analysis, seeing the interconnectedness of things, recognizing that it is a global problem.

2. The fact that the analysis is being made at all! We are beginning to agree that there are problems! Recognizing the problem and talking about it is the necessary first step towards a solution.

3. The inclusion of the "moral" nature of the present social, economic problem.

4. The challenging, "upsetting," almost prophetic dimension of the analysis of these young people given to a crowd much more at home with profit.

5. The assessment that consumerism and greed are not the answer: ours is "a society richer than ever," but resulting in more and more people deprived, on the moral and material margins of society.

There are indeed many signs of hope present in our social and cultural context. Discernement is called for to recognize God's presence today and the possibilities these moments and events present to us for evangelization. What are some of these signs of gracious presence in our contemporary social and cultural context?

Solidarity and Interdependence

In the encyclical *Concern for the Social Order*, Pope John Paul

II notes that, even though conflict and division seem to be the dominant traits of global society, there is also very much present:

> The conviction of a radical interdependence and consequently of the need for solidarity which will take up interdependence and transfer it to the moral plane. Today perhaps more than in the past, people are realizing that they are linked together by a common destiny, which is to be constructed together, if catastrophe for all is to be avoided.
>
> [#26]

This is the sense of interdependence the four high school students bring to the Empire Club! Signs of solidarity are abundantly evident elsewhere: the proliferation of conscientization groups focusing on peace, justice and environmental issues; the response of Canada and, more importantly, individual Canadians and groups of Canadians to the plight of peoples struck by disasters — famine, earthquakes, floods; the extraordinary commitment of many Canadians to welcome refugees and challenge our government's measures to restrict and limit this hospitality; the new sense of responsibility assumed by some of the critical role models of young people — rock stars — seen in their music and in their concerts for human rights, the unemployed, environmental causes, etc.

New Windows of Opportunity

Certainly, the relationship between the two great ideological powers is changing. Positive indications of this change are seen in the Soviet Union. Arms limitation dialogue is receiving new impetus. The global debt crisis is making the bankers of the West consider the debt relief option and the implementation of a more just global trade treaty. *Our Common Future* — a United Nations study headed by the Norwegian Prime Minister, Gro Harlem Bruntland — spells out in detail the interconnectedness of Third World poverty, the devastation of the ecosystem, and the fragile foundation of peace and security. The Bruntland report is a clarion call for a new global order which can only be achieved interdependently, through solidarity with one another — rich-poor, North-South, East-West — and a new creative solidarity of people with their environment. And the Church continues to play the role of critic and conscience: John Paul II, through his global visits and encyclicals *On Human Work* and *Concern for the Social Order*, and conferences of bishops (for example, Canadian and American) in their teaching on peace, justice and human rights.

84

The Quest and Thirst for Meaning

While most of the evidence seems to be that we are all busy in our present "circumstances and situation," creating our own gods — banks and office towers have become cathedrals; malls and shopping centres, the neighbourhood temples and churches — a contrary movement is actually underway based on the fundamental conviction that our creator is Other and Greater! A growing number of us are dissatisfied.

Negative evidence of this is the mushrooming of cults, sects, and fundamentalism; positive manifestation is seen in the growth of meditation and prayer groups, new forms of community and increased efforts at community-building in more traditional institutions such as parishes and schools, and the elaboration of counter-cultural spiritualities and lifestyles.

Quality of Life

To be genuine, any authentic quest for meaning in life today must result in action on behalf of life. The anti-abortion movement, made up of thousands of Canadians, is in the forefront in the struggle for life. In a society so prone to dehumanizing and depersonalizing by its very structures and values, a voice of conscience and prophetic critique are absolutely essential if we are to be faithful to the gospel. Right-to-life groups provide that conscience in a radical and courageous way. The sacredness of life is defended too by individuals and groups embracing the concerns of the handicapped and the elderly and the poor and the disenfranchised.

As a teacher, a religious educator, I have welcomed the "Seamless Garment theology" of Cardinal Joseph Bernardin of Chicago. The pro-life position of the Church is a consistent and comprehensive ethic of life.[9] Cardinal Bernardin acknowledges the dominance of technology in our social and economic life today, a technology that can be devastating when applied, as is all too often the case, to defence systems and militarization. Through the ever-more sophisticated development of nuclear weapons, human life and the very life of our planet are threatened. At the same time, technology, when applied to medicine and to the life sciences, has been miraculous in the care and new opportunities it provides. Yet, here too, the very technology that can promote life can also threaten life: "abortion takes life daily on a horrendous scale."[10] The position of the Church is clearly and unequivocally pro-life from womb to tomb:

> The case for a consistent ethic of life — one which stands
> for the protection of the right to life and the promotion of

the rights which enhance life from womb to tomb — manifests the positive potential of the Catholic moral and social tradition. It is both a complex and demanding tradition : it joins the humanity of the unborn infant and the humanity of the hungry; it calls for positive legal action to prevent the killing of the unborn or the aged and positive societal action to provide shelter for the homeless and education for the illiterate. [11]

The clarity, forcefulness and depth of passion in this consistent and comprehensive ethic of life is very much a gracious moment today, a moment that confers deeper quality and meaning onto the human journey.

And finally, the last federal election fought on the free trade issue raised to a new consciousness "the Canadian quality" of our social and cultural life : we are not Americans; we have a history and social quality to our national life that we do not want to lose.

* * * * * * * *

Ours is a formidable social context. The newspaper and the Word of God together reveal the barriers to grace, the obstacles to evangelization, and the invitations to grace, the signs of hope for evangelization. As evangelizers in the Catholic high school, our task is very much to take our context seriously, to work at understanding this context ourselves so that we might better offer our students the necessary skills and attitudes for understanding and interpreting our social context.

For the Church, evangelizing means bringing the Good News into all the strata of humanity. It means to work at transforming humanity, as we observed in the third meditation in Chapter 2. A sincere, honest and intelligent attempt to understand our own social context is the necessary first step to begin working at the transformation of humanity. That is why this type of social analysis is so essential for the evangelization project in the Catholic high school.

And what does this social analysis look like in practice? The next chapter proposes just such a model.

NOTES
Chapter 5

1 Louis J. Luzbetak, *Catholic Evangelization Today*, edited by Kenneth Boyack, CSP (New York: Paulist Press, 1987), p. 78.

2 Suggested resources for an analysis of the cultural context — Canada, 1990!

* Bishop Remi DeRoo, *Cries of Victims — Voice of God* (Ottawa: Novalis, 1986). A very readable and convincing expression of the Church's social teaching for the North American social, economic, political and cultural context. Some wonderful insights into the relationship of gospel and culture.

* Pope John Paul II, *Concern for the Social Order* (Sherbrooke, Quebec: Éditions Paulines, 1988). Pope John Paul II writes on the occasion of the 20th anniversary of Pope Paul VI's *On the Development of Peoples*. A global analysis concluding that there is more poverty in the world now than there was 20 years ago, and more concentration of wealth. A vigorous critique of the dominant ideologies of both superpowers: Marxist collectivism and liberal capitalism. Particularly pertinent is his analysis of "superdevelopment" (as opposed to underdevelopment) and how it makes people slaves of possessions and immediate gratification.

* Michael Czerny, SJ, and Jamie Swift, *Getting Started — On Social Analysis in Canada* (Toronto: Between the Lines, 1988). A very practical and necessary presentation on the principles and concrete application of social analysis in the Canadian context. The bias is clear, and it is gospel-coloured: to look at social problems from the point of view of the underclass.

* E. P. Sheridan. SJ, ed., *Do Justice* (Éditions Paulines and The Jesuit Centre, 1987). A comprehensive collection [1947-1986] of the significant social teaching of the Canadian Conference of Catholic Bishops.

* SARC — The Thomson Report: Recommendations of the Social

Assistance Review Committee chaired by former family court judge George Thomson (Queen's Park, Toronto: Ministry of Social Services, 1988). A thorough study of Ontario's welfare system by the SARC with 274 recommendations for improving this system. It must be significant when even financier Conrad Black joins many grass-roots community action groups in supporting its recommendations.

* John Francis Kavanaugh, *Following Christ in a Consumer Society* (Maryknoll, New York: Orbis, 1981). A penetrating critique of the anti-personal values so inherent in the dominant ideology of liberal capitalism.

* Robert N. Bellah *et al.*, *Habits of the Heart — Individualism and Commitment in American Life* (New York: Perennial Library, 1986). While this study focuses on individualism and commitment in American life, it is equally applicable to English Canadian society, since we share a common North American culture. A very readable book, invaluable for diagnosing creative individualism and ambitious, selfish individualism. Particularly apt for research into the middle-class context.

* The Word of God — the Bible! Absolutely essential: to be immersed in and challenged by the ideal that "a new creation" represents; to meet and understand the little ones, the marginalized, the weak, the victims in our world, and the Church's preferential love for them; to personally and in the Christian community encounter Jesus and his gospel.

* The newspaper — a record of the social, cultural, economic and political events that form our context. But read critically, mindful of the built-in bias of most papers and media.

3 Pope John Paul II, *On Human Work* [*Laborem Exercens*], 1981. Also refer to the Pope's homilies and speeches during his 10-day visit to Canada in 1984: *Canada: Celebrating Our Faith* (Boston: St. Paul Editions, 1985).

4 Pope John Paul II, *Concern for the Social Order* [*Sollicitudo Rei Socialis*], 1988, pp. 56-57.

5 Bishop Remi DeRoo, *Cries of Victims — Voice of God* (Ottawa: Novalis, 1986), p. 112.

6 Robert Bellah *et al.*, *Habits of the Heart — Individualism and Commitment in American Life* (New York: Perennial Library, 1986). Much of the discussion on the ideology of individualism which follows is based on this book.

7 *Ibid.*, p. 295.

8 Allan Bloom, *The Closing of the American Mind* (New York: Simon and Schuster, 1987), p. 25.

9 Cardinal Joseph Bernardin, *The Seamless Garment* (Kansas City, Missouri: National Catholic Reporter Publishing Company, 1984).

10 *Ibid.*, p. 10.

11 *Ibid.*

CHAPTER 6

A REFLECTION ON EXPERIENCE —
TEACHERS ON THE
SOCIAL CONTEXT

Question: Based on your experience and your own perception of our society, talk about the dominant social, economic and psychological forces that make evangelization so difficult.

This was the question that was framed to have teachers identify the barriers to grace in our contemporary social-cultural context. The analysis of the previous chapter is not only confirmed but brought into even sharper focus by the deftness of perception and the depth of meaning found in the unique experience of committed Catholic educators. Again, what is important for our reflection on the social context is the source of this analysis: the wisdom, the faith, the commitment — in a word, the lived experience of the reflective Catholic educator.

OBSTACLES TO EVANGELIZATION IN
CANADIAN SOCIETY

A Broad Cultural Analysis

Chairperson of English department:

> ...the whole notion of the consumer culture that the students have been fed from so many different sources... and which to a large extent they have bought! This makes it really hard. It's a very significant factor in the classroom. And the whole notion of success having nothing to do with the Christian ethic that we want to present — their ex-

90

perience is the antithesis of that: "We are what we own!" "We are what we can amass!" "We are identified by labels!" And it is a very individual notion of success, anti-Christian even — not: "How can I make this society better?"

And along with all of this, the powerlessness you sense when students start talking. For example, the economic system: "What can I do about it?" They've had no experience of what they can do about it, or they have no models presented to them, so they give in to hopelessness very quickly! Instead, they fast-track it, take courses which are going to get them ahead, which really perpetuates the cycle. They feel powerless, but they are very focused on themselves.

The background many of us came to school with — practising Catholics, an experience of religious practice, liturgy, grace before meals — so many don't seem to have that. We are starting at different points. Things — for example, religious symbolism that we could take for granted in the past — I don't think we can now!

This is excellent synopsis of the fruits of liberal capitalism, our dominant ideology. The salient points of the critique are consumerism, the operative idea of success, the depersonalization, the hopelessness. The critique is enriched by the recognition of so much religious illiteracy, a fruit itself of a society thoroughly secularized.

Principal:

I guess the fundamental principle of our society is the promotion of self-fulfilment and the politics of greed and an economy that enthrones the principle of market forces. It presents the "American Dream" in full flower, and it is pretty damn attractive to everybody, not just to the adolescent — but it sure is to the adolescent! So it is incredibly difficult to present the gospel as an attractive option. But that's the reality. I sat in a business class the other day... The question was: "What kind of budget would you need when you leave school and are out working?" The consensus: $45,000 to $50,000 a year for starters! Big Gino needed 50 thou, and I said: "That's with wife and children?" "Oh no, no! I could never do that on 50!"

This analysis adds the greed factor and elaborates further on the extent of a negative individualism. And the question, the challenge to the Catholic high school, is put very clearly: it is "incredibly difficult to present the gospel as an attractive option!"

* * * * * * * * *

A Fragmented Social Context

Religion teacher:

> I think part of the problem, too, is the "delivery." They get everything in fragments. For example, news items, analysis — unconnected piecemeal fragments! News is a prime example of that. Our kids get their data, their material, the way they experience everything, but there is a real lack of connectedness. I had my students time news clips: everything is 45 seconds, from an earthquake to a hockey game! Forty-five seconds! So the most atrocious thing has no bearing on their lives because they have the same time frame and therefore relevance as the weather or "Stars Tonight" news. No wonder there is a lack of passion. Our data delivery, communication delivery is completely piecemeal and bereft of passion. There is no central myth, nothing to integrate for them!

This is an extremely helpful insight, which underscores for our teaching and our evangelization the need for skills and techniques in media analysis and interpretation. This critique points out the lie of the ideology of relativism: that personal taste or choice alone renders a thing good or bad, true or false, important or irrelevant. The rate and flow of data will only increase in years to come. How to process it? How to discern? How to get at the necessary and important? How to present Jesus, the gospel, a world view based on beatitudes, as the centralizing myth and point of integration for our students? Again here the challenge for the Catholic high school is further defined.

* * * * * * * * *

A Consumer Society: Some Aspects

Principal:

> The materialism of our society is something that we are constantly dealing with. A concrete example would be the

kids at our school who are involved in jobs. A lot of this takes away from the school: studies and school spirit. It's frightening: the kids working up to or over 40 hours a week! Some students work up to 15 hours a week, maybe 30 percent of our kids; 5 to 7 percent of the kids work 40 or more hours a week! Also: "I need $90 Nikes!" "I need the Sun-Ice or Far West" — $280. coats that are popular now! A necessity! Or the latest CD or Doc Martens boots! How do you motivate kids to help out at St. Vincent de Paul or a soup kitchen or volunteer here or there, when their concern is to get to a part-time job because "I'm saving up for a Sony Walkman that is going to cost me $200." From the evangelization angle, to create a sharing-caring atmosphere... materialism and family brokenness challenge us daily!

Chaplain:

Competitive at what cost? Some kids are working 40 hours a week. In class from 9 to 3, work 4 to midnight. When do they have time for socialization with family or peers, extracurriculars, the academic work that is demanded? That is all part of the competitiveness that we have to challenge.

English teacher:

Success and the meaning of success — this is a huge challenge for us! There's a lot of pressure on kids: if you are "advanced," you have to strive for "enriched"! And with success comes "the image"; for example, the other night, a parent-teacher night, a mother cried in front of me. She didn't know what to do. Her son wanted three, not just one, but three Ralph Lauren shirts! The boy in Grade 11 said she didn't love him if she couldn't get three for him, and she was sobbing! And I said to myself: "What's happening here?" I felt sorry for the woman who obviously wants her child to be successful, but what a perversion "success" has become! What and where are our *values*? Ralph Lauren shirts? That 30-year-old yuppie phenomenon has hit these kids at 17. They want it all! Now!

It's all there! The materialism, competition, instant gratification, perverse meaning of success, the feeling that "I have a right" to this materialism. Feel sorry for the Ralph Lauren shirt mother, yes! But, we also need to take a hard look at ways adults consciously or unconsciously promote these values. And as teachers, in our own lives, how much critical distance is there between consumer values and gospel values, and how much creative energy do we spend sharing our ideals and critiquing the dominant ideologies?

* * * * * * * * *

Family Brokenness

Physical education teacher:

> Also the family unit or lack of family! Again, this is frightening. We have kids coming to school who are coping with family situations, brokenness, that many adults couldn't cope with. And then, you have a few kids who have to work and have a terrible home life. What a combination!

Chaplain:

> There is a real poverty in terms of family experience. Many of our kids have money, but they don't have family experience. I saw a kid give up graduation: he had a job and was going to make $30 that day. Here we have a key moment and day in the kid's life: he gives it up to make $30. The whole value system is kind of upside-down.
>
> And yet, these kids themselves know that pain! It's funny. And a lady comes to the school to ask for volunteers for a latch key program because all of the parents are working, and even though the kids see it, it isn't registering! They continue the same routine of their parents.

Religion teacher:

> Also, what we stand for and teach really challenges the way life is lived at home; for example, the permanence of marriage. Two-thirds of the class is in a second marriage family or live-in situation! We say that the ideals are valuable, but they are so challenging to their reality. Years gone by we had family support, but today the family is under siege.

Over and over again "family brokenness" surfaced as an essential element in the description of our social, cultural context. How different from a mere 25 years ago when the family was the solid lead player on the social-cultural stage, receiving support from the Church and the school. The contemporary reality is that the school is charged with many of the socializing functions formerly expected of the family. This is most evident in values and religious education, in the socialization process into our Catholic tradition, and in the nurturing, counselling, healing functions, years ago exercised in the family, but now needed because of the brokenness and violence in so much family life.

* * * * * * * * *

Insights into Individualism

French teacher:

> ...to get a hard look at our culture, it helps to get outside of it. Last summer, I spoke with some very aware people from Peru who commented on our culture from their point of view! Their conclusion: we are an extremely individualistic people, and we are dying as a culture because we have no common project.

Chairperson, religion department:

> As educators today we get caught up in bureaucratic jargon: "Be *professional!*", etc. But another one is "Realize potential!" This sounds wonderful, but what does it mean? It sort of assumes that basically education is very, very narrow and individualistic, centring on the person, and it neglects any sort of commitment "to learning itself" or any commitment to a wider community. I find a lot of that in "gifted education." I don't think I can continue in gifted education after this year. I think it is too elitist. It has its points, but the real flaw for me is "realize personal potential," and the "other" — the wider community dimension — never enters into it.

I don't know whether this French teacher or religion head has read or even heard of Robert Bellah *(Habits of the Heart)*, but both, from their own experience as Catholic educators, give flesh and meaning to Bellah's critique of individualism. Our culture is threatened by the absence of community: a shared history, a common project. And the biggest obstacle to community is the narrow individualism so characteristic of the "human potential" movement.

* * * * * * * * *

The Trivialization of Commitment

Guidance teacher:

> Look at the adult world...! I think of kids who are in and out of the guidance office all the time. One thing is for sure: it is very hard for us to hand down the faith to kids who are not living in homes where there is living faith.

> Our generation — the adult generation — we are having a very difficult time with relationships, and kids are suffering from this...! Kids talk about not wanting to spend another weekend visiting a father who has a new live-in girl friend.... How to talk about God in this?

> And in terms of relationship... so much sexual overtone in almost all of the media and all advertising.

English and drama teacher:

> Some of these kids are not on a journey: they are on a "superstrada"! They are on a highway, trying to get there as fast as they can! In a flash! The thing that scares me most is the "familiarity." In Italian we say *confidenza*! I don't think there is a word in English. It's "contemptuous familiarity!" Some kids are too familiar: too familiar with intimate relationships, too familiar with sex, too familiar with alcohol and drugs, too familiar with labelling, too familiar with so much! It stops being a dalliance and experimentation and becomes a way of living: a way of life they will carry into adult life! It is all part of this rushing-ahead thing! So much of it has to do with lack of respect! It is contemptuous familiarity! I've seen it. I've heard kids say: "I've done it! What's next?"

> I had a class of Grade 9s... They talked about premarital sex and the meaning of intimacy! Incredible! The consensus for them was that intimacy was a "right," a nice way to top off a relationship, like a *cappuccino*! It's not a commitment, not a new way of life! It's just a way to top off a night! It's this familiarity thing! Sexual immorality is really widespread. We need family life education. Grade 12 is too late! Hell! Grade 8 is too late! The stats are that 51 percent of Grade 9 kids are sexually active! So many kids are so wrongly sophisticated, so pseudo-sophisticated!

> In a hyper-consumeristic society such as ours, in which *wants* be-

come *needs* and must be satisfied "immediately," it is almost inevitable that the notion of person becomes commodified, that the "person" takes on the qualities of a "thing": "What are the things I need to make me happy, to fulfill me?" Thus, relationship becomes an exercise in selfish, expressive individualism: there is a contract of sorts, but it is based on individual wants. And of course, the idea of "permanent commitment" — with its emphasis on "the other" and characterized by its capacity to embrace pain, suffering or loss precisely because the other is valued more than the self — becomes a major casualty in society today.

The "contemptuous familiarity" behaviour is a learned reflex: young people today have more than a few role models in the adult generation who have been so thoroughly co-opted by negative individualism as to lose the sense of "the person." This is all such a clear reminder for Catholic education: this imperative to found our education on the true meaning of the person — as Image of God, brother and sister of Jesus, with the mission of stewardship in our world — and the imperative to be a creative agent, co-operating with the Holy Spirit to bring about "the new creation."

* * * * * * * * *

And Also...

It was a privilege to listen to the teachers' reflections and to be escorted through some very profound moments and experiences of evangelization by means of the sharing that takes place in such reflection groups. Their analysis of our social context was rich and varied. As clearly illustrated in these testimonies, their experience confirms that certain social and cultural obstacles to evangelization — consumerism, individualism, relativism and hopelessness / helplessness — are very entrenched in the psyches and experiences of our students. Their testimonies also identified other challenges to evangelization inherent in our social context which the search for effective methods of evangelization must take into account:

- One of the biggest problems in the social context touching our kids is alcohol.

- There is a mentality in society to deal with symptoms rather than causes. Look at the pro-abortion mentality: pregnancy is inconvenient; it's a problem; quick solution! But what about social conditions causing the problem? What about the moral understanding of life? It's not touched! It's just symptoms and easy solutions! Solve effects, not causes!

- ... The process of change tied in with technology; the rate of change; the demands it puts on us; the pressures and fears it creates — this is a huge social thing to deal with. What they say now is that our students will have seven career moves in their lifetime! And the speed of it all: they say 80 percent of those careers don't presently exist; they are to come.

- I'm concerned with the amount of sensationalism in society and how it is tied up so much with violence. A friend and colleague commented on some kids' attitude: "They would sleep through the Second Coming!" I'm convinced now that the simplicity of the gospel message and the gospel way of life has great difficulty competing with the sensationalism we are bombarded with.

- But there is an arrogance here in Ontario that I have discovered after 15 years in Atlantic Canada: we know it all! No one can teach us how it should be done ... or even how to do religion. Our system is the best. It's hard to break down that arrogance.

- In economic terms, look at the last federal election.... We see a real orientation towards business, and we have the sense of business controlling society and being where the power is.... There is a new stratification here: haves / have-nots, count / count-nots!

- Another thing that scares me — perhaps it is on a wider sociological scale, I don't know — there is a real growing trend towards small-c conservatism: of the worst kind because it comes from fear. I'm not sure where the fear comes from, but it is not conducive at all to the risk that faith requires! And sometimes it produces a superficial religiosity which to me is worse than no faith at all.

- The prevailing attitude in North American culture in which Ontario participates: the ultimate goal of life is to have no pain; to strive to live only in the comfort zone. I wouldn't say it's hedonistic pleasure in that sense, but it's the absence of any pain or suffering promoted through materialism: a false sense of belonging and attachment to possessions, even to persons. All of this puts people in a middle position! I see a society which is passionless by and large. Humanity is reduced, and as teachers, we participate in this as people in the culture! Our schools then sadly participate in this. It is very hard to do any evangelization if there is an avoidance of Good Friday Christianity... and then a false understanding of Easter Sunday Christianity.

* * * * * * * * *

One of the reasons I am so taken with the commentary of these committed Catholic teachers is that their commentary is very much grounded in experience. The analysis we attempted in the two previous chapters takes on fresh meaning when it is applied to the actual practice — the doing of evangelization in the Catholic high school. While no real answers or solutions are spelled out, certainly the difficulties and obstacles are described and clarified, and that, in itself, is the necessary first step for any attempt to strategize and propose answers and solutions.

But there is more! There is more than evil structured into our social and cultural context. There are invitations to grace and definite signs of hope.

Question: Based on your experience and your own perception of our society, talk about the elements of our social life / fabric that are positive and can be helpful in evangelization.

Here again the context was examined, but this time from the angle of the possible: what movements, trends, even ideas and social-cultural currents can we exploit on behalf of the gospel?

THE EVANGELIZING POTENTIAL
IN CANADIAN SOCIETY

Instructor of theology, faculty of education:

Another thing I see as a positive thing because of the last election and free trade: there is a new consciousness as to what is significant and good about Canadian society — for example, our social net: health care, unemployment insurance, etc. We can capitalize on this. A lot of our social net really has come out of the social gospel movement in Canada.

Guidance teacher:

> ...Focus on the possibilities in our society. There is a Canadian social life and responsibility which are part of our structure; for example, the free trade debate! We see ourselves as qualitatively different! Also, look at the numbers of volunteers in our country: agencies that work in behalf of the Third World, Canadian concerns, local community needs. There are a lot of possibilities to present to kids who come in and say, "I want to work with people!" We also have freedom — opportunity to live the *good news* — and we have incredible access to education, which puts pressure on us as to the content and the focus of the education we propose in a Catholic high school.

Religion teacher:

> Our society is starting toward integration, like bringing the retarded and handicapped into schools, and that has an effect. Kids are becoming much more tolerant. This offers us some wonderful teachable moments, and even the tough or difficult kids respond. Also, there are a lot of "helping people and organizations" — volunteers — around today. We can introduce kids to this reality.

It doesn't take much imagination or biblical scholarship to see the harmony that exists between the Sermon on the Mount and the social measures structured into our society to protect the little ones, the victims, and the poor. An awareness of this link between the gospel and the marginalized should be part and parcel of a Catholic high school education. There are models to propose and programs of action to present to our students that are definitely in contrast to the models and programs of the dominant ideology.

* * * * * * * * *

A Brokenness to be Exploited

Principal:

> What makes evangelization clear and easy? The ones who are really in need, and we have them in spades! The ones

who are down — the hurting: from family breakdown, abuse, drugs, alcohol. There are a lot more people at the bottom than at the top.

Religion teacher:

So we look at the social structures that break the family down. The flip side here is the opportunity for the pastoral side of schools to meet and tend to the broken side of humanity in our schools.... So chaplaincy teams, teachers who might volunteer, guidance departments and others are working now with kids from separated and divorced families, and there are some peer ministry efforts too that are ways of addressing so much of the negative and broken-down. And out of this come some strong leaders... who have been helped in their moment of crisis! This presence is really important — to be with kids in their brokenness. They are the victims of the negative social and cultural things we talked about.

What energy is needed to do pastoral care or chaplaincy in the Catholic high school today! What creativity is called for to elaborate an effective program: one which makes use of as many pastorally gifted teachers as possible; one that co-ordinates administration, guidance, religious education and chaplaincy; one that can wisely inspire and animate young people to minister to each other. There is so much brokenness. Consequently, there is so much need for an evangelization of compassion and healing. It is so encouraging to see the proliferation of chaplains in our schools, but unless there is energy and creativity in our pastoral care, we cannot even begin to reach those who are broken.

* * * * * * * * *

Media: An Instrument for Evangelization

English teacher:

The media: it's an elusive thing. You're always going to have these extremes: the abusive use... the constructive use! We really need to teach kids critical awareness skills: "Assess! Don't just sit! Ask questions!" Offer alternatives. Give them critical skills. Make them perceptive and aware.

Principal:

There must be a way to use media to advantage. Let's face

it! Kids are more informed now. There is more of a possibility for a social conscience. There really are extremes! I've seen kids who are much more materialistic than ever, and other kids who are much more spiritual! And I think the media bring out potential for these two extremes.

If there was ever a place for evangelization across the curriculum, media education is it. English, history, politics, screen education, music, economics and business, religious education, and there are more possibilities, I am sure. "The Bible in one hand; the newspaper in the other!" But the questions are: how to read the newspaper with an eye to sin and grace in our culture; how to critique different ideologies as they manifest themselves through the media; how to take advantage of the abundance of worthwhile television and videos that are so readily available.

* * * * * * * * *

A Consumer Society that Really Can't Deliver...

Religion teacher:

> I think another positive thing is that the consumer society really can't deliver on its promises... There are contradictions involved, and I think that people do see the idolatry of it all. This really should be a goal for our teaching: to have kids see that.

Religion teacher:

> One positive thing: there's a healty dose of skepticism kids have that can be wonderfully refreshing! And you really wish you could focus it more effectively on other things as well, like the "American dream."

Principal:

> Look at the contrast between gospel simplicity and many of the experiences kids have. The contrast is of great value. The simplicity stands out in greater relief. You know that some of the kids are searching for something simpler, something more authentic than what they see around them and the phoniness they recognize. That contrast really is a value.

"The consumer society really can't deliver on its promises" because the human person by nature is ordered to the Transcendent. Status, money, things do not give one happiness. There is so much evidence of "brokenness" and dissatisfaction, especially at that level of society where people in a material way live very comfortably. "Superdevelopment" can only make us slaves of possessions, as John Paul II has reminded us. In contrast, there is such beauty in the message of the gospel, such power in its challenge, such truth in the person of Jesus. The task of our evangelization is to nourish the nascent skepticism of youth, to have them level that skepticism at the empty promises of our consumer society, and to allow them to experience the radical simplicity of the gospel.

* * * * * * * * *

The Idea of Interdependence, the Ideal of Solidarity

Principal :

> That image of the earth the astronauts took from outer space has changed our vision of the world and humanity. It has made us recognize two things. One, people of the earth are human family — we live on the one planet, and we share, and we have to learn to live with one another. And secondly, it gives an image of a planet that is a living, breathing organism, and we can't continue to engage in a kind of gang-rape of "mother earth" as we have done for two or three hundred years. And I think kids are recognizing that. And with us, we have the impact of immigration and the multi-cultural mix of our schools. This brings home to kids that there is a multiplicity of people on earth — all one family but a variety of forms and overt features — and the kids experience it every day. This is very positive because it can help eliminate old patterns of racism and nationalism. There is a lot of potential here for evangelization.

There is a timely, almost evangelical convergence taking shape today around the notions of interdependence and solidarity. On the one hand, we have the social teaching of the Church. Since Vatican II, the Church's social teaching has been peppered through with the interdependent reality of our world : the poverty of the South is linked to the superdevelopment of the North ; the ideologies of the two superpowers have negative repercussions on the rest of the world. Solidarity, too, has been an ideal central to Pope John Paul II's thinking : a new global unity ; a new sense of global responsibility. On the other hand, from

103

many different sources in the world today, the same sentiments of, and desires for, interdependence and solidarity are manifest in movements: for a safer and saner environment; for human rights; for various justice and peace issues. Such movements received added impetus and inspiration through different aspects of popular culture such as art, cinema and music. Our evangelization efforts should take full advantage of this fortuitous convergence.

* * * * * * * * *

Public Catholic Schools in Ontario

Priest-principal:

> Living in Ontario we can forget how well off we are even in relationship to other Canadians. Another positive thing: our schools provide us with a platform from which to evangelize — a real gift in comparison with other parts of the country. And look at the resources we have: money, programs, qualified people. A huge amount of thanks is owed to religious communities who kept the high schools afloat in the hard times!

Instructor of theology, faculty of education:

> I have a friend who teaches religion in university — a former president of the Canadian Council of Churches. His own children go to public school. He has remarked how his own kids don't have the "vocabulary to talk about religious issues." That vocabulary and the ideas and ideals behind it are non-existent in the public system. They can't even ask the religious questions. So I think we are going to have secularized children, atheistic in a sense, because there is no God-talk. We are going to enter a world where our graduates should come out with some God-language as part of their normal understanding of the world. We often complain how religiously illiterate our kids are, but at least we can use religious language and ask important faith questions.

How important it is to get distance! Such a perspective — viewed from the vantage point of other provinces which do not have publicly-financed Catholic schools, or from the stance of concerned non-Catholic Christian parents who are profoundly convinced that faith education should be part and parcel of education but do not have that option — confirms again how fortunate we are and what a marvellous instrument for evangelization the Catholic high school is. It is as well a further invitation for us to use this blessing to the fullest! Not to squander it!

* * * * * * * * *

In bringing to a close this analysis of the social and cultural context in which we do Catholic secondary education in the 1990s, it is important to reiterate the need for such analysis to take place at the local level. "Local experience must be the determining factor [*The Religious Dimension of Education in a Catholic School*]." The intention here was merely to sketch some of the broad social and cultural trends that are obstacles to evangelization, and to identify a few of the possibilities for evangelization inherent in the contemporary social and cultural context. The hope is that this outline may serve as a methodological help, an idea for a point of departure for the analysis and reflection that could take place in each Catholic high school.

To conclude Part Two, let us look briefly at the Church context. We evangelize through the *Catholic* high school, so the Church, too, must be looked at as part of our context.

CHAPTER 7
THE CHURCH:
SOME CONSIDERATIONS

Catholic education is a participation in the evangelizing mission of the Church. This was the central reflection in our meditation in Chapter 2 on the links between the mandate of evangelization and the purpose of the Catholic high school. The document *The Religious Dimension of Education in a Catholic School* elaborates further on the importance of the Church for the Catholic school:

> Just as the Church is present in the school, so the school is present in the Church; this is a logical consequence of their reciprocal commitment. The Church, through which the Redemption of Christ is revealed and made operative, is where the Catholic school receives its spirit....

> ...Concretely, the educational goals of the school include a concern for the life and the problems of the Church, both local and universal.
>
> [#44]

Since the educational goals of the school should include a "concern for the life and the problems of the Church, both local and universal," it is apparent, then, that the Church contributes in a significant way to the context in which we do Catholic secondary education.

My purpose in this chapter is to propose only a few points of ecclesial analysis, as there are readily available some very important critical assessments of the relationship of Church to society and of the functioning of the Roman Catholic Church in particular.[1] My conviction is that reflection at the local level about what it is to be Church and how the Church helps or hinders evangelization in the Catholic high school is far more beneficial than any detailed analysis I might present here.

106

An individual or a small group of teachers might, for example, grapple with any number of questions to facilitate such reflection. "What three things about the Church would you change if you could?" "What are three things you would absolutely hold on to?" "When you reflect on your disappointments, where is the Church more a burden than a help in our evangelization project in the school?" "And, what is positive — what are ways in which the Church is supportive and effective in our evangelization efforts?" "At the personal level, being critical, what gifts do you bring to the Chruch?" "And how, by holding back or through indifferent participation, do you impede the Church in its mission of evangelization?"

This is a most significant type of ecclesial analysis, because if it is done in genuine communal discernment, the sharing that takes place can only encourage us in our evangelizing mission in the Catholic high school. As well, it can lead to a more profound personal ownership of faith and awareness of one's membership and commitment in the Church.

A COMMENTARY ON THREE ECCLESIAL TRENDS

A Crisis in Ministry

Thirty years ago a certain parish in downtown Toronto was staffed by four priests. Today there is one priest, in his late sixties. In any city in Ontario there are suburban parishes with four thousand or more families and two priests — if they are lucky! There are fewer priests today by far. There are comparatively few seminarians. The average age of Canadian priests is close to 60 years. There is indeed a crisis in ministry since so much of the theology of ministry has been centralized in priesthood.

Dean Hoge, a sociologist at the Catholic University of America who was commissioned by the United States Bishops' Conference to study "the priest shortage," reports on it in his very important book, *Future of Catholic Leadership*.[2] Hoge's premise is that the priest shortage has more to do with the institution than with faith. From the sociological data collected and analysed, he proposes to the leadership of the American Church 11 possible options. And of these options he privileges three in particular as being practical and viable: ordain married men, expand lay ministry and continue traditional recruitment. It is the promotion and formation of the laity, in particular, teachers in the Catholic high school, that now realistically demands our attention.

In that same downtown parish, years ago served by four priests, there are now two lay ministers. This is the positive side of the priest shortage: increasingly, ministry and Church responsibilities are now exercised by the laity. We see it in the Catholic high schools, which years ago were almost totally administered and staffed by religious — priests, sisters and brothers. Now the direction of these same schools is in the hands of the laity.

And yet, even though lay persons are assuming roles in ministry and tasks of leadership, the crisis prevails and can be seen in different ways: in the lack of training or formation of the laity; in the confusion over their roles; in the exclusion of the laity from decision-making; in the absence of leadership — the animators are not being sufficiently animated. Through the 1990s lay ministry will become even more critical if the Church is to evangelize as it is called to do. Nowhere will this be more crucial than in the Catholic high school. We will return to this question of the vocation of the teacher as minister in Chapter 12, when we consider the agenda for evangelization in the 1990s.

The Crisis in Institutional Religion

If religion is to interact effectively with culture, then it has to be able to transcend culture so that it has something to bring, and be responsive to culture, so that it knows how to bring it. If religious groups think they have nothing unique to bring to culture, then the future of religion in Canada and the modern world looks bleak.[3]

This is the conclusion of Reginald Bibby in his extraordinary 1987 study, *Fragmented Gods*. We have already seen the insidious effects that our culture — and its supporting ideologies of consumerism, greed, individualism and relativism — can have on a person's system of values. Bibby contends that religious consumerism — choose a belief here and a religious practice there to fit your own personal needs — is taking the place of integrated religious commitment. He sees the churches now — and religion — as simply mirroring contemporary culture instead of shaping and molding society and culture.

I believe that Bibby's analysis is especially relevant for many Christians who fall victim to the easy way; who want a Good Friday-less Christianity; who will pick and choose what is conducive and comforting and safe (i.e., baptizing, marrying, burying), but will avoid the difficult, the uncomfortable, the prophetic. As Christians we are called to critique our culture, to transform humanity. We compromise this critical and transforming capacity the more we are co-opted by our culture and its enticements. It is hard, but then an authentic following of Jesus must always cost. The task for the 1990s, for believers and for the Church, is willingly to pay the price for being counter-cultural.

The Privatization of Faith

In our earlier social and cultural analysis, we explored some of the aspects of unhealthy individualism: an emphasis on the self to the exclusion of the other, and very little sense of responsibility for community or the larger social project. Today in the Church we see a similar phenomenon when we consider faith: faith in Jesus for many believers is predominantly if not exclusively very much a private thing. Private believers seem to have very little desire or felt need to share faith in dialogue and prayer. They do not seem to consider active participation or involvement in the life and mission of the local Church necessary or important. Their sense of responsibility in the Church is more a personal responsibility to God rather than a responsibility for the Church itself and the Church's mission.

For private Christians, the gospel, Church teaching and practice are primarily applied to personal interior life. Consequently, it is difficult for them to appreciate either the gospel that critiques injustice and social sin, or the Church and communities of Christians that take a prophetic stance. Sensitivity to social sin usually goes hand-in-hand with appreciation for community, for being part of a community of saints and sinners and, therefore, for being accountable and responsible for the blessed common life of a people and the sinful common life of that same people.

It is easy to see how comfortable privatized faith might be with the consumer religion Reginald Bibby describes. Faith is but a discrete part of life, almost a commodity. It does not pervade the whole of life. It is not integrative! Yet, to some degree, privatized faith certainly characterizes many of us in the Church today. How do we confront that privatizing tendency in each one of us: to ignore the exigencies of the believing community, the Church, to discern together, worship together, and collaborate together in the evangelizing mission of the Church? How do we develop faith communities inviting and hospitable so this can happen? How do we effectively challenge denial of the social demands of the gospel?

A REFLECTION ON EXPERIENCE —
TEACHERS ON THE ECCLESIAL CONTEXT

Question: How do you feel we are doing regarding evangelization in the Church? As one who is at the same time a Catholic educator and member of the Church, make some "professional" assessment as to the areas in which the Church needs to be evangelized, and the ways in which the Church is effectively evangelizing.

In this reflection the idea is to bring together, in a very practical way, Pope Paul VI's theology on evangelization — "the Church is an evangelizer, but she begins by being evangelized herself" — and the theology of *The Religious Dimension of Education in a Catholic School* — "the educational goals of the school include a concern for the life and problems of the Church, both local and universal." A very efficacious and realistic way of considering this theology is to tap the faith experience of committed Christians. This will again be evident as we theologically eavesdrop on reflections that took place in the teachers' groups; this time, their analysis of the Church, the ecclesial context in which we do Catholic education in Canada in the 1990s.

The Church Begins by Being Evangelized

1. The Need for a Nourishing, Relevant Proclamation of the Word

Business and economics teacher:

> I would really change the way the homily is done. It is "bad news," not "good news" — the Word we receive in so many parishes. I moved here a year ago. I've gone from parish to parish for something to nourish me. Nothing! Why can't we have some thoughtful lay people do the homily, people who are reflective, who can communicate, who can speak to real life?

Vice-principal:

> The sacrament is fine, but the Word, the homily, this is an instrument that we don't use well. Our priest is wonderful, devout, but horrible at homilies! My kids — that's what turns them off, the homily!

Chairperson of English department:

> ... Really, what is spoken about at Mass is totally irrelevant to what is going on in the world! It has been years since I've heard about anything socially or communally we could be involved in as believers.... Instead, it is too personal and spiritual! The only really social thing is to shake hands at the sign of peace, but even this is superficial. We could do that if we got involved with others as believers in some social action, but there is no impetus, no leadership to urge that.

The Church is so divorced from our experience in this society. The gospel should be a leaven for us, but it isn't.

Guidance teacher:

> But where does adult faith formation happen today? Very little in the parish. Mine happens with friends... other people on staff. And then look at us! How are Catholic teachers going to be evangelized? We need a model, but I don't see it coming from our clergy and the Sunday preaching. Most of the time I feel an amazing amount of condescension: someone is talking to me as though I am of very minimal intelligence with even more minimal interest and almost total irrelevance.

Principal:

> But where the Church does a bad job is in educating adults, developing the faith of adults. There has to be another model! I have trouble with autocratic structures in education. I have trouble with them in the Church. The model — it's where people own the Church, own their faith. People have to participate, not observe. How do we get them to participate?

> Evangelization is not going to work in the school unless the staff is evangelized. It won't work in the parish unless people are evangelized. To go out to the unchurched you need evangelization yourself.

This widespread disenchantment with preaching in the Church is consistent with my experience with other Catholic educators and groups of adults over the last 20 years. Yet, as Pope Paul VI remarks, proclamation is at the heart of evangelization:

> The Good News proclaimed by the witness of life sooner or later has to be proclaimed by the word of life. There is no true evangelization if the name, the teaching, the life, the promises, the Kingdom and the mystery of Jesus of Nazareth, the Son of God, are not proclaimed.
>
> [E.N., #22]

The truth of the matter is that as Church, in that valued and privileged moment of our Sunday worship, the liturgy of the Word, we fall well short in the ministry of proclamation. For too many believers in too many instances, the Word is not leaven. Homilies fail to nourish! Unfortunately, in more than a few cases, the homily actually frustrates.

What a wasted opportunity!

I have often heard priests, parents, teachers and trustees debate and discuss the ways and means of how the parish might be more influential in the school. Usually, people tend to agree on "presence" — the priest should visit the school and spend time with the staff. Now, I don't doubt the wisdom and importance of such a strategy. But after hearing lay people, and Catholic teachers in particular, talk about their faith and their need for faith nourishment, I can't help but conclude that well-prepared, relevant, sincere Sunday preaching is much more important. "The evangelizers must be evangelized!" And it is Sunday Eucharist that is the primary source of faith nourishment for the majority of women and men in our Catholic schools. To experience the gospel, to have one's life critiqued and healed, challenged and consoled by the gospel message, to have the proclamation of the Word serve as a focus — all of this can be wonderfully nourishing for the faith life of Catholic teachers, and can only render more relevant the evangelization these women and men are engaged inin the Catholic high school. Regrettably, in too many instances, this does not happen. "The Church begins by being evangelized herself."

* * * * * * * * *

2. The Inconsistency of Words and Actions

Chaplain:

> I see lay people now having more to do in ministry. This is good! More inroads have to be made into the clerical stronghold. But where lay people are excluded you can see the frustration. These people will leave a parish where there is no life or possibility for growth!

Physical education teacher:

> I'm not sure that the clergy today understand that the adult population is much more highly educated than in years gone by. Also, women: we are more than 51 percent of the population. Our experience is different from the male, but we are excluded from so much! There is a lot of confusion and tension and pain for women, and as a woman Catholic teacher I have to evangelize. But it is a little difficult to do that with the Church's record on women.

112

Vice-principal:

> I agree: the message is right! Jesus and the gospel! But as Church there is confusion! There are mixed messages. For example: social justice and the social teaching of the Church! We are becoming more conscious of that, and yet we see injustice within the Church. For example, we can't have altar girls; the role of women in the Church has been far too limited, and that is regarded by many as an injustice. So the Church sends out a mixed message. And it is far more difficult in a democratic society. We just don't pay attention if we haven't had a say. And we aren't being listened to.

The premise for this discussion on the ecclesial context for our evangelization in the Catholic high school is that we are the Church and that we have all received the mandate to evangelize:

> ... the whole Church receives the mission to evangelize, and the work of each individual member is important for the whole.
>
> [E.N., #15]

The critique rendered by the teachers is very much in the spirit of an owned faith, a sense of responsibility for our evangelizing mission. Their love and respect for the Church is clear and unequivocal. Their anxiety and frustration, however, have to do with "the way" we are Church. There are apparent inconsistencies. To a person, each had nothing but admiration for the prophetic, counter-cultural social teaching of the Church elaborated since Vatican II.

But in certain areas, such as the situation of women and the inclusion of the laity, the actions and practice of the Church do not ring true with its own teaching. The above testimony of the physical education teacher and the vice-principal is very much to the point. There is much pain and frustration. Some women in the Church experience this acutely. What impact has Pope John Paul II's *On the Dignity and Vocation of Women* had on some of the male, clerical mentality that produces guidelines and instructions and makes the decisions in Church offices and parishes? And this mentality, centuries in the making, unfortunately crosses gender lines. There are some women co-opted by the male, clerical mentality who tend to look at governing in the Church and leading in worship in the Church as something intrinsically masculine.

What is inconsistent in such a mentality, indeed, what may be

113

sinful about it — sexism is a sin — is that the feminine dimension to life is either undervalued or totally ignored. The inexhaustible potential for good in the feminine dimension that should be counted on in ministry, in decision-making and in prayer and worship, is hardly tapped. Consequently, the mission of the Church to evangelize is deprived of much wisdom, energy and talent.

Such inconsistencies make it more difficult to evangelize. "The Church begins by being evangelized herself."

* * * * * * * * *

3. An Ineffective Reading of the Signs of the Times

Religion teacher:

> What would I change? First, the power structure of the Church. Allow lay people with gifts to get responsibly involved.

Guidance teacher:

> I guess our most common experience of Church is the parish. Here so much depends on the priest, and I agree: there is too much irrelevance and too much mediocrity to preaching. But on the other hand, look at the enlightened social teaching of Pope John Paul II: the recent encyclical *Concern for the Social Order*, for example. It doesn't filter down to us. Similarly, some of the documents of the Canadian bishops... very prophetic! I've heard this from people from outside Canada! But it doesn't filter down.

Principal:

> The Church lags in keeping up with society. A problem is that so many of us older Catholics were expected to be passive. It's tough to break out of that attitude. Society has changed so much that the Church really is no longer a vital part of people's lives anymore! Is it a part of young people's lives? I don't see many in their twenties at Mass! I say, "Thank God for Catholic schools! Where would kids get any contact with faith without them?"

Religion teacher:

> People will turn off the institutional church if it continues to speak a language of power. It will become irrelevant in peo-

114

ple's lives. But if "the servant Church ideal" comes through, it will really speak to people because it is grace, it is gospel, it is genuine. A church that lacks humility poses an enormous credibility problem for Church. And so, if there is arrogance and condescension in our parishes with the preaching, it will turn people off.

Again, in these varied reflections, the issue is not "What's wrong with the Church?" but "What is wrong with the way we are Church?" Surely it is a question of implementation. So much of the theology is in place: the empowering of the laity (refer to Pope John Paul II's 1989 apostolic exhortation, *Vocation and Mission of the Lay Faithful* [*Christifideles Laicii*]); the Church's teaching on justice and peace issues; a renewed theology of ministry based on collaboration; the invitation to read the signs of the times and dialogue with our social and cultural context! But it is not filtering down, and in many cases the lived faith experience at the base is not percolating up. "The Church begins by being evangelized herself."

* * * * * * * * *

The Church Is an Evangelizer

1. The Beauty, the Simplicity, the Power of the "Message"

English teacher:

> The Church does a good job basically because of the message — Jesus and the gospel.

Physical education teacher:

> There are some positive parish experiences.... My parish experience is very positive.... The homilies have been nourishing for me, but then, I feel very fortunate! I know what the others mean.

Vice-principal:

> One very positive thing is the Church's affirmation of the elderly... [and its presence in] dying and grieving. I go to a non-Catholic funeral: it is so empty! Void! I go to a Catholic funeral, and I feel different. There is faith and celebration and affirmation.

Voice from group:

... but please, dear God, let us not have to wait for death to meet the best of Catholicism!

Religion teacher:

> What's hopeful about the Church is the inclusion of such diverse elements. Prophetic voices are not silenced even when they are silenced.... And popular theologizing today is more widespread and relevant. The *Toronto Star* almost daily covers the Church in some way... which does indicate, I guess, the social relevance or influence of the Church. I think there are hopeful signs. Empires have risen and fallen over 20 centuries. For some reason Catholicism has survived, and that has to be because of the Holy Spirit. It certainly hasn't been because of men!

While there is frustration and impatience with some of the ways of the Church, these teachers are very much at home in the Church and comfortable and enthusiastic about their ecclesial vocation of Catholic educator. They see the hopeful signs — many of them are that to one another. Jesus — the Message — gives meaning and direction to their personal lives, and the proclamation of Jesus is the rationale for so much of what they do in school and outside of school.

An historical perspective is perhaps useful here. Our time for evangelizing is certainly most interesting, and the Church's dialogue with our culture is more relevant and important than ever: much more meaningful than Pierre Berton's *Comfortable Pew* church of the 1950s and the "God is dead" times of the 1960s. With so much psychological uncertainty and insecurity about society today, the role of the Church can become even more meaningful through the 1990s. In their angst and confusion people will look to "the Church as the evangelizer," because it is through the Church that the Message of Evangelization — Jesus — is proclaimed:

> The Church exists in order to evangelize, that is to say, in order to preach and teach, to be the channel of the gift of grace, to reconcile sinners with God, and to perpetuate Christ's sacrifice in the Mass, which is the memorial of His death and resurrection.
>
> [*E.N.*, #14]

* * * * * * * * *

2. A Prophetic, Relevant, Counter-cultural Teaching

Vice-principal:

> One great strength in the Church is the courage to oppose
> so much of the secularizing, dehumanizing tendencies in
> society. There are great examples of this "prophetic" nature
> of the Church.

Religion teacher:

> I'd like to say this: there really are some very profound and
> pertinent things in the recent teaching of the Church, from
> the Pope and bishops, that we don't really know about. For
> example, Pope Paul VI's line: "The Church is an evangeliz-
> er but she begins by being evangelized herself." This is a
> new model of Church for me. I would like to see it realized
> more in parishes, schools, and Catholic school boards and
> chancery offices.

In his study, Reginald Bibby warned of the danger of the Church
making too many accommodations with our culture, thus compromising and watering down the gospel, which should instead be critiquing
the injustice and dehumanizing forces inherent in so many of our social
structures and cultural attitudes. While many believers risk making these
accommodations in their personal and communal lives, there is little
evidence of this taking place in the teaching Church.

One need only review the social teaching of Popes Paul VI and
John Paul II and some of the documents of the Canadian Bishops. The
teaching Church, in fact, incurs at times the wrath but most of the time
the indifference of many believers with its vigorous defence of life and
critique of the dominant ideology of liberal capitalism. Such teaching
does not make for easy evangelization. As we have frequently seen in
the testimony of different teachers, "the Canadian dream" is a very attractive package, and it isn't easy to present an alternative option which
embraces "toil and suffering, a life lived according to the Gospel, abne-
gation and the cross, and the spirit of the beatitudes" [E.N., #15]. As
the Church wends its way to the millennium, increasingly our efforts at
evangelization must be looked at as being something very "counter-
cultural."

* * * * * * * *

3. The Extraordinary Attraction of a Humble, Servant Church

Principal:

> I like the idea of a humble Church... a servant Church.
> The institutional Church has got to see itself as a servant
> Church. I'm hopeful that this process will continue.

Of the images or models of Church that speak most clearly and significantly to the people of our times, *the Church as servant* is perhaps the most striking. This is the case, it seems, because the image of servant is most at odds with the spirit of our times, a spirit in the North American context, anyway, that champions power, prestige, privilege and pleasure. In contrast, there is the counter-cultural servant, represented most often in both the secular and religious imagination by a Mother Teresa ministering to the dying or orphans, or Jean Vanier throwing in his lot with the mentally handicapped, or Bishop Oscar Romero giving up his life because he dared speak for the poor and oppressed. It would be wrong, however, to think that service is the prerogative only of contemporary faith heroes or saints. The symbol of foot washing is essential to the gospel, and Holy Thursday reminds us of the pre-eminence of serving — of washing feet — if we are truly to be followers of Jesus. It is good to look again at our faith communities — school, parish, ecclesial community — from the perspective of Holy Thursday. Service is operative and the servant Church is realized in parishioners taking a turn at a soup kitchen, or a hospitality committee welcoming refugees, or volunteers working at an AIDS hospice or visiting the sick.

Every faith community would do well to reflect on Pope Paul VI's description of the humble Church we encountered in the second meditation of Chapter 2: the Church is often tempted by idols and needs to be cleansed; the Church always needs to be called afresh by God; the Church is in constant need of being evangelized. This is the necessary starting point always if the Church wishes to serve and empty herself as Jesus did.

But how would this servant image of Church, this service model of authority operate in the faith community of a school or a Catholic school board? With great difficulty, experience unfortunately seems to indicate. The blessing of bureaucracy is supposed to be efficiency. The curse of bureaucracy for Catholic education, undoubtedly, is its tendency to impersonalize, to dehumanize. In Chapter 2 we remarked that the bureaucracy of Catholic education and some aloof, impersonal principals, administrators and trustees represent a formidable obstacle for the evangelization project in the Catholic high school. Jesus tells us that

118

it is hard for the camel to get through the eye of the needle, and for the rich person to get into the Kingdom of heaven. It is not impossible, mind you, but very difficult.

Perhaps Jesus might say today : it is so hard for a gospel of mercy and compassion and forgiveness, a gospel of justice and peace and solidarity, a gospel that sees real power and authority in foot washing to be welcomed and embraced and given priority in the technocratic bureaucracy of most school boards that are the nerve centres, and represent leadership, for our Catholic high schools. Not impossible, mind you, but very difficult. The "theology" or "philosophy" part of our school mission statements (to be true to the gospel) should enshrine "service" as the model for leadership; the "Catholic" dimension of Catholic education (to be faithful to the gospel) should privilege "service" as the model for authority.

Working from a "service" model of authority, how much easier it is for every person to take on ownership and responsibility for the Catholic high school. And how much easier it is to listen to the experience of the victims of our society and the marginalized. And how much easier it is to minister to the brokenness which is so much a part of our social context! If not easier, at least more consistent. And the "service" model of authority is counter-cultural. It absolutely flies in the face of the "power-prestige-privilege-pleasure" syndrome which motivates so many in our time and place.

Again here, it is *the way* we are Church, *the way* we do Catholic education. The theology is there : from the top, the texts we have reflected on; and from the bottom, in the lived faith experience of more than a few Catholic educators. The challenge for the 1990s continues to be implementation. We all begin by being evangelized ourselves.

* * * * * * * * *

There are other important elements of the ecclesial context that must be considered.

- In Chapter 3 we noted that "the students' lack of participation in the parish was a genuinely perplexing question for everyone."[4] Indeed, the traditional parish-school-family partnership and perspective must be reviewed at the local level in the light of the recent analysis of the Ontario bishops:

Given the increasing fragility of families and *the overextension of parishes*, it is becoming more obvious that the school, for some, is often the primary place where young people experience the Church as an alternative community which is shaped more by faith, hope and love than by the values of our consumer culture.[5]

We will explore some of the ramifications of this analysis in Part Three and Part Four.

- Throughout these reflections, I have drawn heavily on some of the Church's bold, prophetic theology to critique society, to point out and condemn the structured evil and injustice in many of our social institutions and systems. But a humble Church mindful of its own need "to be evangelized" must be ready to hear and accept society's critique of the Church. Here I simply pose the question: as Church — as faith community in a school or parish or diocese or, indeed, congregations and offices in the Vatican — what is the level of our openness to external critique?

- And still on the question of critique, a teacher offered this challenging and insightful comment:

> Can we also prepare the kids for disappointment with their church? Evangelization is a radical task. Is the institutional Church ready for an evangelized youth? Will it welcome them? Will they feel at home in it?

* * * * * * * * *

This sketch of some of the elements that contribute to the cultural and ecclesial context for the Catholic education project in Ontario in the 1990s is just that: a sketch. Hopefully the sketch will invite those who are committed to Catholic education to broaden and deepen the analysis. I return again, however, to the element of local experience: "Local experience must be the determining factor." A reflection on the obstacles to evangelization in our culture can be very helpful in identifying just what it is we must evangelize. A similar reflection on the signs of hope prevalent in our time and place makes it easier for us and allows us to take advantage of some very positive cultural forces in our evangelizing activities. An appreciation of some of the strengths and limitations of our Canadian Church today can only give us more understanding and meaningful insight into our mission, as Church, to evangelize.

But the real challenge is at the local level. By doing some social and ecclesial analysis of their own, a group of teachers will inevitably find themselves sharing their faith and their hopes and fears as followers of Jesus and Catholic educators. They will, in fact, evangelize each other. Such an experience can only enhance the overall evangelization efforts in their Catholic high school, an evangelization addressed particularly to young people. And that is an enormous evangelizing challenge — as we shall now see.

NOTES
Chapter 7

[1] Refer to : " The *Toronto Star* Poll : On Roman Catholics in Ontario — Attitudes on Religious Practice, Church Discipline, Some Church Teaching ; Sexual Morality, " *Toronto Star*, August 23, 1987, p. 1.

Also : Reginald W. Bibby, *Fragmented Gods : The Poverty and Potential of Religion in Canada* (Toronto : Irwin Publishing, 1987).

And : Dean Hoge, *Future of Catholic Leadership — Responses to the Priest Shortage* (Kansas City, Missouri : Sheed & Ward, 1987).

[2] Hoge, *op. cit.*

[3] Bibby, *op. cit.*, p. 260.

[4] Chapter 3, p. 53.

[5] Ontario Conference of Catholic Bishops, *This Moment of Promise*, p. 16, emphasis added.

PART THREE

Youth — The Beneficiaries of Evangelization in the Catholic High School

CHAPTER 8
REFLECTIONS OF THE CHURCH ON YOUTH

I like order. Now, I don't think that I am terribly compulsive about it, but an ordered work environment — for example, a desk, an office or a classroom — seems to add clarity to a project: what I'm about, where I'm going. It gives me more assurance. Walking through an empty school at the end of August before Labour Day, or in the evening when the kids have gone home and the custodians have spiffied the place up, I sometimes catch myself thinking: "This is the way it should be! There is room to move! The place is clean! I can get from Point A to Point B, and I know exactly what I am going to do once I get there. There are no interruptions; there is no confusion; no chaos! There are no kids!"

Such wishful thinking can be therapeutic — occasionally! Too much of it, however, can be bad news for the teacher, and especially bad news for the kids! The kids, our students, are really what we are all about in the Catholic high school! The interruptions, the confusion, the chaos; the questions, the hurts, the dreams — all of this constitutes the immediate context for evangelization. This is the normal environment, and indeed, given the spontaneity, enthusiasm, unpredictability and raw energy of teenagers, this is pretty much the way it should be. The kids, our students, are the beneficiaries of evangelization in the Catholic high school. And, as we have already seen, our whole purpose, our raison d'être, is to share our experience of Jesus and our understanding of the gospel and our tradition as Roman Catholics with these young people:

Finally, the person who has been evangelized goes on to evangelize others. Here lies the test of truth, the touchstone of evangelization: it is unthinkable that a person should accept the Word and give oneself to the kindgom without be-

124

coming a person who bears witness to it and proclaims it in turn.

[E.N., #24]

My intention in Part Three is to facilitate a multifaceted reflection on young people as the beneficiaries of evangelization in the Catholic high school. Continuing with the methodology of "theological eaves-dropping," we listen first to the teaching Church. Several recent documents and statements offer some very rich insights that will be helpful for us when we search for strategy to evangelize our students more effectively. Then we listen to the beneficiaries of evangelization, the kids themselves, by "eavesdropping" on some 40 young people, students from five Catholic high schools, as they share their own impressions of evangelization in the Catholic high school. And finally, we listen once again to the teachers we have already met in Part One and Part Two, this time as they reflect on their own experience as evangelizers and on the young people in their evangelizing care.

I am convinced that "listening" is the apt methodology to employ here even though some might want to focus more on "proclamation"; that is, on the preaching and teaching techniques best suited for the evangelization of young people and getting the message across to our students. But, as we shall see, listening is the necessary first step. Listening means that we are attempting to really know and understand our students; that we respect the subjectivity, individuality and personal journey of the young person; that we are sensitive to the adolescent's preoccupations, felt needs and aspirations. It will become clear, then, that the best evangelizer is not necessarily the best preacher, but rather, perhaps, the best listener!

LISTENING TO THE CHURCH

"But where does adult faith formation happen today? How are Catholic teachers going to be evangelized? We need a model!" This was the query of a guidance teacher we encountered in the last chapter. The same sentiment was expressed by a principal:

> But where the Church does a bad job is in educating adults, developing the faith of adults. There has to be another model. I have trouble with autocratic structures in education. I have trouble with them in the Church. The model — it's where people own the Church, own their faith. People have to participate, not observe. How do we get them to

participate? Evangelization is not going to work in the school unless the staff is evangelized.

There is a certain irony here in that our primary consideration is the evangelization of adolescent students by adult teachers. Yet, from whatever starting point we choose, we keep coming back to the basic truth that "the evangelizers themselves must be evangelized"; that the most effective instrument for the evangelization of young people is the evangelization of their teachers. So of course the central question becomes: "How are Catholic teachers going to be evangelized?"

Listening to the teaching Church is an indispensable tool for becoming informed and growing in understanding of one's faith. We have already indicated that an unfortunate obstacle to evangelization is the gap between theory and practice and between theology and reality. This gap is manifest in how much very nourishing, challenging and critical Church teaching does not filter down to the base, the members of different local churches. Paul VI addressed his exhortation *On Evangelization in the Modern World* to "the Bishops, Priests and Faithful of the entire world." But, how many of us even knew this document existed? And again, Pope John Paul II's encyclicals — *The Redeemer of Man* [*Redemptor Hominis*], 1979; *On Human Work* [*Laborem Exercens*], 1981; and *Concern for the Social Order* [*Sollicitudo Rei Socialis*], 1988 — were all addressed to "Venerable Brothers and *dear Sons and Daughters*," but how many of us received these communications? His exhortation on *The Vocation and Mission of the Lay Faithful* [*Christifideles Laici*], occasioned by the Synod on the laity and published in 1989, is the most recent very challenging teaching of Pope John Paul II. But will it reach us? Will it filter down?

Perhaps it is an adult education problem. Perhaps it's a communication and public relations problem. Perhaps it's a preaching problem. Probably it is all of the above and more! But the result is a lack of nourishment and challenge for so many Catholic followers of Jesus. This is even more unfortunate when we know that such nourishment and challenge exist!

The teaching is there in a content that is filled with wisdom and relevance — both theologically and pastorally — but we can't get at it! These documents, this teaching, for all the impact they seem to have had, might never have left the confines of the Vatican and the cellars of Polyglot Press where they are first published in Latin. It would seem, in talking to Catholic teachers and administrators across Ontario, that a similar fate befell some key documents of the Vatican's Congregation for Catholic Education. *The Catholic School*, 1977; *Lay Catholics in*

126

Schools: Witnesses to Faith, 1982; *The Religious Dimension of Education in a Catholic School*, 1988 — all contain some wonderfully rich theological insights for the visioning of, and the doing of, Catholic education. As well, they include suggestions and examples to facilitate the application of their theory within the context of local churches and particular school communities. Yet, for the most part, they are sources for evangelization that have gone untapped. They have not filtered down. So the critical question remains: where does the adult faith formation of the teacher happen today?

Though such documents are not the only sources of evangelization for the evangelizers, they are very important, necessary and worthwhile sources, especially for evangelizers who are also teachers in a Catholic high school. It is for this reason that I have deliberately chosen to highlight some of this "top-down" theology throughout my discussion on evangelization in the Catholic high school. To have a text before me, to let it speak to me and challenge me and critique me, then to listen to the comments, ideas and ideals of fellow teachers occasioned by a reflection on the same text — such an experience has personally always been a profoundly rich one.

We are Catholic educators! A sign of competence and professionalism in any educator is the habit of reading, of keeping current not only in one's academic specialization, but in movements, trends and ideas in education in general. For the educator in the Catholic school, competence and professionalism are further marked by attention to the faith ideas and ideals that give Catholic education its distinctive character and mission, and by a strong desire to integrate them into the classroom and into the total school environment. We ought to be familiar with recent Church teaching on issues such as evangelization, the mission of the laity, and Catholic education. We ought to return to them frequently for ongoing formation and inspiration. Now we turn to selected texts from these documents and listen to what they have to say to us about *the adolescents* who are the beneficiaries of our evangelizing efforts.

Among the themes I have discovered in sifting through the Church's teaching on the evangelization of adolescents, there are four that invite special consideration in the elaboration of any strategy for evangelization in our Catholic high school.

1. THE NEED TO ADAPT OUR EVANGELIZATION

In *On Evangelization in the Modern World*, Pope Paul VI speaks very frankly about the necessity of "adapting evangelization"; that is, taking into consideration the actual people to whom it is addressed. Keeping in mind that it is "the kids" — our students — that we are addressing in our evangelizing efforts, let us listen more intently to Paul VI's ideas on adaptation:

> The individual Churches, intimately built up not only of people but also of aspirations, of riches and limitations, of ways of praying, of loving, of looking at life and the world, which distinguish this or that human gathering, have the task of assimilating the essence of the Gospel message and of transposing it, without the slightest betrayal of its essential truth, into the language that these particular people understand, then of proclaiming it in this language.

> The transposition has to be done with the discernment, seriousness, respect and competence which the matter calls for in the field of liturgical expression and in the areas of catechesis, theological formulation, secondary ecclesial structures, and ministries. And the word "language" should be understood here less in the semantic of literary sense than in the sense which one may call anthropological and cultural.

> The question is undoubtedly a delicate one. Evangelization loses much of its force and effectiveness if it does not take into consideration the actual people to whom it is addressed, if it does not use their language, their signs and symbols, if it does not answer the questions they ask, and if it does not have an impact on their concrete life.
>
> [E.N., #63]

Several points should be made on this critically important teaching of Paul VI.

1. Our English Canadian Church is unique. Indeed there are differences, some slight, others more pronounced, from local Church (diocese) to local Church. Each local Church has "the task of assimilating, transposing and proclaiming" the gospel into the language; that is, the social and cultural language of its people. This brings us back to our earlier reflection on the context — social and ecclesial — and the need to know and understand our society, our local Church: "its aspirations, riches and limitations."

2. For the adolescents in our Catholic high schools, it is necessary that the gospel be transposed and proclaimed in religious education

128

and liturgy that speak to them. Paul VI uses the word "language" in a cultural way. The challenge for us is to understand and communicate in their language. There is always a fine line between "adapting" the gospel and "watering it down." The call, though, is very clear: *to adapt.* This we must risk. The task is to listen and to understand both the exigencies of the gospel and the "signs, symbols and questions" that constitute the language of our students.

3. To paraphrase: evangelizing in our Catholic high school loses much of its force and effectiveness if it does not take into consideration the kids, the actual people to whom it is addressed; if it does not use their language, their signs and symbols; if it does not answer the questions they ask, and if it does not have an impact on their concrete lives. I don't think it is so much a question of knowing what's cool or uncool regarding the latest fashion or the current week's *Muchmusic* charts. Mind you, such knowledge wisely used is not at all a trivial matter, and some of the more thoughtful social commentary music around today can be an effective means of evangelizing. Rather, the important thing is the listening — being aware of the needs and preoccupations of the 15-year-old girl or the 17-year-old boy, their struggle for identity, and the most important concerns in their young lives (which are not likely to be first and foremost religious or Church questions!): their need for acceptance and friendship.

4. How does Pope Paul VI's teaching on "adaptation" play against what we are about in our schools? Certainly there is an emphasis on the need to be sensitive to the intellectual and psychological capacity of our students regarding the nature and content of the religious education we propose. In a way this calls to mind OS:IS and the streaming of our education content and strategies into advanced, general and basic levels. (My intention here is not to debate the merits of the streaming model for religious education although such a debate is necessary and should be engaged in at the local level.) Each level — advanced, general, basic — has its own demands, its own understandings, its own strategies.[1]

I have taught advanced senior level classes. One of my regrets is failing to challenge them sufficiently. Many of those students would have been capable, for example, of a study of John Paul II's *Concern for the Social Order.* So what if it required two or three readings! Surely the degree of difficulty would be no greater than some of the content they would encounter in advanced science, math, economics or literature classes. But my strategy was to synthesize the text and feed it to them in little pieces. I don't believe I negotiated "adaptation" very well in this instance.

Once when visiting at a Catholic high school, I spent time in a Grade 9 general level religion class where for 70 minutes a day for a full semester the students worked away at a textbook on Church history designed for high school seniors! Why? It was easier for the teacher: he needed a textbook, and he was primarily in the history department! The content of that course didn't address the needs of kids: insecure, frightened coming into high school, growing in and confused by their own sexuality! "Adaptation" was not at all operative here!

Nor does "adaptation" take place if we choose to impose on a group of basic Grade 10 students essentially the same academic program but watered down, complete with units of work, tests, papers and exam that we might use for general and advanced students. Opting for this model instead of creating an experience-reflection model that would speak to these students, to their questions and their needs, is still another way of failing at adaptation.

And remembering that evangelization is a responsibility and goal in every class and in all facets of Catholic high school life, it is important to scrutinize how much consideration we give to adaptation in key aspects of the more global Catholic high school program.

For example, liturgy is a regularly-scheduled activity in all Catholic high schools. But we need to ask: how much of the liturgy we do actually belongs to the students? Is it adapted? Are the students included in its planning and preparation? What about our efforts at animation, at encouraging participation?

And for want of a better term, what about our witness language, "spoken" by every single teacher in any Catholic high school? Our students, as noted earlier, are masters at detecting hypocrisy! "Witness language" is something they understand at the core of their young beings, even if they cannot easily articulate it. Our witness language certainly belies our professed values (school mission statements, morning prayers, liturgies, etc.) — and the kids quickly see it — if the energy, attitudes and actions of teachers are indifferent to the demands of the gospel. On the other hand, as we have already seen, "authentic life witness" is a most excellent means of transposing, adapting and proclaiming the gospel.

* * * * * * * *

2. A DESCRIPTION OF YOUTH: SOME COMMON CHARACTERISTICS

The Congregation for Catholic Education's 1988 document, *The Religious Dimension of Education in a Catholic School*, proffers a useful description of youth as we begin the last decade of the 1900s and head toward the millennium. Some thoughtful reflection and mutual sharing on the characteristics proposed here can be invaluable for evangelization in the Catholic high school.

Many young people find themselves in a condition of radical instability. On the one hand they live in a one-dimensional universe in which the only criterion is practical utility and the only value is economic and technological progress. On the other hand, these same young people... seem to have a desire to be released from this narrow universe.

[#10]

Others live in an environment devoid of truly human relationships; as a result, they suffer from loneliness and a lack of affection.... Young people today are notably more depressed than in the past; this is surely a sign of the poverty of human relationships in families and societies today.

[#11]

Large numbers of today's youth are very worried about an uncertain future. They have been influenced by a world in which human values are in chaos because these values are no longer rooted in God; the result is that these young people are very much afraid when they think about the appalling problems in the world: the threat of nuclear annihilation, vast unemployment, the high numbers of marriages that end in separation or divorce, widespread poverty, etc. Their worry and insecurity become an almost irresistible urge to focus in on themselves, and this can lead to violence when young people are together — a violence that is not always limited to words.

[#12]

Not a few young people, unable to find any meaning in life or trying to find an escape from loneliness, turn to alcohol, drugs, the erotic, the exotic. Christian education is faced with the huge challenge of helping these young people discover something of value in their lives.

[#13]

Educators cannot be content with merely observing these behaviour patterns; they have to search for the causes. It may be some lack at the start, some problem in the family background. Or it may be that parish and Church organizations are deficient. Christian formation given in childhood and early adolescence is not always proof against the influence of the environment. Perhaps there are cases in which the fault lies with the Catholic school itself.

[#17]

There are also a number of positive signs, which give grounds for encouragement:
  — young people outstanding in every way; ...
  — excellent family background; ...
  — searching for deeper meaning; ...
  — committing or recommitting themselves to the
    Christian way of life...

[#18]

A first reading of this description can leave even an optimist a mite despondent. Review the descriptives: instability, devoid of human relationship, depressed, uncertain future, escapist! Is this really an accurate description of that mob of adolescents we observe daily in the cafeteria and corridors or at a pep rally? It would seem not. But then when we pan the crowd of kids with the isolation camera and start fixing on individuals as they develop over four or five years, we begin to sense the depth and the extent of "the poverty of human relationships" that many experience today. And as our social analysis indicated, the "one-dimensional universe" (the materialism, consumerism, utilitarianism all hitched to the only value: economic and technological progress!) really does imprison many of our young people. Catholic educators indeed are faced with the immense challenge of helping these young people discover meaning.

The Religious Dimension of Education in a Catholic School urges special analysis of the religious conditions in the world today and specifically calls upon Catholic educators to do such realistic analysis in order to pay particular attention to the religious situation of young people:

> Whatever methods they employ to do this (analysis), they should be attentive to the results of research with youth done at the local level....

[#7]

132

One such piece of "local research" is the critically important study completed in 1985 by Reginald Bibby and Donald Posterski, *The Emerging Generation — An Inside Look at Canada's Teenagers*.[2] This fascinating and invaluable resource based on a survey of more than 3000 young people across Canada focuses on values and provides an overall impression of where teenagers (15 to 19 years of age) stand on such questions as: values, happiness, troubles, intimacy, relationships and beliefs. To add to the description of the young people in our Catholic high schools, I have culled some of the more salient conclusions from the research of Bibby and Posterski:

- In the teen years, *friendship* and *being loved* are the most important values for young people. Next come in order: *freedom, success and comfort, privacy, family life,* and *acceptance by God.*

- What makes teenagers happy: *friendships / relationships* followed by *music* and then *boyfriend / girlfriend, one's mother, sports, one's father,* and in position 15 and 17 on a prioritized list of 17, *school* and *Church!*

- What troubles teenagers: *employment after graduation* — the uncertainty; *finances* — to live well; *school,* which causes pressure and induces stress; *time, appearance, purpose of life, loneliness, sexuality* and *family life.*

- Concerning how teenagers feel about *sexual intimacy,* the Bibby / Posterski assessment is that teenagers today reflect very much the attitudes and values of their parents. More than 50 percent of teenagers may be engaging in premarital sex. As for extramarital sex, the vast majority are opposed. The conclusion is that young people still believe in traditional monogamous marriage. On the broader issue of adolescent sexuality they report:

The new-found biological ability of teenagers to procreate is fuelled by a society that sanctions sex as a recreational option. Our visual world has pushed the creed of "the more the better." Soap operas, TV, movies and home videos have been intent on breaking the barriers of nudity, rape and incest. Many of the most popular television shows seem to gain their status from the frequency of the sexual innuendos in the script. Enticing, erotic ads send the message to "get active" sexually. As adults, we have offered adolescents a sex-oriented society that drives for immediate gratification. At the same time, many adults still call out for celibacy as the standard for young people. When what is happening inside teenagers is wrapped with the erotica of the daily experiences in our culture, the combination is potent.[3]

- On the significance of *family* and *friends* they have concluded:

The family continues to have a significant impact on Canadian young people. However, influence is one thing, enjoyment another. The survey reveals that many teenagers tend to find high levels of gratification from friends rather than from their mothers and fathers. They consequently place more value on friendships than they do on family life.[4]

- Bibby / Posterski conclusions on the place of *religion* in teenage lives are that belief and practice on the part of adolescents pretty well mirror that of their parents — 85 percent believe in God and the divinity of Jesus. Yet as a value, *belief in God* is rated well below *family* and *friendship*. Their research enabled them to extract a profile on more specific aspects of religion in teenage lives, including *spiritual interest, church attendance, parents and religion,* and *consumer religion:*

Only 10 % highly enjoy church life, but another 35 % highly value acceptance by God. Beyond both of these categories, still another 25 % are concerned about resolving the question of the purpose of life. Thus, some 70 % of teenagers seemingly have clear religious and spiritual interest. To the extent that religious groups fail to captivate young people, it is not because "the religious market" is not an appreciable one.[5]

While almost every young person identifies with one religious group or another, we have seen that by the time they leave their teens, only about 1 in 6 are regular Church attenders. The major reason may not be very mysterious. As we saw earlier, religious groups are not associated with high levels of enjoyment for teenagers.[6]

Some observers maintain that the tie between religion and parents is so strong that adolescents rebelling against parents may use religion as a means of striking out against them. For these young people, the rejection of religion is "a way of emancipating themselves from parents who are not giving them the freedom they seek."[7]

This general pattern of "polite detachment" yet ongoing identification with and consumer-like use of religious organizations mirrors dramatically the nature of adult religion in Canada. It appears that such a style is being transmitted to the emerging generation with surprising thoroughness.[8]

This is but a sketch of an extremely interesting and detailed picture of teenagers today outlined by Reginald Bibby and Donald Posterski. Understanding and appreciating this picture is of the utmost importance as we go about our task of evangelizing in the Catholic high school. And a daunting task this evangelization project is! I was aware of the importance of peer relationships, of friendship, of acceptance. I was not aware of the extent of the seeming non-importance of the Church. But at the same time I was encouraged by the potential of spiritual interest: "Some 70 percent of teenagers seemingly have clear religious and spiritual interests" and the great majority (85 percent) believe in God and in the divinity of Jesus. The "religious market" indeed is rich with evangelizing potential!

And then there is the impact adults and parents have on adolescents. The sexual environment today is frightening, and apart from the struggle every teenager has with his/her sexual development and identity, this is pretty much the sexual environment — hypererotic and promiscuous — elaborated and promoted by adults. Again, this fact takes us back to the social and cultural analysis proposed in Part Two. Our society, our culture impacts on everyone — adults and adolescents. The social and cultural obstacles to evangelization for adults are the same for adolescents; the possibilities for grace in our social and cultural context are the same for adults and adolescents. Let's not be so quick to fix blame on the kids for the violence, low Church attendance, sexual promiscuity, cheating, greed and exaggerated consumerism of our circumstances and situation. All the evidence points to the fact that they are only aping their elders, even to the point of buying into the consumer approach to believing and practising their faith.[9]

To conclude this description of youth, I would like to refer briefly to a recent investigation into the attitudes and activities of youth that both updates the Bibby/Posterski study and confirms the key points of analysis in Part Two — on the social and cultural context: adolescents tend to adopt the values and imitate the actions of an adult generation that is very much into materialism, and although young people are concerned about some serious problems (nuclear war, Third World poverty, environment), the complexity and immensity of it all renders them helpless, while the strong attraction of the North American dream paralyses them.

135

*From the *Toronto Star*, February 25, 1989, p. H1:

[headline] **Youth into the 1990s Living in a material world**

As we approach the last school term of the last year in this decade, The *Star* looked at youth and their world — a decidedly material world, in which they're becoming material boys and girls.

[Youth] are traditional, conservative conformists, experts say. Politically, they're quiet, worrying about issues like acid rain, but not acting out in protest. They respect police, believe in God, and dream more of personal gain than social justice.

Though a few do talk about the environment, free trade and Third World poverty, most think about money: where to get the good paying jobs, the great jackets, CDs, and those big, clunky, black, expensive boots called Doc Martens.

"They want the good jobs, the status symbols," says Decima pollster Allan Gregg, "but they have personal values, too. They think they can have both designer jeans and nuclear disarmament."

Young people today are stressed and pampered: stressed because they know how important it will be to make money when they grow up; pampered because many of them are earning it already, flipping burgers and stocking the local grocery shelves while mom and dad supply the home and meals.

As is always the case, this new generation manages to puzzle and frustrate the one preceding it. This time, it's not so much because they won't listen to us or because they're doing wild and crazy things, but rather because they seem to be doing just what we're doing — taking it to an extreme, obsessed with making it in the material world.

In this same *Toronto Star* report on "Youth Into the 1990s," on the same page, Donald Posterski further elaborates on youth values:

Youths are "enthusiastic consumers," Environics Research reported, buying things "almost compulsively, sometimes just for the pleasure!" It happened when the hippie uprisings petered out, says Donald Posterski, a researcher and youth consultant. Instead, he says, kids saw that student revolt "was crushed eventually, and they walked away from trying to find solutions to problems, and opted instead for personal pursuits."

They don't worry so much about nuclear war, as they did in the mid 1980s, says Posterski. Instead, he says, they worry about whatever the media worry about: the environment, AIDS. But they worry quietly. It's not that they don't care. They just don't act.

* * * * * * * *

3. THE INVITATION TO YOUTH TO PARTICIPATE IN EVANGELIZATION

We have already alluded to the intrinsic role of the Catholic high school as very much an *extension* of the Church. But some features of the present ecclesial reality in Canada — low attendance rate or irregular practice of many Catholics, "the overextension of parishes," plus "the increasing fragility of families" — has resulted in a shift of role acknowledged by the Ontario Bishops in their recent pastoral letter on Catholic education, *This Moment of Promise*, when they spoke about the Catholic school as having become for some students the primary place for experience of the Church. Immediately following this observation, the bishops, referring especially to teachers, state: *"In this situation, those involved in Catholic education have an awesome privilege and responsibility."*[10]

I very much like the way they describe the task of evangelization — an awesome privilege and responsibility! It *is* a privilege and responsibility to be a counter-cultural community of believers and to invite large numbers of young people to embrace gospel values rather than to be sucked in by the dominant values of our consumer culture! It *is* a privilege and responsibility to be ministers of the Word, channels of compassion, instruments of justice and peace; it *is* a privilege and responsibility to be the preaching, healing and prophetic face of the Church for students in the Catholic high school. Indeed, it *is* a privilege and responsibility to speak on behalf of the Church and to invite young people to participate in the process of Catholic education, and to participate by playing an active role in the evangelizing activity of the Church.

What *is* the Church saying to young peole?

In *This Moment of Promise*, the bishops of Ontario, well aware that Catholic education is at a pivotal moment in its development, speak eloquently to our students, recognizing them as a partner group involved in the process of Catholic education:

Students,

We invite you to become active participants in the process of Catholic education. We urge you to bring your energy, enthusiasm and generosity to the task of building a Catholic community within your school and to shaping the vision of Catholic education. Your strengths and your weaknesses, your joys and your fears, your struggles and your searchings will be welcomed in this community. Whatever your age, you are not too young to assume responsibility with and for your fellow students. You are a most significant educational influence on each other. You can help each other become disciples of Jesus Christ or you can hinder each other from becoming everything you are called to be. How you are with one another now will significantly influence how you will be with others as adults. The future of the Church and its mission of service in the world will be yours. For this you will need courage, self-discipline and all the love you are able to give. Take up the challenge of growing into a sense of who you are as Christians so that you can develop the talents you have been given and bring the best of yourself to the society in which you will be living. [11]

A Commentary

• The tone of this invitation to our students is certainly parental, but it is not at all paternalistic. The students are what our shools are all about: they are partners, along with parents, teachers, administrators and trustees. The bishops readily acknowledge the students' importance in this partnership.

• The students are invited now — at this very crucial moment of promise for Catholic education — to actively take part in building Christian community and in giving shape to the vision of Catholic education, to the way we describe ourselves and define our mission as a Catholic high school. This fact, then, presents a pair of challenges. First, this invitation *must* be extended, delivered, communicated to our students! How will this be done? And, second, once the invitation is extended, how will the students participate? Creativity, risk, imagination and openness — these are qualities we must have as the adult partners. In a word, we must be willing to allow our students to participate in more than a decorative way.

• The real strength of this invitation is found in the manner in which the bishops understand the influence of friends and peers. Undoubtedly they have studied Bibby and Posterski! The Bishops stress the students' influence on and responsibility for one another. This is a relational influence, but it can also be a social, educational and "ministerial" influence: "You can help each other become disciples of Christ, or you can hinder each other from becoming everything you are called to be." This is a direct challenge to our pastoral and chaplaincy teams to be creative in the development and expansion of peer ministry.

• Like the parent entrusting the family business and the benefits and responsibilities that go with it to the daughter or son, so the bishops challenge our students to prepare to take on the Church's mission of service to the world. It is now, and will be even more so, a countercultural mission. It is not at all understating it to say that courage, self-discipline and love will be needed in abundance to stay the countercultural course! How do we as the evangelizers in the Catholic high school assist our students in cultivating courage, self-discipline and love? What do these things — courage, self-discipline and love — mean in today's culture?

What *is* the Church saying to young people?

Pope John Paul II also has a special invitation to the youth of today to become "leading characters in the evangelization and participants in the renewal of society." In his exhortation, *Vocation and Mission of the Lay Faithful*,[12] Pope John Paul II addresses youth as the hope of the Church:

> …youth make up an exceptional potential and a great challenge for the future of the Church. In fact the Church sees her path towards the future in the youth, beholding in them a reflection of herself and her call to that blessed youthfulness, which she constantly enjoys as a result of Christ's Spirit. In this sense the Council has defined youth as "the hope of the Church."

> Youth must not simply be considered as an object of pastoral concern for the Church: in fact, young people are and ought to be encouraged to be active on behalf of the Church as leading characters in evangelization and

participants in the renewal of society. Youth is a time of an especially intensive discovery of a "self" and "a choice of life." It is time for growth which ought to progress "in wisdom, age and grace before God and people." [Luke 2:52]

The Synod Fathers have commented: "The sensitivity of young people profoundly affects their perceiving of the values of justice, non-violence and peace. Their hearts are disposed to fellowship, friendship and solidarity. They are greatly moved by causes that relate to the quality of life and the conservation of nature. But they are troubled by anxiety, deceptions, anguishes and fears of the world as well as by the temptations that come with their state."

The Church has so much to talk about with youth, and youth have so much to share with the Church. This mutual dialogue, by taking place with great cordiality, clarity and courage, will provide a favorable setting for the meeting and exchange between generations, and will be a source of richness and youthfulness for the Church and civil society.

[#46]

A Commentary

• This invitation impresses by its realistic tone. The Synod on the Laity (1987) is the source for much of the realism. Yes, young people are idealistic. There is a sensitivity, and openness to justice and peace questions. There is potential for an unheard-of global solidarity and interdependence. But youth today are troubled, anxious and afraid. There are too many deceptions attached to the dominant ideologies. For our own students the tension is real: the attraction of "the North American dream" can be overwhelming. How do we participate along with our students in the creation of a counter-cultural approach to life?

• Pope John Paul II is very clear: adolescents are not objects! They should not be acted upon! Rather, they should be very much included as agents of evangelization and participants in the renewal of society. As the Ontario bishops look at students as partners in Catholic education, Pope John Paul II insists that we see young people as very capable of evangelizing with us now! Concretely, how does this break down in our evangelizing efforts within the Catholic high school? What is it to be "active on behalf of the Church"; "to be a leading character in evangelization"; "to participate in the renewal of society"? These questions must first be grappled with by adults, and especially by teachers in our Catholic high schools, if we are to serve as effective instruments of communication in inviting young people to become actively involved in an evangelization that transforms.

• Again we have the linking of evangelization and the transformation or renewal of society. The bishops tend to stress the future dimension — that students prepare now "to serve in the future and to bring the best of yourself to the society in which you will be living" — leaving the *now*, the present time, for students to be immersed in school life. Pope John Paul II, on the other hand, accentuates *now* as the time for the transformation of society and is very emphatic that young people, our students, should be very much involved. John Paul II's emphasis is certainly bold and prophetic. And because of this boldness, the adult evangelizers in the Catholic high school are called to review their strategies. How much of our evangelization leads to this type of engagement? How are our students involved in the transformation of society? How are we, the evangelizers, to communicate this bold, prophetic challenge?

• In the original text Pope John Paul II highlights the sentence: "*The Church has so much to talk about with youth, and youth have so much to share with the Church.*" Mutual dialogue! But where does it happen? This is the perennial problem for adults working with young people: to create for young people the opportunity to contribute. Too often, it is on our terms, in our way. But we have to listen! The best evangelizer is really perhaps the best listener. I suppose the best way to set up the mutual dialogue encouraged by Pope John Paul II is to go to the students first: "Listen, Pope John Paul II says the Church wants to hear from you guys! What have you got to say?" In reflecting on dialogue we are in a very real sense talking about power: providing to youth the opportunity to be heard, to criticize, to suggest, to dream. For teachers and priests and bishops and even Pope John Paul II himself, this means risk! Are we really ready to hear what young people have to share with us? The first step in evangelization is listening, and authentic listening embodies the risk that our preconceived assumptions and strategies might have to change when tested by the truth of our partners in dialogue — our youth.

* * * * * * * * *

4. AN EVANGELIZATION THAT RESPECTS ADOLESCENT EMERGENCE

The final idea I would propose, emanating from the experience and wisdom of Church teaching regarding the evangelization of adolescents, is the imperative to respect the phenomenon of "emergence." Adolescence is a process, a time for personal evolution. An adult is being born from the stuff of childhood. Many of us, parents and educators alike, might well lament the fact that it seems to be a nine-year gestation period rather than nine months! But, increasingly, that is the reality!

In *The Emerging Generation — An Inside Look at Canada's Teenagers* by Reginald Bibby and Donald Posterski, the thesis that "adolescence is a time of emergence from child to adult" is convincingly demonstrated.[13] Yet too often our efforts at formation, education and evangelization are insensitive to this time and this process of emergence. There are very definite developmental tasks that preoccupy the adolescent and should command our awareness and understanding: the mastering of new relationships with both sexes and growing in these relationships socially; coping with physical development and growing confidently in one's sexual identity; becoming independent emotionally and psychologically from one's parents; assuming personal control of self and making personal a set of values or ethical priorities which guide one's behaviour; taking ownership of faith in Jesus Christ and membership in the community of believers, the Church; and preparing for the future — career option and vocational option (single / married).[14]

The Church, too, recognizes this unique segment of the life pilgrimage that is termed adolescence. In the documents we have just considered, there is a surprising sensitivity to the process of adolescence and especially to the phenomenon of *emergence* and all that entails.

- The Ontario Bishops

  On allowing Time and Space for Struggle
  and Searching:

  ...your struggles and your searchings will be welcomed into the community of the Catholic high school.

- Pope John Paul II

  On Respecting Subjectivity and Individuality:

  Youth must not simply be considered as an object of pastoral concern for the Church.... [The emphasis here is on

142

what is **not** said : namely, to respect the subjectivity and individuality of the young person.]

- Pope John Paul II

On Privileging Adolescence as a Time for
Intense Personal Discovery :

Youth is a time of an especially intensive discovery of a
"self" and of "a choice of life." It is a time for growth which
ought to progress "in wisdom, age and grace before God
and people."

[Luke 2:52]

- Pope Paul VI

On Adapting Evangelization
to Respect the Culture and Questions of Adolescence :

Evangelization loses much of its force and effectiveness if it
does not take into consideration the actual people to whom
it is addressed, if it does not use their language, their signs
and symbols, if it does not answer the questions they ask,
and if it does not have an impact on their concrete life.

What are some of the implications of an evangelization in the
Catholic high school that is respectful of adolescent emergence? I
would suggest five considerations.

1. Freedom

While all of life might be looked at as "emergence," the time of
adolescence is critically so. Teenagers need room to develop, to assume
more and more personal control over their own lives. To be sure, this
will be a time of trial and error. It will be a time of mistakes and disappointments. One can't really travel the road from childhood naivete and
innocence to adult responsibility and discernment without detours,
breakdowns and even an accident or two along the way. Adolescents
must have the room and the time to make their journey.

2. Assistance

But they also need assistance. There is a bit of poster-theology that says: "We give our children roots — and wings!"[15] This idea captures well the essence of an evangelization strategy respectful of emergence: we want to share our values, our faith, our experience of Jesus the Lord and the richness of our Roman Catholic tradition. In a word, we want to hand down to our students everything that "roots" us — nourishing us and giving us a sense of purpose and meaning. And yet, we want to respect the uniqueness and individuality of each young person. Perhaps the most effective assistance we can provide is an evangelization based on listening and characterized by understanding and encouragement. There is indeed a time to be directive and a time to let go, and that is the real trick, the dynamics of which vary from one young person to the next. The foundational question for us to ask ourselves year in and year out is how to share our "roots" while respecting their freedom.

3. Awareness of our culture's negative, counter-gospel socialization

In some respects, as adults and parents we have already been more than successful in some of the socializing attitudes and habits we have handed down to our adolescents. Unfortunately, this has often been an unquestionably negative achievement. I refer here to "the enthusiastic consumerism," the greed, the "me first" approach to life, the readiness to relativize anything that comes in the way of personal pursuit and instant gratification. As we have already seen, many young people have bought the non-gospel consumer values espoused and promoted by adults in our culture hook, line and sinker. So "emergence" must take on another more urgent meaning, and it applies equally to adolescents and adults: how to escape, how to gain independence form this plastic bondage of consumerism and greed that can so enslave us. As we make our way into the 1990s, this increasingly becomes the central question for all evangelization in the North American context.

The well-known American specialist in youth ministry, Michael Warren, describes the evangelizing task of the Catholic high school which is serious about confronting this negative and anti-gospel socialization thrust of our society today:

> ...the role of the Catholic high school is to be a voice in the wilderness, that is, to offer quality education in the context of counter-cultural values based on the gospel. One of the

144

problems all schools face is that they represent a socialization thrust of society, by which the rising generation is induced into the mores and values of the culture. It is very easy for the schools to become the cheering squads leading the cheers for the contemporary culture. The best schools raise serious questions about this culture, critique it, and put it in perspective. They offer some critical distance from which to view culture. Catholic education should do this in a special manner, since it is based on Jesus' extensive set of principles that turn popular wisdom on its head.[16]

4. Teachers and the Catholic high school

It is very much incumbent on us as teachers in the Catholic high school to understand 'the nature of adolescent emergence and to respond to it in our evangelizing efforts. The model of Jesus in the gospels is of enormous benefit here. The adolescent is a person and has the uniqueness and dignity of every child of God. The dignity accorded each person means that the adolescent deserves to be reverenced and respected. Adolescents are people who matter. Their struggle and searching, too, call out for our attention, understanding and support.

Consequently, our curriculum, whether it be in religious studies or in any other discipline, should be made to correspond with their interests and needs and to meet the challenges — (so many of them non-gospel challenges) — of the world we live in. Today an absolutely crucial component of a Catholic education serious about evangelization is the ability for critical reflection. Again it is opportune to refer to Bibby and Posterski:

> If not committed to a respect for individuality and critical reflection, in addition to the mastery of existing material, our major institutions will function as socialization assembly lines. In the words of one writer, schools in particular will simply see young people as "empty bottles on the assembly line of grades — each grade [filling] the bottle up a little more, the bottle representing the child's memory." Teenagers and others will hold "the right ideas" and follow "the right" rules, yet largely be void of individuality.[17]

If adolescents are to own their faith in a mature way, they must do so from the realization they gradually develop of their own freedom and individuality. If they are to live that faith in a commitment that is both meaningful and relevant, they must acquire the skills to critique the obstacles in our culture that prevent the living-out of the gospel. And they must acquire the wisdom to discern the opportunities present in our time and place for service and for advancing the gospel. These are "the roots" we share with our young people in the Catholic high school. This is what Pope John Paul II has in mind in proposing Luke's description of Jesus' youth and adolescence as a model for today: "It is a time for growth which ought to progress 'in wisdom, age and grace before God and people.'" [Luke 2:52]

5. The Catholic high school: an evangelizing community

I have heard students describe the impact of teachers on their own lives. I am always quite taken with their perception of "community" — its place and importance in making the Catholic high school a real alternative to the public high school down the road. One observation runs like this:

> It's different now. We're so big. Two years ago when we had only 700 students here there was a genuine spirit of community. There were a number of teachers with the same values and commitment to social justice questions and to this Catholic high school of ours. It was not just one person, not just the odd teacher, but a group of them. It was a core community of teachers. We could feel it. Now, we are more than 1600 students and twice as many teachers as before. We are too big! We are losing the sense of community. These teachers are still here, but because of numbers and work load, they seem to be lost or isolated. It is harder. We don't experience the real Christian community we had just two years ago. It is impersonal, too much like a factory.

The above discussion actually took place. The seven students from that school who participated were profoundly aware of the absolute primacy of the Christian community in the passing on of faith. That core group of committed teachers touched them in several ways. Living the gospel and having one's life based firmly on gospel values is not something peculiar. Many people do this. The students experienced that. And when there is this "gathering" of committed women and men, evangelizers in the Catholic high school, good things do happen: there is spirit; compassion and encouragement flow more readily and impact on the life and workings of the school more consistently; the possibilities for a genuinely alternative education, based on critical reflection and Jesus' teaching, become more abundant.

In *This Moment of Promise*, the bishops of Ontario, as we have already seen, confirm this very point on the primacy of building the Christian community within the school:

> [Emphasis added.] . . . Those involved in Catholic education have *an awesome privilege and responsibility*. They are called not only *to create an authentic faith community in the school* but also *to bring that community into community with the parish and the wider Church community.* [18]

It is probably impossible to recall too frequently the phrase, "awesome privilege and responsibility"! And put very franlky, it *is* a privilege and responsibility to make of our schools authentic faith communities. From the point of view of the adolescents, such a faith community speaks to them: it can be of great benefit in assimilating and making their own the values and ethic upon which they will base their lives and actions; it can give a clear gospel focus to the things, the questions, the issues they will deem important; it can allow them to see that the Church is most relevant and has a significant contribution to make to the ways and means we opt to organize ourselves in our society and in the world.

As I noted earlier, much of the problem in evangelization is implementation and communication: the combination of filtering down (transmitting the bold prophetic social teaching of the Church to people) and percolating up (channelling the needs of adolescents and questions of the laity to the teaching Church)! A dynamic, vibrant Christian community in the Catholic high school, animated by committed men and women aware of this "awesome privilege and responsibility" will be of enormous assistance to our students as they negotiate the exciting but unpredictable roadways of adolescence. Such a community is the face of the Church — the Church listening, encouraging and leading by example. Indeed, this type of evangelization is most sensitive to adolescent emergence and, therefore, has the best chance of inviting young people to participate now in the evangelizing mission of the Church.

* * * * * * * * *

Theological eavesdropping, then, can be an enlightening, nourishing and challenging experience for teachers in the Catholic high school. It is clear that the teaching Church is an invaluable resource in our attempts to understand the faith development of adolescents and to strategize; that is, discern the essentials of evangelization and to work out the possible approaches for our evangelization project with adolescents in our schools. In our reflection on the different documents, we can't help noticing how the teaching Church privileges "adolescent participation": *the bishops* — "We invite you to become active participants in the process of Catholic education; and *Pope John Paul II* — "The Church has so much to talk about with youth, and youth have so much to share with the Church." Our next step, then, is to advance this participation, this dialogue. Let us listen to some of our students as they reflect on the evangelization project in the Catholic high school.

NOTES
Chapter 8

1 For an invaluable resource for an understanding of Ontario's adolescents and the implications of such an understanding for advanced, general, and basic students, see: A. J. C. King, *The Adolescent Experience* (Toronto: Ontario Secondary School Teachers' Federation, 1986).

2 Reginald W. Bibby and Donald C. Posterski, *The Emerging Generation* (Toronto: Irwin Publishing, 1985).

3 *Ibid.,* p. 93.

4 *Ibid.,* p. 112.

5 *Ibid.,* p. 66.

6 *Ibid.,* p. 125.

7 *Ibid.,* p. 126.

8 *Ibid.,* p. 127.

[9] Refer to the discussion of Reginald Bibby's *Fragmented Gods* in Chapter 7, p. 108.

[10] Ontario Conference of Catholic Bishops, *This Moment of Promise*. A Pastoral Letter on Catholic Education in Ontario (Toronto, 1989), p. 16

[11] *Ibid.*, p. 22.

[12] Pope John Paul II, *Vocation and Mission of the Lay Faithful* [*Christifideles Laici*] (Montreal: Éditions Paulines, 1989).

[13] Bibby and Posterski, *op. cit.* "Emergence" is considered in detail in Chapter One and Chapter Ten.

[14] *Ibid.*, pp. 50-57.

[15] *Ibid.*, p. 200.

[16] Michael Warren, *Youth, Gospel, Liberation* (San Francisco: Harper & Row, 1987), p. 55.

[17] Bibby and Posterski, *op. cit.*, p. 188.

[18] Ontario Conference of Catholic Bishops, *op. cit.*, p. 16.

CHAPTER 9

LISTENING TO YOUTH — REFLECTIONS ON THE CATHOLIC HIGH SCHOOL

In the first week of March, 1989, I set out with my Sony Stereo Cassette-Corder in search of some enthusiastic, opinionated, but reflective adolescents — students in our Catholic high schools. My intention: to hear them talk about their experience in the Catholic high school, their impressions of what we are about, and their assessment as to how we are doing.

I visited five schools. I listened to 40 students. I engaged in some "theological eavesdropping," and I do not hesitate to use "theological" as the descriptive in this instance because the students I listened to, with but three or possibly four exceptions, were serious about their faith commitment as followers of Jesus. It became obvious, too, that they loved their particular Catholic high school, and they appreciated the ways in which the school could help them deepen their faith commitment. When followers of Jesus reflect on life, on their condition and situation, their practice and experience, and when personal faith and the gospel serve as a fundamental point of reference, then something "theological" takes place. It is surely *fides quaerens intellectum*: faith seeking understanding. And that is theology!

I do not consider these 40 students typical of the vast majority of students populating our Catholic high schools. Would that they were! To work out a profile of the typical Catholic high school students from the data of my sample would be inaccurate — I think! The students I listened to were senior students — Grade 12 and Ontario Academic Credit (OAC) students. For the most part, they have enjoyed their Catholic high school education and are enthusiastic talking about it. They are confident and quite articulate. Most of these young people intend to go on to college or university. As for family background, only

150

15 percent have parents who are separated or divorced. More than 60 percent of them work — on the average of fifteen hours a week. For the vast majority, belief in God and in Jesus Christ is a significant part of their lives. Fifty percent participate frequently (more than twice a month) in Sunday Eucharist; 25 % infrequently (once a month), and 25 % rarely (once or twice a year or on special Church occasions; e.g., weddings, funerals, etc.).

In line with the Bibby-Posterski findings, "friendship" is perhaps the most powerful experience in their lives. Music, too, is very significant, but time spent watching television is minimal. "What are some of the things that make it so hard to be a Christian in our society today?" It was unanimous: materialism, greed, cheating, the pressure to get ahead and be "successful." And confirming the importance of peers and friendship, when asked, "Who or what has most influenced your own faith development during high school?" again not surprisingly, it was "friends" or "a friend" followed distantly by "a significant teacher," "a chaplain," "a retreat experience."

The impressions and reflections that follow, then, find their source and inspiration in some thoughtful and concerned adolescents describing their experience in the Catholic high school. They talk about their ideas and ideals, their critique and suggestions, their hopes and fears for Catholic education. I am confident, however, that while the depth and maturity of their faith commitment disqualifies them from the label "typical Catholic high school student," what they express does represent the concerns and feelings of more than a few of their classmates.

As it happens, this was the propitious time to listen to these particular students. They are unique! They are the first generation of a fully-funded Catholic high school education in Ontario; yet, they have memories of the way it used to be in pre-full-funding days. A few years back, when they were in Grade 9, they remember "the private school" — the spirit, what was experienced and emphasized. Of that year or two — before the private school went the way of the dodo bird — they have recollections and a point of comparison that can be very beneficial for all of us elaborating strategies for evangelization and an agenda for our Catholic high schools in the 1990s.

This was an exercise in reflection. There was some preparation: an explanation of "evangelization in the Catholic high school" was proposed in advance, along with some questions on "how we seem to be doing" in this evangelization project. For this eavesdropper it was a fascinating, enlightening and encouraging experience. Indeed, it was fun

— so much so that I found myself wondering: "Why haven't I done this before?" Group reflection of this type, I am now convinced, can be done with any grade level or academic level of student. It is "an integrating" sort of educational experience that gets at the roots, the foundation of a Catholic education.

Through the years, I suppose, I just seemed to take for granted that the kids were not capable of thinking in any depth about "Catholic high school education" — or that to engage in such an exercice would bore them to death. The latter explanation, I think, would probably be true if such an exercise is carried out routinely in the classroom. But "declassroomize" the experience and the questions — create the situation where the students know that their views and experience count for something — and design an atmosphere where they can probe "philosophically" into their own feelings and opinions, and I believe we have the makings of a significant educational and evangelizing moment for these students. It is in such moments that maturity develops and ownership of faith is personalized. We need many more of them.

As we have seen, the bishops of Ontario have invited our students "to participate actively in shaping the vision of Catholic education." In the pages that follow, I share some of the results, the fruits, of 10 hours of reflection on the Catholic high school on the part of these thoughtful students. I believe that reflection of this quality contributes significantly to shaping the vision of Catholic education in the Catholic high school. Any teacher or administrator with even a modicum of wisdom knows well that students can teach us much! The same dynamic obtains in evangelization — listening to our students reflect on evangelization in the Catholic high school becomes for us a moment in which the evangelizers are evangelized. We learn much from our students.

Our primary concern in the Catholic high school is to pass on our faith, to assist our students to grow deeper in their knowledge of, and commitment to, the Lord Jesus. We listen, first, to the students reflect on the different ways they know Jesus, what it means to follow Jesus, and how they pray. Then they explore the purpose of Catholic education: what they perceive to be the vision of a Catholic high school education. Finally, they evaluate the ways in which this vision is lived out.

ON KNOWING AND FOLLOWING JESUS...
AND, ON PRAYER!

Question: What is it about Jesus and the gospel that speaks most profoundly to you?

Forgiveness

We must be doing something right when it comes to something wrong; that is, we're handing down to our students that there is a sense of the wrong! I have often heard that our young people today do not have a sense of sin. That may very well be true, but it was not the case with the young people I listened to. By far, the most intimate and profound experience these young people have of Jesus is forgiveness. The rule of thumb for the spiritual life is that you can only experience authentic forgiveness if you know and experience yourself as sinner. The evidence is clear: these adolescents have a sense of sin. They so admire and enjoy Jesus' forgiveness.

Angela, 18:

> Jesus' willingness to take you back when you do something wrong. This really hits me. It doesn't really matter who you are or what you did. For me the story of the prodigal son says everything about Jesus — forgiveness.

Curtis, 17:

> What speaks most profoundly to me is that Jesus had an unconditional love: like the apostles hiding at the crucifixion... Peter denying Jesus three times... Judas... Mary Magdalene...! Jesus didn't stop loving, ever! Mary Magdalene was the most significant example for me. She was a prostitute! Jesus knew about her reputation, but Jesus protected her; he spoke for her. It is this Jesus who loves me.

Biff, 17:

> The thing I like is the way Jesus goes to the sinners, to individual sinners. He really cares. Everyone has a chance to enter the Kingdom of God.

James, 17:

> ...You read the stories and parables, and you can't understand how someone can be that good, that perfect, like Jesus! Automatically there is a sense of respect — and what I like is that most perfect person will be there to forgive you.

When there are hard times, that lightens things up for me.

* * * * * * * * *

The Vulnerability, the Humanity of Jesus

A human, vulnerable God is very much a relational God! The humanity of Jesus speaks in a large and meaningful way to our young people. This is how one student describes it:

> I am awed by the fact that Jesus was sent by God, that he is God, but I relate to him as a person more than as a distant God.

And a personal God is a God who struggled, who questioned, who doubted. Struggling and questioning are very much the stuff of the teen years, as Lynn, 17, relates:

> Jesus suffered the pain of frustration, I see that. He questioned; he had doubts!

Marie, 18:

> It is Jesus' humanity! Pain and frustration were a part of his life. This comes through in the gospels. He questioned! It is really nice to know that! A lot of times I question, and I have doubts. It is nice to know Jesus did too.

Wally, 19:

> What amazes me is that every time Jesus was looked at as God, he was human; and when looked at as human, he was God! There is always this element — especially the humanity of Jesus. He was tempted. I can relate to this human, vulnerable God better.

* * * * * * * * *

Jesus, True to Himself — A Role Model

I have mentioned before how quick students are to see through hypocrisy. The flip side of hypocrisy is authenticity. They are equally adept in recognizing authenticity. For some, Jesus' faithfulness to himself is so significant that Jesus becomes the role model.

154

Marie-Claire, 17 :

> Jesus is so authentic and so true to himself. He is a role model for me.... He was always honest... and his ability to love and do what he thought was right at all times — this is how I see Jesus in the gospels.

Michael, 19 :

> "And Jesus wept" — to me this shows very much that Jesus is human. This I like. Jesus knew what he had to do. It was a real problem for him... and yet he did it. He responded to that challenge with his life. This idea I like also.

* * * * * * * * *

Jesus' Invitation to Love: Self, Neighbour and the Poor

As young people make their way through the teenage years, there is a preoccupation with identity : an autonomous self is struggling to emerge. Sometimes accepting the self and feeling good about self are difficult things to do for a young person. There are so many doubts, so much feeling of inadequacy. Faith in Jesus and understanding who Jesus is helps enormously.

Kathryn, 17 :

> One thing that amazes me about the gospel is that Jesus loves me, and that, whatever happens in my life, I will always have Jesus to turn to or go back to.

Angela, 18 :

> One thing I really like is that Jesus did not force people ; he didn't push people. He said : "Come, follow me!" And he said : "Love one another as I have loved you!" For me, Jesus loves me ; I have to love myself. But some people don't love themselves a whole lot!

And one's neighbour! "The Good Samaritan story I like very much. My responsibility to my neighbour is very clear here." Another teaching surfaced several times : "Do unto others as you would have them do unto you. This is so simple, but it says so much."

With Jesus there are no outcasts. Jesus' preferential love for the little ones, the marginalized, the voiceless, the powerless deeply touched several of the students.

Christina, 18:

> It was Jesus' personality... so open-minded! For example, to the lepers and children. He spent time with those who didn't count for much. It's easy to relate to Jesus because he was so human.

Marie-Claire, 17:

> I like the way Jesus spread his love for everyone. He showed he cared, no matter if they were poor or rich or sinners or sick. Jesus gave them a sense that they were wanted, they were loved, they belonged. There were no outcasts. Also, it hurts me to see that Jesus had to suffer so much... for us.

I found the above reflection profoundly challenging. It really does come from the freshness and wisdom of teenage experience: the strong conviction that all are equal; the need for a person to be loved, to belong; the need for community; the disdain for a system or social structure that produces "outcasts"; and the sensitivity to Jesus' suffering and the suffering of others.

* * * * * * * * *

Question: What part of Jesus' teaching challenges you, and you don't know if you are up to it or not, or, you are timid in accepting the challenge?

Accepting Responsibility for One's Life as a Follower of Jesus

Any definition of maturity must include the critical element of "responsibility" — assuming the direction of one's life and the consequences that follow. It is this successful acceptance of control, and the internalization of the laws, customs, rules and modes of behaviour that were once externally imposed, that is our usual measure of healthy adulthood. I believe the same is true in faith development or maturity in faith. It is the internalization or assuming personal ownership of one's faith that is most challenging to the students. One student very candidly described the challenge this way:

> ... Entering the Kingdom of God is hard! You feel sometimes that you don't want to grow up — you want to stay young where you're somehow less responsible.

156

Many of these students are certainly at the threshold of adult faith. I would even say that they are further down the road of a mature following of Jesus than many adults, including, probably, some of their teachers. They have amazing self-knowledge. They are given to personal reflection. They know God's love for them manifest in their own gifts and talents. And because of all of this they appreciate the personal responsibility at play in following Jesus, and the insecurity and mystery of it all!

Kathryn, 17:

> I think my fear is the responsibility! If Jesus loves me so much, asks me to be Christian, to be Christ-like — this is a huge responsibility. To remember the way he loves me and the way I am to love others — that's the challenge! And if Jesus loves me, then I should love myself, and I find that difficult a lot of times.

Biff, 17:

> The thing that sort of scares me is... like what exactly you have to do to enter the Kingdom of God! I'm not exactly sure what has to be done. I want to do it, but it's how to get there... that's the problem.

Marie, 18:

> The thing I find challenging is that Jesus is so hard to know. I know when I search for a strong spiritual force in my life that it is not going to be easy! It's going to be hard. It takes a lot of self-evaluation and that is scary for me. To find that stuff inside you... to establish a relationship with Jesus... I find hard.

* * * * * * * * *

Following Jesus in a Material World

In the description of adolescents proffered in the last chapter, reference was made to recent research claiming that teenagers today are "living in a decidedly material world, in which they're becoming material boys and girls."[1] The students I listened to, judging by the quality of their reflections and insights, are acutely aware of their material- consumer context and the challenge it is to follow Jesus: to let go and trust, to not use the overwhelming materialism of our society as an excuse, to choose to serve in the materialistic world.

Denise, 18:

> Jesus was so loving. He did not rely at all upon material possessions. And he says: "If I can do it, you can do it too!" I don't know. I find it difficult to let go of material possessions, to let go and to trust! That is really hard!

William, 17:

> The challenge for me is to give up... give a cloak or turn the other cheek. Now our society is so selfish! I find myself caught up in it. It is really hard to do. But then I can't use society as an excuse. I guess though I am afraid of taking up the challenge of going the extra mile, because for me, selfishness in a way is security. You don't want to leave it, but then that's the challenge to do what Jesus said — to do that little bit more. And for me, it's just hard.

Marie Catherine, 18:

> Jesus was such a servant — giving and doing for others — and even when he was hurting and struggling himself. I shouldn't blame it on materialism, but it is so hard today to serve. I am always struggling myself. I wonder how can I serve, how I can help someone else? For me, that's the challenge today — to serve in our materialistic world.

Bill, 18:

> I live in a society that gives me so much opportunity to have fun. I mean, it's incredible the material things we have... the opportunities!... But then I have to keep in mind that just next door to me — or on the other side of the world — there are people in dire need... starving. There is a balance I have to keep: satisfying myself, and yet to be responsible for others. This for me is the challenge.

Angela, 18:

> Something that I am fearful of: "The first shall be last and the last shall be first!" Right now, in our society, in the First World, we are the first! What does that mean? I find that really frightening in a way — and challenging.

I am very struck by the above words of William: "I guess though I am afraid of taking up the challenge of going the extra mile, because for me, selfishness in a way is security. You don't want to leave it, but then that's the challenge of doing what Jesus said!" I don't know that

158

the challenge to the First World Church and First World Christians could be put any more succinctly — or insightfully. It is a theology of letting go, of leaving the false security of material things and believing and trusting in a God who calls us to go the extra mile, to respond to him in the poor, the outcasts.

There are other challenges too!

• *Forgiving and Accepting Forgiveness*

It's this forgiveness. It's really hard. I can't forgive some people. I've got someone I haven't forgiven in eight years. I find it very hard to be kind to people who are not kind to me. If I'm rejected, I'm very hurt...

I feel sometimes that there is nothing I can do to be forgiven, even though I know God forgives. This scares me.

• *Reconciling Science and Faith*

Is there the resurrection? I'm scientific. Once you are dead, you're dead! I'd like to believe it, to take that one extra step!

There are so many questions, so many things about the Bible that do not jibe with science. A lot of that bothers me!

• *Being Fair*

It is tough to be as true and honest as he [Jesus] was to other people. The ability to be non-judgmental is really hard. It seems we are always biased. That's an immediate reaction! It's hard to treat everyone the same.

* * * * * * * * *

Question: What about prayer for you? How do you pray? Who taught you how to pray?

I was just about to embark on my mission of listening to the five different groups of students when I received the following communication from a friend who is keenly interested in youth ministry and religious education in our Catholic high schools:

A key question which confronts us is the distinction between sharing knowledge about God and giving a true experience of God. We are generally not succeeding with our young people in bringing them to a genuine experience of

159

God and that may be because we have not accepted fully the responsibility of teaching them how to pray. We can no longer assume that Catholic high school students know how to pray. The only legitimate assumption is that there exists a longing, however inarticulate, to do so.

This observation literally blindsided me! I was not at all expecting such an assessment. If this is true, I reasoned, then we are much more secularized than I had thought, and we really can't do much more in the Catholic high school than some very elementary pre-evangelization. But then, I continued to reason, "What does he know about teenagers that I don't know?" My instinct coming from deep down in the caverns of my gut told me that he was wrong. Kids pray! I know it. They have talked to me in the sacrament of penance about their prayer. "Are you praying?" is a question I inevitably ask. And many of them are quick to share: for some, they "are not sure; it's hard!"; for many, "Yes!" — but too much of it is of a pre-teen quality. And for a surprising number, indeed, they do pray and are not at all reluctant to relate how important prayer is and what support they find in their prayer. And that was my instinct.

But then I reflected on my praxis. And I thought: "He's right! In all my years teaching religion, have I ever taught kids *to pray*? The *what* of prayer, the *how* of prayer?" And I began to worry. He's right! I, for one, "have not accepted fully the responsibility of teaching them how to pray." I have prayed with them in class. On numerous occasions I have, as a priest, led them in prayer, and I have even talked about my own prayer and the place prayer has in my life. But to teach them formally the what and the how? No! It is a painful and perhaps shameful admission I have had to make to myself.

So it was important for me, then, to add the above impromptu question on prayer into the mix of preparatory questions I served up for the students' reflection. I am happy I did. Their sharing on prayer certainly made for an evangelizing experience for me. As for my friend's hypothesis, "We can no longer assume that Catholic high school students know how to pray," I believe that he is more wrong "now" than he is right. But my fear is that in the not-too-distant future, he could be more right than wrong. I will explain.

The students I listened to pray, and their prayer has an extraordinary quality and variety to it.

- *Prayer as Awareness*

For many of the students the internalization of childhood prayer

160

had already taken place. It very much reflects the struggle we have already seen of accepting responsibility for one's life as a follower of Jesus and the struggle it is to follow Jesus in the material world. "To stop, ponder, and reflect on my life" is how one student spoke of prayer, a prayer that nourishes and gives perspective. It is in such prayer that one feels belonging — "you are not alone."

Marie, 18:

> I think prayer can be on a lot of levels: a simple appreciation of nature, gifts we have, or friendship. I think even sitting down and writing your feelings is a form of prayer. You're not alone! You sense that. I think there is prayer in everything we do where we are searching.

Biff, 17:

> I think prayer is basically when you speak to God. I don't think prayer has to be like a ritual, really. I think it should be more personal than that. That's the problem with memorized prayers.... I don't think many of us — like with the Our Father — take the time and stop and think of what we are saying. I think prayer is more meaningful if we say what we mean and not verses and psalms...! I think we should just stop and ponder and reflect on our personal lives. For me, that's prayer.

Marie-Claire, 17:

> It is a relationship. In prayer I think the *real me* is at work. I get to see myself... by talking in my mind to God. It really is a way for me to cope with life and my problems. Talking to God for me is like talking to a friend.... And listening, too, is important, like listening to a friend.

Kathryn, 17:

> It's true I do pray in need: exams, a volleyball game, a tough situation. And for me, prayer just blurts out: "Gotta help me, God!" But for me, prayer is balanced out. As I get older I realize that prayer is more than just reciting something. At night, I recap my day. I think. I thank God for little things. That's prayer.

Peter, 19:

> Really, prayer is thinking! I put music on to mellow me out — like U2 — and I think, and I philosophize, I guess, with

God. Formal prayers are harder. For me... my prayer is in my own words.

* * * * * * * * *

- *Prayer as Relationship*

Prayer is personal! Communication with God in prayer is very much talking to a friend.

Adrianna, 17:

> Well, there is the formal prayer — Church and Mass. But now more important for me is talking to God like a friend.

Lynn, 17:

> It is the relationship I have with God... more than prayer at church or here at school. For me it's every night. And I feel that there is a need for it, a need to maintain my relationship with God, and that's what prayer does. I don't think every once in a while we check in — knock on the door and say: "Hi, I'm here!" I think it should be daily — and worked at.

Tom, 19:

> Prayer to me is communication with a friend. Songs help me. I pray every night. It is not only if I need something either. I thank God. I talk to God in a personal, friendly way about my life. God is a friend, someone I can lean on, someone who is beside me, at my level.

* * * * * * * *

- *Prayer: Acknowledging God as Source of All Life*

This was the type of prayer that I found truly admirable — the prayer of dependence. It is such a difficult attitude to cultivate in our material world: a dependence not on consumer goods but on God.

Christopher, 17:

> For me now prayer is... more than just asking! What really can I ask for? Really! Material things! I have so much. I owe everything I have to God. Prayer for me is recognizing

this . . . . It is admiration and thanking God.

Allan, 18:

> I feel that prayer is any method or means to communicate with God. Retreats have helped me. A song, for example — the words help me a lot. I can wake up and feel good on a beautiful day, and I know that God is responsible . . . That can be a prayer to God.

Wally, 19:

> For me prayer is attaching anything to God — a beautiful day, friends, luck, gifts. For me it is to see God as *the source* and not taking it for granted.

* * * * * * * * *

- *The Lord's Prayer?*

While formal and memorized prayers are often difficult for the students to personalize, one student indeed had discovered the incredible richness in the prayer Jesus taught:

> For me, everything you want to say is in the Our Father, whether it is forgiveness or thanks or praise. Everything is in there.

- *Who Taught You How to Pray?*

Here I must return to my friend's hypothesis: "We can no longer assume that Catholic high school students know how to pray." As I have said, the students who shared with me would not fit well into the profile of the *typical* Catholic high school student — if, indeed, there be such a profile. On prayer, their reflections are as eloquent as they are insightful. I believe, however, that the really crucial years for these students were their early childhood years. This is where they were introduced to God, to Jesus, to the idea of prayer. And their parents, especially their mothers, for the majority of these students served as their first spiritual directors, their primary evangelizers.

And what was initiated in the home was enhanced at school. I have acquired a richer, deeper appreciation for our Catholic elementary schools. Much of the creativity and personalization of prayer is very much the fruit of grade school years where kids pray via their experience of para-liturgies and prayer writing. Indeed, it was not only the teacher in the Catholic grade school who served as prayer mentor:

163

My mother helped, but I think I learned more about prayer in school, especially from a janitor I got to know. She taught me a lot!

As we enter the 1990s, we are entering foreign territory, especially as far as the family is concerned. Even 15 or 17 years ago, when these students were in their early childhood, the family was more intact, and family life was less secularized. The question is: will families today and tomorrow introduce their children to God in prayer? Through the 1990s, will this be a priority, or will it be just another parental responsibility passed on to the jack-of-all trades teachers, just like the socialization process already is. This teaching is already operative:

Where did I learn to pray? Not at home! Prayer really wasn't that important.

I never prayed when I was little! My parents did nothing for me, but I started talking to God because I had a good religion teacher in Grade 2. Then, I would talk to myself, and now, for me, prayer is being quiet, reflecting. I burn a candle in my room, maybe some incense. I pray to God for direction for my life, to get through my confusion.

Again, we see here the urgency in the Ontario bishops' analysis:

Given the increasing fragility of families and the overextension of parishes, it is becoming more obvious that the school, for some, is often the primary place where young people experience the Church....[2]

And, we might add, where students experience Jesus and prayer! It is this "fragility of families" that makes me think that my friend's hypothesis might soon prove to be accurate. And yet, we still have that very rich and meaningful resource, the Catholic grade school. More and more, Catholic primary education will have to function literally as "schools of prayer" — the starting point for evangelization.

And in the Catholic high school, teachers like myself will have to "accept fully the responsibility of teaching them how to pray."

A final note here that we will develop in more detail in Part Four is the importance of the retreat experience: "I really learned a lot about prayer on a SEARCH weekend." Several times a type of retreat experience was mentioned as the key moment for maturity in prayer. Some of these experiences took place within the high school context; some were outside. What is abundantly clear, though, is the critical importance of both the experiential and the relational — both central components of a youth retreat. If we are to teach prayer, then more and more we must promote, encourage and develop such retreat experiences as an integral part of the evangelization agenda in the Catholic high school.

* * * * * * * * *

• *And Do Your Friends Pray?*

This question was discussed ever so briefly, almost in passing. The intention, simply, was to try to ascertain just how representative these students are. The consensus was that most students do pray — in one form or another.

Chris, 17:

A lot of people who say they don't pray... have a misconception. They think it has to be something formal or ritual, but prayer is in everything. It is personal! Many people do it indirectly — without even realizing it.

* * * * * * * * *

ON THE VISION OF THE CATHOLIC HIGH SCHOOL

In Chapter 8, we explored the Church's invitation to young people to become active players in the evangelizing mission of the Church. To the students in the Catholic high school the Ontario bishops extend this invitation:

We invite you to become active participants in the process of Catholic education. We urge you to bring your energy, enthusiasm and generosity to the task of building a Catholic community within your school and to shaping the vision of Catholic education.[3]

As we have already indicated, one very real problem in all of this is *the how*. It is nice theory, a fine ideal, but the reality is that adolescents generally, and our Catholic high school students in particular, have such little power. How are they to be heard? Who will create the forum at the school level or separate school board level for students to have genuine participation in shaping the vision of Catholic education?

And there is a further consideration. Shaping the vision is often a much easier endeavour than getting others to share the vision or converting the vision into reality. This is the hard part. To their credit, the bishops render an important service in identifying the key players — the partner groups as they are called — in the Catholic education project in Ontario at "this moment of promise." The challenge is now very much at the local level to bring together the different partners to shape the vision of Catholic education. It goes without saying that such an experience needs to be repeated often to keep the vision focused and relevant; to have people feed into the vision and in turn be nurtured and challenged by it.

Shaping the Vision

What is it that our students might tell us about shaping the vision of Catholic education and the living out of this vision? This question was formulated in terms of *the difference* the Catholic high school purports to represent over and against the public high school.

1. Describing the difference

Question: What is the something different you expect in a Catholic high school that you would not expect to find in a public high school?

It was surprising to discover how many of these particular students had had some type of experience in both systems. This was not expected.

Denise, 18:

> When I went to public high school, I remembered what my sister who taught in a Catholic high school said about students being closer, and there being more of a community atmosphere in the Catholic high school. When I moved here and came to this Catholic high school, I expected this atmosphere; along with the religion classes, supportive students, supportive staff, closer relationships — and that's what I found.

Louise, 18:

> When I went to public high school, I really thought religion classes here would be just pious — really holy prayer-type classes. But they are really interesting, especially discussions about life and problems.

Christopher, 17:

> I've experienced a public high school and a Catholic high
> school, and here I really do feel there is a stronger sense of
> community. Also, there is emphasis put on the communi-
> ty outside the school: the city, those in need, our respon-
> sibility as Christians for the poor, etc. None of this was
> emphasized in the other high school.

And there is an instance where there was no distinguishable
difference whasoever.

Maria, 17:

> I don't see any difference. I went to a public high school.
> Their attitudes are the same as ours. Just because you put
> a uniform on doesn't make us different.

A minority view surfaced as well that one was at the Catholic high
school simply because of one's parents.

Anna, 17:

> To be honest, I didn't expect anything different. It was more
> my parents who expected a more enriched environment in
> education. I really had no say. My choice would have been
> a public high school.

Most of the obvious external differences were noted: the uniform
— everyone looks the same, it's easier, cheaper, you don't have to pick
out clothes every day, you avoid competition; the presence of priests,
sisters and brothers was appreciated; religious symbols — the chapel,
crucifixes, pictures; and liturgies — the Eucharist, penitential services
were deemed very important.

It was, however, the sense of community that was the outstanding difference. "Spirit," "bonding together," "family," "a common atmosphere based on our faith" are all descriptives used to sketch the
difference between the Catholic high school and the public high school.

The students are quick, too, to underscore the critical role the
teacher plays in creating and maintaining the community atmosphere
in the Catholic high school.

Louise, 18:

> The difference is the teachers! A couple of my friends went
> to the public high school, and came back here... because
> of the teachers. They find our teachers care more... they

are more friendly.

Adrianna, 17:

> I think a big difference is the number of teachers who help us create a real community here. There is a caring atmosphere.

Curtis, 17:

> I look for a sense of community between staff and students. Also, Lent and Advent we have daily Eucharist. I'm always surprised at how many teachers participate. And then there is concern for the world around us, action on behalf of the larger community.

Allan, 18:

> It is like a big family to me. There are kids and teachers here I can talk to about my problems, especially the chaplain.

Throughout this discussion, faith education and religion class were frequently mentioned. While there was a negative edge to their critique as we shall see later, the students were also positive in their assessment of religion class in the Catholic high school. They noted particularly: that respect is attached to human life — to the person, to the individual; that values and ethics are emphasized in other classes besides religion; that for their own development, very practical and realistic discussions about life are appreciated; that opportunities for retreats are provided; and that the possibility of discussing and questioning faith is constantly available. As well it was pointed out that faith is more than a chapel activity or a classroom subject. A Catholic high school education should foster awareness of the world and social responsibility. This ideal was expressed realistically in this way.

Marie, 18:

> In a way we should be different, but remember, we are in society, and I guess on a smaller scale we function just like society! We can't really expect to be the community we would like to be. I would expect, though, that we should emphasize more social responsibility to the larger society and awareness of the world we live in and the things that go on there... here in our school. I know we are still a young school, but I think this is what we should work at.

We can teach religion; students can learn it. But faith needs doing, experiencing! In our Catholic high schools that happens as much

168

outside the classroom as inside.

Wally, 19:

> There seems to be a greater sense of unity in what we do.
> The public school had a cancer drive on a school day. Kids
> were to canvass, but very few took part. They stayed home.
> Here we take a Sunday every year for our Third World pil-
> grimage. More than three-quarters of the school turns out.
> That is a real sense of community. There are other exam-
> ples of genuine action: a toy drive, food drives. It is more
> what we do than what we say that makes us different.

* * * * * * * * *

2. Enhancing the difference

*Question: To enhance the difference — to make our Catholic high
schools really serious about "evangelization" — what changes would
you make?*

At this point the discussion zeroed in on three central concerns:
students, teachers and religion classes.

Students

Selectivity is the issue here. Several students remarked that there
are kids at the school "who don't really understand who we are or why
we are supposed to exist." The following exchange between John and
Ann shows how nuanced the students are in their understanding of
Catholic education.

John, 17:

> Be more selective in the students who come to the school
> — in this sense: they should make some option for faith
> and religion; at least to have a willingness to give our
> religion classes, our activities, our liturgies a chance.

John is genuinely concerned about the quality of what goes on
in religion class. He is disturbed at the noise in the gym during liturgies.
He feels there should be more personal investment on the part of the
students.

Ann, 17:

> About being too selective: we have to remember that Jesus was for everyone! We can't look at people's hearts. We can't choose or select who comes. Some who don't care at first do grow to love the school. I know kids like that. I did myself. I think we need a wider variety of religion classes and liturgies for kids who are at different levels in their spiritual growth. And by that I do not mean advanced, general, basic.

Ann has a very adult faith. She knows well our schools cannot become elitist in the sense that they keep out, they exclude people. "We can't look at people's hearts." Ann has gone to school on her own experience. She knows well that change is possible because it happened to her. She has exceptional insight in her prescription for a variety (not OS:IS categories) of religion classes and experiences in liturgy.

A third student summarized the challenge in this way:

> "We need to educate the students that it's not uncool to believe."

Both John and Ann are in agreement with this.

Teachers

Just as the students are connoisseurs as to the qualities of teachers — authenticity and commitment — so they are expert critics when it comes to identifying mediocrity!

> Change the way certain teachers are.... Get teachers who obviously believe in the gospel, who care about you, and are not just there for the job.

> Most students are influenced quite a bit! If you want students to believe, the teacher has to believe too.

> Our faith has to be personalized, for both teachers and students.

> If this baby is going to fly... that is, the Catholic high school will work if the teachers are genuine! The one change I would make: change the mediocre teachers.

It should be noted here the students were not addressing the subject mastery or technical competence of the teacher, but rather the teacher's faith commitment. One can't help but recall Pope Paul VI's often-quoted words from his exhortation, *On Evangelization in the*

170

Modern World:

> Modern men and women listen more willingly to witnesses than to teachers, and if they do listen to teachers, it is because they are witnesses.

[#40]

Religion Class

On the question of faith education and religion classes, the students had several very rich and pertinent suggestions.

- We could be integrating our faith and Christian values much more than we do now... in other subjects; for example, English and economics.

- My religion classes have been boring and irrelevant. Memorizing Old Testament facts does nothing for me. So what? What has that got to do with my life now? This year is different. At last we are discussing life. Memorization is not good. Understanding is what we should be working at.

- One problem I see is that some of our religion teachers do not seem to be very confident or competent!

- We need better learning methods for religion! Talk more about the present and the future than the past.

- I guess we have to talk about religion, but we need to do more than just talk. We need to do something where we can apply it! For example, visiting and helping needy people... and retreats!

And there were other imaginative changes proposed as well that demonstrated a genuine care for, and understanding of, what the Catholic high school is all about.

On community:

> If community spirit is so important — and I believe it is — our school is getting too large. We have to recapture the smallness and the spirit we had two or three years ago.

On a unifying project:

> We can't lose the ideal. We need one concrete thing to unify us. For us here it is a commitment to the Third World and our school pilgrimage. This is a common ideal — a

common project. Look at us here. After 13 years, the Pilgrimage is still the main thing that happens. That's four generations now of high school kids who have touched and been touched by this project.

On the grade school and family:

One of the things, you know, is the grade school and the family. If there is not much emphasis on faith or religion in the grade school and family, you can't expect too much here! I know! My family background — my parents are split, no emphasis on Church — is like that. What influenced me was a retreat here at school... But most kids don't have those experiences. I just think you have to reinforce the foundations: grade school and family.

The final change I present here is in many ways the most profound. Biff, 18, is wise beyond his years when he says that our Catholic education is more than classes and credits. Rather, it has to do with a gospel outlook on life. It has to do with the challenges of our cultural context and its notion of success. Biff, to my mind, proposes an education that transcends and integrates the bits and pieces, the modules and credits that a student accumulates over four or five years. So much of this education is disconnected. Or if there is coherence to it, the glue that seems to hold it all together is our culture's contemporary understanding of success, which is the acquisition of wealth and privilege. A Catholic education should offer a different "glue" — a different integrating perspective. And that obviously is the gospel. So Biff suggests that we be philosophical "and focus on the long run." His challenge to Catholic education is the radical challenge to be different in the gospel way.

Biff, 18:

One thing would be to focus more on the long run. What about our notion of success! We come to school thinking we have to make it big in the business world. You have to have a lot of money. This is the attitude I want to change. Make money less important. Look at the gospel!

* * * * * * * *

3. The difference and the future

Question: What about 20 years from now: what difference would you see in the Catholic high school for your children?

The autonomy and independence emerging in the teen years is certainly a dominant trait — one that many adolescents will go to the barricades (figuratively speaking) to defend. Certainly this was the case when the students were asked if they would send their children to the Catholic high school 20 years hence! Many of them insisted that they would leave the choice to the individual (thus respecting teenage independence and standing tall for the democratic way!). But then most of them proceeded to wax eloquent on how much they personally have enjoyed the Catholic high school experience and would want that same experience for their children.

But not all were positive. One student was particularly articulate on what she perceived to be the limitations and drawbacks of the Catholic high school.

Anna, 17:

> I wouldn't send my kids to the Catholic high school. I would send them to the public high school. I don't feel that there is anything very enriching. In the public high school there is more variety and exposure to different people. It is not as protective an environment and I think that would give my child a more realistic approach to life. I wouldn't inflict a certain religion on my children.

And there is the yuppie factor! For a couple, "quality education" has more to do with the academic fast track than it does with gospel principles.

Joseph, 18:

> Another consideration is the reputation, the quality of the school. If it is good, okay. If the public school's education is better, I would send them there.

Jayne, 18:

> When the time comes I will discuss it with them. French immersion will be important. Being Catholic may not get you a great job, but having French will, especially in Canada.

The students also have a sense of history — at least of the recent past. It is ironic that projecting into the future was an occasion for several of them to root around in the past. The question of full funding came to the fore. It is important to remember that most of these students have an intuition into, and experience of, the pre-full-funding Catholic high school in Ontario. (Remember Michael's assessment at the beginning of Chapter 1.) And while they certainly do not mean to pronounce definitively on the wisdom and merits of full funding, they do have their hesitations and some fears as to the impersonalization of the school, the loss of community and a watering down of the Catholic difference. Their comments go a long way in helping us grasp the full meaning of the timeliness of the Ontario bishops' pastoral letter on Catholic education, *This Moment of Promise*. Entering the 1990s, Catholic education is at a very critical moment.

Bill, 18:

> The real thing for me is the sense of community, belonging. I'll have to look at it. If my child is going to be a number, and not a person, or if the Catholicity is watered down, I'd send my kids to a private Catholic high school! But I still am more hopeful than skeptical!

Ann-Christine, 17:

> I would really be wary. I've enjoyed my years here, but with this full funding business, there has been a change. I am concerned about our standards — not only academic but the community, the atmosphere, the dedication of the teachers. I really wonder if my kids are going to be short-changed!

The overwhelming response to the future, however, was positive: "Yes, I would send my kids to the Catholic high school."

Yes... because of the sense of community!

James, 17:

> Yes, I would send my kids to the Catholic high school. I want them to feel the sense of a family. You learn more if you are comfortable.

Lynn, 17:

> I would like for sure to send my kids to a Catholic high school, not only because I went to one, but I'd like them to receive the sense of individuality, yet the feeling of togetherness; that you have someone there for you! Here we have a community where you care about each other. Maybe not everyone does, but I think you have a good portion who do.

174

Yes... because of the faith education!

Curtis, 17:

> I think the important thing is not just to know what Jesus said but also to practise it. The Catholic high school gets us to take part, to think; for example: "What's wrong with our society the way it is?" You analyze the political or economic structure, think about it, point out what's wrong, try to find a solution. In the public high schools I don't know. I don't think they do this. We are encouraged to do this from our faith... the gospel. They sure don't do that.

Christina, 18:

> Yes, I believe religion is very important, not so much in the Bible sense or religion class sense, but in understanding who you are as a person. We are brothers and sisters. We need to understand this and question things: why are they the way they are. Going to a Catholic high school, I should have a hope and some expectations that my child will get this in return from teachers.

Kathryn, 17:

> I think a lot of things would be different for me. I went to a junior kindergarten Catholic grade school only because of the program. I find that religion and faith learned along the way have become really important for me. Because this has been so good for me, I would want it for my kids. I have Catholic friends at the public high school, and they go to church, and their parents are good. But our school really does add a lot more. It makes my religion and faith richer.

Yes... because of the teachers!

Marie, 18:

> Yes! But I think I am realistic. That doesn't mean that I think they are going to stay Catholic and so on, true to their faith, but I think they will have a better chance here than anywhere else. Hopefully they'll get guidance and direction to carry with them the rest of their life, even if there are only one or two teachers that they can look up to... as I do here. I mean, use them throughout their life as an example. That would be great! The chances of doing that here are better than anywhere else.

175

Yes ... because of tradition and the family!

Adrianna, 17:

> My parents came here. They have sent me here, and my
> sisters. It is just natural. I'm very happy. The Catholic high
> school really helps me to make a connection between life
> and faith. It helps me understand how life comes together.
> I'd want my kids to have this.

Angela, 18:

> I would send my kids here because of the values the edu-
> cation tries to instill; because of the type of staff, the exam-
> ple! I would want the values I teach my kids to be
> reinforced.

These adolescents certainly have an understanding of the key in-
gredients that go into the formulation of the vision of "Catholic high
school education." The next line of questioning, then, was designed to
analyse the dynamics at play in our attempts at implementing the vision
and making real our ideals in the Catholic high school.

* * * * * * * * *

LIVING THE VISION

Question: How is the difference best communicated to you?

It really does work — this Catholic high school ideal, that is!
There are, indeed, moments and situations in which the ideals are realized. The community atmosphere was again emphasized: the friend-
liness and caring. The school's activities: liturgies, penitential services,
consciousness awareness experiences, peer tutoring, the integration of
the developmentally handicapped, the variety of extra-curricular clubs,
sports and cultural pursuits, and the special spirit in which all of this un-
folds. And faith education — the religion class — was also felt to be a
special means for communicating the difference, especially a faith education sensitive to the person and the person's life journey, and focused
on the world and the awesome challenge of following Jesus in our time
and place.

The following reflection sums up much of the spirit and the activities that constitute "the difference" in the Catholic high school.

Michael, 19:

> The difference is communicated in a number of ways: our
> activities — food drives, toy drive, school-wide experience
> for the Third World. The teachers and administration work
> hard here at making us aware of the outside community
> and outside world — a global awareness. And then there
> are the liturgies, and like today, the sacrament of reconcili-
> ation in the gym. And the real difference, I think, is appar-
> ent in teachers who care about the well-being of students;
> and the administration too.

One special feature of the Catholic high school experience that
was mentioned several times in different schools was the spiritual and
healing ministry so readily available, especially at times of crisis!

Peter, 19:

> One thing is crisis! Two years ago we lost two classmates in
> a car accident. It was really hard here, but what we did: we
> had a special liturgy in the gym, and that really helped so
> many of us. That shows in a nutshell one of the great differ-
> ences between us and a public high school.

The outstanding dimension by far, however, is the dedication and
commitment of the teacher. The qualities, values and attitudes of
teachers who are genuinely and generously committed to the ideals of
a Catholic high school education powerfully transmit their faith in Jesus and the meaning and richness of our Catholic tradition, as the ef-
fusive testimony of the students attests.

On transmitting values

Angela, 18:

> One of the best ways... teachers! It's much easier to adopt
> certain values and ideas when you see someone else doing
> it, someone you admire, trust and know. This is clear in the
> teachers who work at helping us increase our own social
> awareness, our Christian responsibility.

The qualities that are tangible, that speak volumes to the students,
are very likely postures and gestures that many teachers take for granted: understanding, respect for the student as a person, patient listening, honesty and fairness, friendship. One student aptly described the
impact a teacher can have:

177

It comes through as plain as day that they are happy about being a Christian.

On handing down the faith through witness

Marie-Claire, 17:

> There are a few who are really committed. God and faith or values... will come up in class... any class; for example, math or French! Also, the ones who give us confidence — a compliment to build up our inner strength. And for these people, it's not a drag! Teaching seems to be fun!

Kathryn, 17:

> For me it is the teacher whose faith comes through — in the corridor, in no matter what class they teach! It is obvious: faith is a part of their life. Also, you see them at Mass and in the parish.

Adrianna, 17:

> They are just genuinely good people, not superficial in any way. They like to get involved. For me, they really are the basis for what makes the school different. Faith comes alive for me through these people.

Wally, 19:

> The good teachers in this school are more personal, and they really do teach us by their actions, through example. There is a work atmosphere in class, but it is not independent from our faith or from the gospel. Faith is lived out. It isn't a Sunday thing... or a church thing. I pick this up from these teachers. This is the something more, the something different we discussed earlier.

Jane, 17:

> They take the time. They have time for you in class. They say hello in the hallway. They are personal! Most of the teachers who are concerned about the gospel are less concerned with stupid little things like rigidly applying the dress code or uniform rules. I can tell. Teachers who feel that Catholic education is special — it comes through: it doesn't matter what the subject.

Andrew, 18:

> For me there have been three or four teachers who have really impressed me with the way they integrate their faith in all that they do. They openly discuss issues, bring their faith to them, [explain] how this relates to the lives of the students. Besides, they will admit that they don't know it all.

Ann, 17:

> It's a personal thing. A particular teacher is a mentor... encourages me. Someone found something in me before I found it in myself. I think they were seeing me through the eyes of Jesus.

Angela, 18:

> What impresses me about these teachers is that I can learn something from them beyond the subject; that is, totally separate from school. They teach something about life. You don't have to separate the teacher from the person. Also: integrity, authenticity; there is a passion about faith and Catholic education. You just know it!

* * * * * * * * *

Question: In what ways are we weak in the Catholic high school in getting the difference across to you?

But our very strength — the aspects of a Catholic high school education that differentiate us from the public high school and help us create an alternative education based on the gospel — can also be our weakness. While the quality of the school community and gospel-inspired involvement and faith education tend to give substance and depth to a Catholic education, the absence of these evangelizing dimensions is generally debilitating and compromises all of our efforts to provide a genuinely alternative education. The students noted three obstacles in particular that diminish our evangelizing efforts in the Catholic high school.

Counter-witness of the teacher as obstacle

Adrianna, 17:

> There are a few teachers who just radiate indifference. They don't seem to care, so why should I? They give me no encouragement or interest to learn... no Christian stuff at all.

It's a job for them — nothing else — and it becomes a chore for me.

Elizabeth, 18:

> Some kids and teachers really don't seem to know why we are here or what we are about as a Catholic high school. And there are teachers who just teach their subjects; they never talk about life or faith. You notice this because there are teachers who do this very well. No matter what the subject, they will talk a little about life in general and even their faith.

Bill, 18:

> I really think a lot of teachers are just too busy leading their own lives, and if Jesus or the gospel isn't part of their lives, there is no way it will come out in school — classes or wherever. There are some teachers like this. They stand out in contrast to the dedicated ones.

Jayne, 18:

> I think some teachers aren't chosen well enough. I don't think they all have to be Catholic, but they should have to go along with what we're doing here in the Catholic high school. They should have a class or something where they learn how to handle the views that will come up in the Catholic high school. You've got kids who are trying to learn about their faith, and if teachers can't help, then they are an obstacle.

Christina, 18:

> Here, at lot of the teachers who have been here — older ones who have been here a long time — emphasize the tradition of the school! Some of the younger ones — it seems that the school is just a place to work. Teaching is a job.

Largeness as obstacle

Andrew, 18:

> I guess realistically you can't say that the Catholic high school has to cut down on the number of students, but the problem is we have gone from being a community to being a large institution. And the problem with being an institution is the lack of the personal approach and personal care — especially for the student. I look around here: we're so big,

180

but there are some really good teachers trying to foster community. But it is overwhelming, like pounding your head against a brick wall. And they burn out.

Angela, 18:

> Things have definitely changed since our earlier years. It's not that the effort isn't being made now. It's just that the job is so much harder because we are so big now — 1500 students. It is so much harder to create a sense of community. Also, we see this at school Mass. I think it is due to the size of the school, but there just seems to be a lack of respect. You have to wonder how many kids in the cafeteria where we have Mass actually go to church, because they just are not respectful! I think it's because they don't understand what the appropriate behaviour is.

Religion classes and religion teachers as obstacle

We have already touched on the difficulties here: the lack of confidence and even of competence of some religion teachers; a curriculum that is out of touch with the spiritual and psychological development of the student; a reluctance to challenge the students with "the hard words" of the gospels; and the wide faith background of the students which can vary from the baptized pagan to the mature committed believer.

Marie, 18:

> ...the religion program! Maybe it was me, but I took classes and didn't think much about my relationship with Jesus. I really don't think I was challenged to think about my personal relationship with Jesus. I think this is missing.

> And the religion teachers: some of them are insecure. They stay with the content in the book but don't reveal the struggle there is in religion or the continuing challenge it is in your life.

These student reflections on the strengths and weaknesses can serve as a mirror for every teacher in the Catholic high school. These kids — our students — desbribe us. They first catch us with their slow-motion camera, and then they play us back, diagnosing and explaining "what we do" and, especially, "how we act"! And from their replay they get a very accurate picture of "who we are" and "what we stand for." They mince no words: what is authentic comes across as such and is appreciated; what is superficial is obvious and is deemed to be an

181

obstacle. These students know it and state it very well: the ultimate validity and credibility of the Catholic high school depends upon the commitment of the teacher; the implementation of the vision of Catholic education — a vision that the kids themselves can help us shape — rests primarily on the readiness of teachers to take seriously their role as evangelizers.

* * * * * * * * *

The intention here has been to listen. As we experienced in the preceding chapter, eavesdropping, listening to the teaching Church reflect on the adolescent faith journey, can be an evangelizing experience. Here, too, eavesdropping on some of our students as they reflect on their Catholic high school experience can be refreshingly beneficial. And the questions we have considered are crucial questions!

- How do our students experience Jesus?
- What is it for the young believer to follow Jesus today?
- How do they pray?
- What is their vision of Catholic education?
- And how do they grade our efforts! What do they see as our strengths and weaknesses as we struggle "in this moment of promise" to give flesh and meaning to the ideals of a Catholic education?

This is precious data — an excellent resource for all of us engaged in evangelization in the Catholic high school. Certainly, for any "visionning" that we do — or philosophizing and theologizing on the meaning of the Catholic high school that we may engage in — the experience of our students must be tapped. As the bishops remind us, the students are indeed "active participants in the process of Catholic education." They must be respected as such.

Eavesdropping of this type is not only morally correct; it is a highly recommended exercise in evangelization.

It is time now to return to our group of teachers and listen in as *they* reflect on the experience of our students, as they discuss the different methods of evangelization that seem to be most effective, and as they share how they themselves are evangelized by the students in our Catholic high schools.

182

NOTES
Chapter 9

[1] Refer to Chapter 8, p. 136.

[2] Ontario Conference of Catholic Bishops, *This Moment of Promise.*
A Pastoral Letter on Catholic Education in Ontario (Toronto, 1989),
p. 16.

[3] *Ibid.,* p. 22.

CHAPTER 10

A REFLECTION ON EXPERIENCE —
TEACHERS ON YOUTH

I admit that the students who have just reflected with us on their own faith and their own vision of the Catholic high school — largely because they have succeeded in making their own the gift of faith received from God and nurtured by their parents — are exceptional. Yet, I am convinced that however exceptional they are, their testimony in Chapter 9 can tell us much about the faith journey of the majority of students in our Catholic high schools and about how that majority responds to our evangelizing efforts. The central elements of teenage spirituality are there: the fundamental stance of recognizing oneself as sinner in need of God's forgiveness; openness and generosity; varying approaches to, and understandings of, the meaning of prayer; the searching and struggle. And, even though the majority of our students may not be capable of profound and articulate reflection on the meaning of their faith and the challenge of following Jesus in our society, there is still enormous potential, so much of it untapped. Recall the conclusion of Reginald Bibby and Donald Posterski:

> Thus some 70% of teenagers seemingly have clear religious and spiritual interests. To the extent that religious groups fail to captivate young people, it is not because "the religious market" is not an appreciable one.[1]

I think that, given the nature of our Catholic school system and the exceptional nurturing of faith that takes place in our Catholic elementary schools, the 70 percent assessment (of teenagers with "clear religious and spiritual interests") might even be higher in our Catholic secondary schools.

The immediate task, then, is to mine a bit deeper this potential for evangelization in the Catholic high school. We have already eavesdropped on the teaching Church and reached several conclusions: that

184

our evangelization should be adapted to the needs of our students; that it should be an inviting evangelization, one that respects the subjectivity of the young person and that considers it an imperative that young people participate as an equal partner group; and finally that evangelization be sensitive to the dominant psychological reality of "emergence" operative throughout the teen years. We have, as well, eavesdropped on some very thoughtful students as they have reflected on the meaning of discipleship and prayer in their lives and what they assess to be the strengths and weaknesses of the Catholic high school.

Let us now return to our group of teachers; this time, to their reflections on "the searching and struggle" in the faith journey of students in our Catholic high schools. Once again these teachers speak of their experience: their observations, their personal successes and failures in evangelization as they have accompanied so many adolescents in their faith journey. Their sensitive reflections reveal a certain wisdom inevitably culled from their own searching and struggle.

1. TEACHERS ON YOUTH: ON EDUCATION AND CATHOLIC EDUCATION

It was ironic! Some of the first reflections of the teachers who agreed to participate in this project were on the topic of "The Social Context" and the role it plays as instrument of, and obstacle to, evangelization.[2] Months later, as we gathered to reflect on the beneficiaries of our evangelization — youth — the groups of teachers consistently found it impossible to discuss general student attitudes toward education apart from the social and cultural context which they believe at the very least strongly influences those attitudes, when it doesn't outright shape them. Consequently, there is a "big picture" that is rather gloomy! The teachers recapped some of the "givens" in our materialist-consumerist value system that so condition both us and our students:

- *The importance of money* — for clothes, cars, stereos, CDs, concerts, vacations, ordinary weekend socializing; money for wants, not needs! Thus, for many students, the importance of part-time jobs.

- *The popular meaning of success:* a sense of worth determined by what we have rather than who we are; a mind-set counter to everything the gospel stands for.

- *Instant gratification* — wanting it all, now! A philosophy that access to the material things we want is a human right!

- *De-sensitized, de-humanized feelings and attitudes* — an ad proclaims: "I love him almost as much as I love shopping!" Consumerism becomes a priority; persons become commodities.

When that is the dominant value system, education is, at best, a necessary means to jobs which assure enough money, success and gratification in the future. At worst, the hours from nine to three on weekdays are an interruption, even an intrusion. The "real world" happens after three and on weekends. And when, in the context of Catholic education, there is an effort to name the dominant consumerist-materialist ideology — to expose its components and its corruption — the proponents of the dominant ideology often respond with denial, resistance, resentment. For the teacher struggling to evangelize in this context, it can seem that there is a cosmic conspiracy to sabotage the effort. An English teacher summed up the challenge of doing Catholic education in our contemporary cultural context this way:

> The media bombard us with a whole vocabulary of values and images of values. It's overpowering, and I'm not sure our students are given tools to critique these values. Where are the images of values to model honesty, integrity, fidelity? Even the Ben Johnson inquiry fails us. It's focused on drugs [who used what, when, administered by whom with whose knowledge]. But what about the prior thing: the value of honesty, the immorality of cheating?

But the testimony was equally loud and clear that despite all the gloom and doom, all is not gloom and doom. The negatives were consistently juxtaposed with irrefutable positives: our students themselves — their intelligence, insight, generosity, searching, tolerance and open-mindedness; a faith which calls us; a Church which teaches us; the reality of the separate school system in our province — we already have a place to do evangelization during a very sacred time in each student's human development; and there are so many teachers in our system who perceive teaching as a vocation at least as much as a profession. Quality Catholic education is happening; students are being touched by it; the potential to do even better is within our grasp.

Certain responses to particular questions posed during the teachers' discussions nuance this summary analysis. Their big picture is sometimes disturbing, other times affirming, and always challenging.

Question: How are our students looking at education today?

The consensus was that for the most part students view education in very practical, utilitarian terms. It's a commodity! For some, it's a ticket to future "success" in the most disappointingly crass, non-gospel sense of that word. For others it's a ticket to a job! It's as clear-cut as that!

Chairperson, English department:

> I think kids see themselves as "workers-to-be" — earning money! I think that is the big focus in our education. "Where am I going to make the most money? What fields are open?" The question, "What would I enjoy doing with the rest of my life?" doesn't seem to be asked very often. "What talents do I have to bring to the world out there?" is not asked. I do see some enjoyment in learning and grappling with issues, but too much of it is: "What's the assignment?" "What's it worth?" "How do I get an A next time? I really need these marks for university!" It's hard to paint all kids with the same brush, but...

This particular observation of our "Chairperson, English department" pulls together several disappointments and concerns consistently voiced by a number of teachers. First, questions of meaning and service and talent seem relatively unimportant for students as they make their way through the dynamics of decisions about post-secondary education and future career ambitions. In fact, many students seem to lack a sense of "vocation" — in the Christian sense of that word: what they might be "called" to do; what talent they might be "invited" to develop; what contribution to our world they might be "inspired" to prepare to make.

Then, there is the realization that too few students ever acknowledge experiencing "the joy of learning" or valuing "education for its own sake" — "education" defined as it derives from the Latin, *educere*: "to lead out of oneself"! That's a foreign concept! Instead students' relationship to the education process is perverted by unhealthy pressure: pressure to end up with at least the previous year's cut off mark for admission into certain limited-enrolment college or university programs, or pressure to just get accepted anywhere; pressure to meet unrealistic parental expectations, or, just as damaging, pressure to meet unrealistic expectations of one's self.

More than a few teachers remarked on the climate of insecurity that haunts many students today.

187

Chaplain:

> I think a lot of kids are desperate now: "Whether or not I
> will get a job; will it be a well-paying job; will I have secu-
> rity?" There is more insecurity now among students than I
> found before.... I think they see education as the key to fu-
> ture security. And yet their sense of insecurity is bigger than
> that. The climate of insecurity is due not only to the un-
> predictability of the employment situation. Other things add
> to it, like family, diseases, the nuclear thing.

And there is another insidious form of insecurity: the student in
search of social relationships that will shore up a terribly fragile self-
concept or will dull the pain of a broken or abusive or otherwise impoverished home situation. This combination of insecurity and pressure
produces a distorted, compartmentalized view of school. On the one
hand, as one teacher commented, "school is the place during the day
where you meet your friends; at night, it's the mall." On the other
hand, it's the place to get marks.

Physical education teacher:

> Their view of education is utilitarian. "What do you want
> me to do?" They'll do it in that way — to get the marks!

And then there is the allurement of, the competition with, the
damnably destructive effects of the part-time job.

English teacher:

> I had a class this morning — an OAC [Ontario Academic
> Credit] class! A student came in looking beat, washed out!
> I said: "Where's your assignment?" He said: "I didn't fin-
> ish it. I was up all night working at the gas station." He said:
> "I have to make money to go to university!" I said: "You
> need this course to go to university." There are so many
> things infringing on their role as student.

The political and economic forces at play in our education system
surfaced frequently enough to suggest the importance of reflecting on
the enormous influence power and the economy exercise on education. There is more than a little evidence that they can be devastating-
ly effective and influential.

English teacher:

> A powerful conditioning into the consumer values of our
> society takes place in — and you can even say because of

— our schools. Kids learn our economic system in school: power, marks, competition. Upwardly mobile kids will do well: they'll go to university. Less well-off kids generally don't do as well.

Principal:

> Education serves as a sorting system for our social structure. Advanced students / OACs are headed for big dollars and good jobs. Basic and general students are headed for hard times and poverty.

In acknowledging that many students are impoverished by lack of flair, imagination and creativity, the teachers shouldered some of the blame.

Principal:

> Generally, the fault is ours. It's the system from top to bottom. As educators we fail to engage their [the students'] intellect and barely attract their attention; and we manage to suppress their enthusiasm. We do it consistently. I find it very depressing.

Guidance teacher:

> It is significant that the question speaks of "education" and not "school"! In some instances "school" should be a prior question because, for some kids whose home life is a battle zone, school is a sheltering, comfortable, even nurturing place to be.

> But the question of students' attitude toward education — maybe it should be asked of teachers: "How do teachers look at education today?" How many of us would want to be taught or counselled the way we teach and counsel? How creative and exciting are the learning environments we provide?

But in the midst of all this negative reality, or in spite of it all, there are, of course, thoughtful students who enjoy their education. And there are kids who grow intellectually and in wisdom as they make their way through the high school years. And there are kids who really do want to "get out of themselves" and explore in creative and imaginative ways life's wisdom and possibilities.

Head, guidance department:

> The degree of maturation that exists in the kids has a lot to

do with it. When kids choose courses, there are certain kids who think about more than what they need. They look at it in a more global way: they would like to do this or that. But these are always the mature ones. It's a process. . . . Hopefully, as they do move through high school, kids learn that education is more than just job preparation. Many, of course, never arrive at this vision.

* * * * * * * * *

Question: How are our students today looking at Catholic education?

The teachers' views varied considerably. Each perspective, however, contained some truth that when pieced together produces a mosaic that probably depicts the range of feeling students have (or in some cases, don't have) about Catholic high school education.

There is, first of all, the realistic view that holds that in too many instances the Catholicity dimension of education is only a cosmetic.

Guidance teacher:

> One thing I find difficult in working with student leadership over the years: here at school some very positive "Christian things" happen with a focus on the poor! A few weeks later, the students' council — in response to severe administration sanctions following a food fight among senior students in the cafeteria — wants to sponsor "an official food fight." "Kids would really enjoy that," they maintained. I don't know. Maybe it is adolescence; maybe it's our times! It is very disappointing.

Principal:

> We seem to adopt all the paraphernalia of the public system. We're so big. It's IBM operational management tactics. This is what becoming a public system has done. Our teachers are "OSSTF-ed"! We will rally to fight a one per-cent hike we have to pay for superannuation, but a rally for justice won't draw flies. Some of our senior kids see that Catholic schools once represented something different, but now, since full funding, the vision is gradually slipping away. I think that 15 to 20 percent of our kids have real values; they see a higher value to the Catholic high school. The majority are there in the first place for other reasons: be-

cause of parents, as a haven from drugs and sex, the discipline is better. They don't see the Catholic high school as a vibrant source of gospel values. I think when kids are exposed to real Catholic values in the school, most of them respond very positively. But if the values, the difference, remain only superficial, nothing will happen, and kids will only identify with externals.

"Parents," "academic reputation," "discipline" and "sports program" surfaced consistently among the major reasons teachers believe too many students choose Catholic secondary education. For such students, our identity as an alternative faith-oriented system doesn't seem to enter into it.

But there is, too, a sensitivity to the affective and intellectual development of teenagers. They are, after all, high school students. There are many realities in life they cannot yet name. There are sentiments and the beginnings of abstract concepts that they cannot yet articulate. A Catholic high school education is one such value. This, too, is being realistic.

Chemistry teacher:

> There are a lot of kids who appreciate it [Catholic education] but can't articulate it. But then you ask them in 10 or 15 years time, and I really think they will be able to talk about the impact the Catholic high school had on them. Maybe I'm just projecting too much from my own experience. I couldn't have formulated this point of view in high school, but Catholic education introduced me to an experience of faith I had not had before. It has given me direction as a person. It shaped my determination to teach in a Catholic high school. So even though I would teach chemistry, I could also hopefully help kids meet the world of faith and meaning I only found in high school.

Religion teacher:

> So many kids are unchurched, and many of them have a funny idea of what it is to be Catholic. Yet when you talk to them, they want "the Catholic thing" we stand for: respect for the person, community. They like the liturgy, the activities. They can't articulate this very well, but I'm sure they want it.

And while the teachers tended to agree that there is not widespread student articulation about Catholic high school education as a conscious preference for a faith-oriented alternative to public high school education, at the same time, they consistently identified aspects of Catholic education they have heard and seen students appreciate. Among the key themes were the Catholic high school as a *community* and the sense of teaching in Catholic schools as a *vocation* or ministry above and beyond being a job or profession. These observations resonated strongly with the student testimony reported in Chapter 9. In talking about a caring atmosphere and concerned teachers, we are, to be sure, talking about ideals, but ideals that have been realized time and time again. The testimony of both the students and the teachers attests to this. This, too, is reality.

It is important to report that a debate took place on the "concerned teacher" theme. A number of teachers were uncomfortable that there could possibly be any insinuation that Catholic schools have cornered the market on caring, concerned teachers. Caring is a humane personality trait identifiable in all kinds of good people. It ought to be an operative characteristic of every teacher. And I, for one, saw the truth of the premise and the reason for caution in the rhetoric.

In response: Absolutely! There are great people teaching in the public schools. But in our schools, over the years, there has been so much emphasis on teaching as a vocation — teaching as a ministry — that it has had an effect. It rubs off on some of us anyway, as it has clearly rubbed off on some of our students. That faith dimension: the call to witness, the call to acknowledge the fact that we are evangelizers — it sinks in! This same emphasis obviously is not found in public systems. And for this position, too, I was sympathetic, and I was confirmed in my own conviction that a gentle but persistent nagging for the sake of the gospel is effective.

Finally, recognizing the dynamic presence in our schools of some very exceptional and committed young people, a chemistry teacher pointed out the critical — the alternative — dimension of Catholic education that is a trait in some of our schools:

> I now know of several Catholic high schools that are doing some very imaginative things with kids in the area of peace, justice and development. You ask those kids who are involved in these projects. They can tell you what a Catholic high school can be.

* * * * * * * *

A Commentary

It is important at this juncture to listen again to the teaching Church. The teachers have reflected that for the most part education is regarded primarily as preparation for a well-paying job. A few teachers observed that our education generally promotes the consumer values of our society and in turn conditions us to accept the dominant ideology of liberal capitalism and its by-products: greed, competition and selfish individualism. It is obvious that a Catholic education should be something other. Ours should be an alternative education founded on the teachings of Jesus and the gospel values of forgiveness, compassion, justice and solidarity.

I believe strongly that discussion and debate on the meaning of education in our time and place is critically important. But where and when does it take place among educators? Looking at my own praxis, outside of a few late-night beer and pizza discussions, I have a hard time recalling any formal or informal staff discussion on the philosophical foundation of education; not airy-fairy rhetoric but fundamental questions like: "What do you mean by education?" "What should education be?" "What is its role in the development of the person?" "What is its relationship to society?" Most practising educators would willingly consign these questions and others that are equally critical to colleagues "given to discussion." (In this context, "discussion" is a polite euphemism for what would likely have been said!) And that is exactly the problem. If as a profession we don't own the questions, how do we address the answers? All around us we experience the consequences of the unexamined life.

On education the Church has a voice, a perspective, that has been developed over the centuries and that reflects a wealth of accumulated wisdom; a voice, a perspective that transcends the viewpoints and values of any particular society; a voice, a perspective that has been formed by listening to God's Word; a voice, a perspective that is a response to being called to interpret that Word to the people of our time. It is imperative that any discussion on the meaning and function of education that we engage in take into serious consideration the perspective of the teaching Church.

I propose two passages of Church teaching on the meaning of education because I believe that this "voice and perspective" speaks directly to the reflections on education we have just considered.

193

- Pope Paul VI: *On Evangelization in the Modern World*

  On an Evangelizing Education that Upsets

For the Church it is a question not only of preaching the Gospel... but also of upsetting, through the power of the Gospel, humankind's criteria of judgment, determining values, points of interest, lines of thought, sources of inspiration and models of life, which are in contrast with the Word of God and the plan of salvation.

[E.N., #19]

- The Synod of Bishops, 1971: *Justice in the World*

  The method of education very frequently still in use today encourages narrow individualism. Part of the human family lives immersed in a mentality which exalts possessions. The school and the communications media stand now even under the power of the established "system" and so they can only form persons in the way they are needed by the "system"... not new persons, but only a reproduction of the traditional types.

  But right education demands a transformation of heart; fundamental to this is the admission of sin in its personal as well as in its social forms. Education must emphasize a totally human way of life in justice, in love and simplicity. It must awaken the capacity of critical reflection on our society and on its current values; it must stimulate the readiness to reject these values when they no longer contribute to helping all persons come to their rights.[3]

* * * * * * * * *

2. TEACHERS ON YOUTH: ON EVANGELIZING AND BEING EVANGELIZED

This common "reflection-on-experience" exercise was a new experience for a few of the teachers. At first there was a propensity on the part of these teachers to look at evangelization as something that happens in the chaplain's office or in the religion classes. Hearing the testimony of colleagues, however, and then delving deeper into their own experience and pondering their own ideals proved to be an expanding and very enriching experience for them. By the time we had reached the halfway point in our discussions (after four and a half hours of group reflection), it was commonly understood that evangelizing in the Catholic high school had many rich and interesting dimensions. More important, though, was the acknowledgement that it is the task or — to use words of the Ontario bishops we have already considered — "the awesome privilege and responsibility" of every teacher in the Catholic high school to evangelize. And so the shared reflections on the methods and challenge of evangelization — while at times touching specifically on the faith education provided in the retreat experience or the religion class — for the most part transcended the confines of the religion department and found applications in the total environment of the school, affecting every teacher, every class, every department.

Question : On evangelizing — what are the methods of evangelization that are most effective with young people?

"Respect the person each of them is!" "Reinforce their sense of dignity and self-worth!" The points of departure for all serious teaching ought also to be, in the opinion of the teachers, the points of departure for evangelizing youth in the Catholic high school. A physical education teacher pointed out how important it was for teachers to keep going back to this "first principle."

Perhaps one of the most critical challenges that full funding has visited on Catholic secondary teachers has to do with the respect, dignity and self-worth of the increasing numbers of students who have entered our system whose preference or need is for general and basic level courses. Prior to full funding, most Catholic high schools lacked the financial resources to develop appropriate vocational and technological programs. We now have those resources; we also have a significant increase in the number of students who want to have Catholic secondary education. Yet we have been slow to demonstrate our profound respect for the dignity and worth of each student by developing different programs, approaches and strategies. We have been slow to adapt.

Having established common agreement about "first principles," the teachers also quickly achieved consensus that the most effective method of evangelization is any exercise or activity that involves students' experience : something hands-on ; something tangible and concrete ; something that allows them to go deeper into discovering more and taking ownership of their faith ; something that needs them to make it happen. As examples teachers shared numerous accounts of student testimony about the value and meaning of particular faith experiences provided in their schools.

High on the list of "most effective" were : retreat experiences — COR, SEARCH and class retreats seem to be inexhaustible resources for evangelizing; school liturgies — particularly the Eucharist and the sacrament of reconciliation, and especially when carefully prepared with the students and then celebrated with creativity, reverence and meaning — have a lasting impact; and the experience of service — assisting at a food bank or a refugee shelter, giving care to someone handicapped or chronically ill — puts the student on the helping end of things. Such experience gives the kids the opportunity to be touched, to experience their own worth, their own capacity to make a contribution, to make a difference. It initiates them into the critically important activity we know as social analysis: they begin to understand and question the social factors at play; for example, "Why are there food banks?" And they deepen their awareness, sometimes even their ownership, of any number of fundamental Christian perspectives; for example, respect for the dignity of every human person or the Christian's call to serve.

Numerous teachers underscored the moment of crisis as especially ripe for evangelization. The human journey cannot avoid crisis. The faith journey of a follower of the crucified Jesus anticipates pain and crisis as part of the cost of discipleship. But teenage years are filled with so much energy and enthusiasm. The individual teenager is caught up in the dynamism of the crowd or the group. Until it is experienced, it is so hard for the individual teenager to conceive of crisis — "the cross" — in whatever form it takes: sickness, death or other personal tragedy for the young person. But crisis happens, and when it does, it has impact not only on the individual but sometimes on friends and sometimes even on the entire school community.

Chaplain:

> In evangelization there is a real need for the person to get
> in touch with himself or herself. You need self-awareness.
> A crisis does this. The young person then looks for help...
> for meaning.

If a teacher lacks the habit of care and concern for students, that teacher can be oblivious at the moment of a student's greatest need and greatest vulnerability. That teacher can miss the moment when "the privilege and responsibility" of evangelization is most acute. The world of crisis — our own or anybody else's — is not our favourite terrain. The caring, concerned evangelizer accepts the awkwardness, the uncomfortableness, and the inconvenience of joining and accompanying a student in a moment of crisis.

We have already seen from the perspective of both students and teachers that the teacher really does make a difference as far as the

196

Catholicity or faith dimension of the school is concerned. It is not surprising, then, that the quality of personal witness is considered to be another very privileged method for evangelizing in the Catholic high school.

English and drama teacher:

> It is so important to remember that we are mentors for the kids! I teach drama. If I do things "dramatic," the kids will mimic. It's the same on the faith level. Kids will see and imitate.

Chaplain:

> It's really not what we say; it's what we are. If I am ever going to teach the gospel, it will be primarily through myself as a person. They'll remember me, not so much what I say. And if they do remember what I say, it will be the times I shared my story, my personal struggle, my faith with them. The kids are bright. They spot phoniness immediately. Really, the vehicle for teaching the gospel is the individual teacher ready to share his or her story.

French teacher:

> A lot of little things — friendship, conversation, personal gestures — are all so important. These are all methods. Maybe they're not seen as terribly effective right now, but they will become part of the student's memory. It really is personal witness. As a teacher I carry with me my history, my values, my view of life. I don't know how it comes across to the student now. My hunch is that kids will look back and say: "That teacher took faith seriously."

It is obvious in reading the above testimony that there is an important oral dimension to personal witness, and that is, the readiness to share something of one's own faith journey. This really is the heart of evangelization. This is what it is to hand down the faith. Essentially it is the readiness to share with others our own experience of Jesus and his forgiveness.

English teacher:

> I think to bestow self-worth or to transmit values, I use the personal story. My own children relate well to the personal story. And in that I am honest. I tell them about my own struggle. I use examples from life. It is intuitive — when I think the time is right or appropriate. I risk sharing with them something of my own journey, which is very much a journey in faith.

Chemistry teacher:

> Humanity — that's the method. Share your weakness, your fragility, your humanity. Making mistakes is part of life. Admit it if you don't know something. And apologize. Ask for forgiveness! This really does model some pretty fundamental Christian values.

Risking to share one's story, one's experience of Jesus, is a most radical gesture. And yet it shouldn't be. It should be the most natural of activities. Recall the words of Paul VI in our sixth reflection in Chapter 2:

> Finally, the person who has been evangelized goes on to evangelize others. Here lies the test of truth, the touchstone of evangelization: it is unthinkable that a person should accept the Word and give oneself to the Kingdom without becoming a person who *bears witness to it* and *proclaims it* in turn.
>
> [E.N., #24, emphasis added.]

Yet, to be ready to share one's faith story means that a person has questioned and pondered and prayed. It means that one is serious about growing in the understanding of his or her faith.

Head, guidance department:

> Bring yourself to the situation. The more we can do to grow in our understanding of faith, the more impact we are going to have on our kids. A guidance principle is: "The more you have it together yourself, the better you will be able to help someone." I think it's the same in evangelization: the more serious I am about my faith, the more it will show and hopefully impact on students.

Unfortunately, as one teacher put it, lamenting the underdeveloped quality of the understanding of faith today, there are some teachers and too many parents who are not "Vatican II-ized"! The negative aspect of this model of faith was elaborated on by a vice-principal:

> A problem in our school is pre-Vatican II type teachers. Not so much teachers who want Latin back or those who are really conservative or traditional Catholics, but the silent types — whose understanding of what it is to be Roman Catholic is still a pre-Vatican II understanding. They haven't grown at all, and the parents of many of our kids are like that, especially the once or twice-a-year church Catholics! They really don't understand the renewed Church, and they give their kids that outdated understanding of religion. For our kids, these are the *models,* and they are not healthy faith or Church models.

There were numerous experiences shared, other methods of evangelization in the Catholic high school that have "worked." "Peer evangelization" was underscored: the prior importance of our listening to students in order to in turn train them in the art of listening and reflection. Students have the capacity to evangelize each other in ways closed to adults. They need our instruction, direction, support and encouragement. In stressing the importance of integrating skills for students, a teacher remarked:

> To help the kids on their faith journey, we need to provide them with a knowledge to integrate what they have and with tools to interpret what is happening.

* * * * * * * * *

Question: On evangelizing — what are the challenging elements of evangelization today, especially for young people?

The teachers approached this question from two different perspectives: the challenge of Jesus' life for young people today and the challenge we face as evangelizers of young people.

* *The challenge to young people inherent both in Jesus' life and in the gospel.*

On self-sacrifice and the cross

Instructor, faculty of education:

> There is no gain without pain. The gospel is about the cross, and that is a hard lesson. The cross is difficult. It is always a

challenge to anyone. The sacrifice of self is most important: following Jesus must cost. Unfortunately, most kids today seem to have little sense of sacrifice. Their parents have done that for them! Sacrificing for others is really not a part of their reality.

A "hard word"

Religion teacher:

You can't really give into their values by giving up your values. You can't always say what you know they want to hear. They have to have a "hard word." They need to be challenged. That's Jesus and the cross. We need to allow kids to meet Jesus. They are attracted to the human Jesus. They can relate to him.

The whole life of Christ

English teacher:

The whole life of Christ is such a challenge! Jesus stepped out of the mainstream of society and lived with the powerless. He went to the little ones. This is the very antithesis of every other message we seem to get in society.

* *The challenge we face as "evangelizers" to help our students grow in faith.*

Serving the other

French teacher:

How often do we propose to the kids — not in a preachy or condescending way, but a good way — that life is more than a good job and material success? How do we present to them "the other"; that you can really find yourself in the other and in service; that doing something for the betterment of the community or society or the world is a more fulfilling thing, a better thing, in the hierarchy of career possibilities.

Instilling a sense of vocation

Guidance teacher:

We need to rediscover the meaning and content of the word "vocation"! In our guidance classes or career counselling sessions, do we challenge the students with critical questions such as: "What gift do you have that could make a difference in our world?"

Ministering to the Broken

Chaplain:

> ...to be present to and walk with too many of our students who are challenged horrendously, day in and day out, by the brokenness, violence and hatred experienced in some families today.

* * * * * * * * *

Question: On being evangelized — how are you evangelized by the students?

In Chapter 8 we read Pope John Paul's assertion that the mutual dialogue between youth and the Church "will be a source of richness and youthfulness for the Church and society." There must be some universal wisdom in that sentiment, for it certainly proves to be the case in the year-long conversation that takes place between some students and teachers in the Catholic high school. Our students are very definitely "a source of richness and youthfulness" for us as teachers. We are taken with their "tolerance and compassion"; we are humoured and at times astonished by their "enthusiam"; we are touched and occasionally humbled by their "idealism" and "sensitivity." Our students evangelize us, as one teacher put it, in the affairs of the heart:

> We get mechanical, in a rut, but the kids keep us in touch. We tend to get away from our heart, our emotions. They bring us back. They keep us in touch.

Teaching is a noble profession. With the added dimension of vocation or ministry, teaching in a Catholic school is also an enabling, an empowering profession. As such it has its own unique satisfaction. When students develop a view of the world based on Jesus and the gospel; when they discover something new and rich about life; when they can be critical of so much of what is sinful and wrong in our society, this, too, is an affirmation, and in its own way proves to be an evangelizing experience for the teacher.

English teacher:

> What keeps me going, saves me from burnout, keeps my faith alive, is that there is a certain satisfaction, even though

I've taught the course many times, in meeting a new group of students and in being able to turn these students on to the world of ideas; to get them to see, to be critical, to see through the idols of society! I think it's a great thing to lead kids to a new understanding.

Religion teacher:

I have always admired John Henry Newman and his idea of the university. He argued: the purpose of education is to give people a view. By that I think he meant a fundamental orientation, a perspective on life. As a teacher, I am encouraged when someone can leave your class having developed or acquired such a view.

In evangelizing their teachers, the students are a mirror. As one teacher put it: "When they allow us to see our own faults they are like a mirror." It is in that capacity of reflecting back to us that they keep prodding us toward honesty. They can do this in a very frank way by nailing us in our hypocrisy:

Someone said: "Kids have a built-in crap detector!" It may take some longer than others, but they spot honesty and phoniness.

But this mirror action on us can be affirming and encouraging.

Head, guidance department:

The feedback I get from the kids, the positive reaction or affirmation — the work, the service, the involvement — all of it is really worth it! Kids are so much better than adults at showing appreciation. That helps me! It makes me think that it is all worthwhile.

Indeed, we can learn a lot about ourselves from our students.

Chaplain:

How am I evangelized? The students force me to be more authentic, to examine my own faith.

Vice-principal:

Some [students] are so kind and sensitive. You might say something sarcastically, and they ask: "Why did you say that?" And really they are saying: "Why are you so unkind?" And I see my shoddiness. They trade me some of their innocence, some of their healthy naivete. They al-

202

low me to see how jaded I am — or can be!

It seems more than anything else, the students are a sign of hope for us, very tangible signs that the Holy Spirit did not go out of business with our generation but is present still, busy concocting in the minds and hearts and spirits of our students some very exciting and no doubt mind-boggling surprises for our world.

English teacher :

Some experiences of students who suffer, who then bring a real sense of hope, and understanding of people, an empathy to others in similar circumstances. This is an experience in evangelization for me.

Principal :

The incredible privilege of working with kids all my life has taught me to be honest, open, authentic; to be able to admit : "Hey, I'm wrong!" They have forced me to be compassionate and forgiving. And wave after wave of keen-eyed kids have taught me to be always hopeful — that tomorrow will be better than today. They make me aware of the gospel which is always hopeful in spite of human weakness. I think kids teach me that.

* * * * * * * * *

3. TEACHERS ON YOUTH : ON FAITH AND PARTICIPATION IN THE CHURCH

An introductory discussion on the question of the religious literacy of our students produced some enlightening and instructive insights, some rich data which can add shape and content to our various evangelizing strategies.

Question : How are adolescents today religiously literate, and how are they religiously illiterate ?

Literacy is certainly a valid question, indeed, a necessary question to discuss in the context of school and education. It is equally valid and important in the context of education that means to guide and facilitate faith development. The dynamics of adolescent faith development should be learned and discussed often by everyone involved in the doing of Catholic education. In their reflection on religious literacy, the teachers proposed two preliminary considerations. First of all, they recognized that there is a comparative dimension possible in this discussion: we can fall into the trap of expressions like "more literate or illiterate now than before." A caveat was expressed, therefore, to avoid claiming qualitative superiority for either yesteryear or the present. Secondly, literacy was taken to include the affective — feelings and attitudes and the doing of religion — as well as the cognitive or intellectual — the academic awareness of things relating to faith and Church. The following testimonies reflect these concerns.

Chairperson, English department:

> If I compare what students know now with what I knew then, there is a radical difference. We knew history and dates and documents and customs and rituals. It was all of a piece in those days 25 to 30 years ago. You couldn't avoid it in a Catholic milieu. Kids today, however, are much more aware of global issues, more aware of links and connections. I think, too, they have a notion of conscience. They know that conscience is pretty much the last thing in making a decision. In many ways they are not literate, but I feel hopeful, for they are aware in ways that we were not.

Physical education teacher:

> Some of the students are very literate. They do more thinking. They appreciate interpersonal relationships. Some are religiously illiterate, like many adults, living a compartmentalized existence. Faith is only a part: sometimes it counts; other times, turn it off. It is not an integrating or regulating principle of a person's everyday life.

There are many surprising ways that our students are literate, that they demonstrate an understanding of what it is to follow Jesus as a member of the Roman Catholic Church:

- There is a tolerance and sensitivity to other churches and religions that surpass the prejudice and narrow-mindedness that characterized many Catholics in the past.
- There is an awareness and appreciation of the complexity of modern moral questions relating to bio-ethics and social justice.
- There is a critical edge to their faith; a questioning of what is right and wrong in society and in the Church. Many are disappointed with the Church's record on the treatment of women. Some see a conflict with birth control and abortion. They will

204

agree with the Church's teaching on abortion, but they also tend to see birth control as a way of avoiding the abortion dilemma.

- There is a literacy manifest in their actions; their generosity, service and idealism are truly admirable.
- There is an openness, a readiness; and among some, a deep thirst to discover more.

English and drama teacher:

I think our mistake is thinking we can give it to them instead of allowing them to do it. We should provide the atmosphere or the environment. For example, my kids danced The Passion liturgically to the music of *The Mission*. They had no Jesus. They had to create Jesus. It was an amazing experience for them. They loved it. I'm sure they grew in their faith.

But there is illiteracy too. Time and time again, the home, the parents, were mentioned: they are either the primary source for, or the primary obstacle to, religious literacy.

Religion teacher:

Some are not getting faith at home. They don't go to Mass. So ultimately, they are not getting much in class. But in class they do get something: some moments for personal growth, opportunities to grow in awareness. But the school can't supply what the home fails to give. Faith is either a personal and family priority, or it isn't! We do our best.

Another religion teacher:

What we have, then, with religious illiteracy is the failure to pass on to our children, our students, the rituals, tradition and symbols that were a part of our parents' world; because there very definitely is a gap!

And where an understanding of faith is handed down, too often it is confused, reflecting pre-Vatican II traditions and perceptions that are outdated.

Religion teacher:

Most young people are religiously illiterate. They don't see the relationship between faith and reality. They all have an opinion as to what the Church says, much of it uninformed! A lot of this illiteracy comes from adults, their parents, most of them in the pre-Vatican II era! Mind you, I think they are well-intentioned, but they talk post-Vatican II and live pre-Vatican II. They like black and white answers. They personally don't invest themselves in the faith, in the Church. Church is too much out there — something other than self.

English teacher:

> It seems to me that many of them have a sense of Catholicism as the out-of-it pre-Vatican II Church. I've had examples. Kids list rules; they say that the Church says what we can do and can't do; they accuse the Church of being legalistic. This stuff comes from parents, and kids have inherited their parents' perceptions. Most of these parents are not regularly at Mass on Sunday.

Much of this negative conditioning regarding faith (or the lack of any conditioning at all) at home makes for a very distorted image of Church. For many the Church is a "rigid, legalistic, inflexible institution concerned only with dos and don'ts." It is not a community of brothers and sisters trying to discern the Father's will and trying to co-operate with the Holy Spirit in continuing to exercise Jesus' stewardship in bringing about the new creation. Their distorted image of the Church and their underdeveloped understanding of what it means to be a praying and serving people are manifest in their appreciation of "holiness" and their attitudes regarding Sunday Eucharist.

Chaplain-priest:

> Many of them are illiterate. They see religion as being very negative — a list of don'ts that takes joy out of life. Also, it's passive. Even for those who do go to Sunday Mass, how involved are they? It all happens to them! Their sense of holy is a woman dressed in black, carrying a Bible and going to Mass on Sunday. That's "holy" to kids! They don't sense *holy* as someone working for the homeless or caring for AIDS patients or lobbying for the peace movement. They don't see that as holy. We have to get Matthew 25:31-46 across to the students. In a way, I guess it's that pre-Vatican II-post-Vatican II thing.

Priest-teacher:

> I assist Sundays in a parish right beside a school of 1600 students. Granted, not all the kids are in the parish, but students are sure not conspicuously present on Sunday! Our liturgy vehicles our language, tradition and symbols. Kids

206

are not getting it at Sunday Eucharist. Of course, only about 30 percent of adults are there.

There is also the history factor! A common complaint with education today is that students have no sense of the past. Memory is important for computers, but for the collective wisdom of the ages, the record of people, events and factors that have shaped the present, there is little interest. History has been "down-phased" in the realm of what should be taught today. This relegation of history as a subject to the periphery of mandatory curriculum happens in faith education as well, and is seen as a source of religious illiteracy.

Ultimately the question of religious literacy is significant because of its relationship to the challenge for faith education in the Catholic high school.

Principal:

> Let's face it! Throughout our entire secularized society today, religion and the Church are just not a high priority. We are a small minority now, a little remnant. But we have to be salt and leaven. And in the high school, we have to start with the kids.

The phenomenon of the number of teenagers who, in the descriptive analysis of one teacher, are "frozen in an early childhood set of religious values," must also be taken into account in evaluating adolescent religious literacy. While on the one hand we are not surprised in view of the number of adults who seem similarly "frozen," on the other hand we recall that one of the tasks of evangelizers of adolescents sketched in Chapter 8 is to facilitate emergence — to provide the occasion for the students to break out of that childhood mentality and internalize their faith in Jesus and all the demands implied in following Jesus.

Religion teacher:

> The real challenge for us in teaching religion is how to lead the students to make the content their own; to internalize their faith. This is probably *the* challenge for teaching adolescents... *period!* It's assisting them to make values and faith their own.

But to perform responsibly as facilitators of emergence, our own houses had better be in order. What about the religious literacy of teachers? Two very direct challenges were issued, touching on our maturity in faith: "our image of God" and "what does it mean to teach in a Catholic school?"

Chaplain-priest:

> I have done a lot of professional development days with
> teachers in a retreat context. We focus on questions like:
> "What are our images of God?" "How do we perceive
> God, relate to God?" This is an important starting point.
> Spirituality really flows out of this. Most teachers, I find, still
> have some kind of image they adopted in childhood. They
> really haven't developed.

Principal:

> I ask the question in interviewing Catholic teachers: "How
> would you make your classroom different if you were
> teaching in a Catholic school as opposed to a public
> school?" Rarely have I ever received any genuinely Chris-
> tian suggestions. I always hear: "teach them with respect,"
> "teach them to be fair!" The public school does this. It
> should do it. That is part and parcel of teaching. What I
> would expect: gospel values, the beatitudes, the Sermon
> on the Mount, the particularly "Jesus things."

* * * * * * * * *

Question: And what about prayer for the students?

The teachers' impressions were rich and varied. The following
random observations probably create a pretty comprehensive profile of
prayer as it is practised and experienced in the Catholic high school —
with its weaknesses and strengths.

> ...the way we have Mass in school with 1400 students sit-
> ting on the gym floor. It can be an experience of commu-
> nity, but is it an experience of prayer?

> Unfortunately, most of the prayers they get at our school
> are through the PA box.

> Some have the sense that prayer is standing and listening:
> words are provided, maybe a thought is triggered, a senti-
> ment is touched.

> I'm always surprised at the great number of students at daily
> Eucharist during Lent.

There are several students who seek out the solitude of the chapel.

The psychology of adolescence has much to do with the meaning of prayer and the shape and form prayer may take. In the teen years it is not unusual for prayer to be rejected much as some teens are wont to slough off the authority of parents and the Church. What prayer does manage to impress upon the psyche and spirit of the adolescent is usually a childhood mode of prayer that has yet to be adapted and internalized.

But as we have seen, the elementary school years can be a very fertile school for prayer, with great emphasis on personalization and creativity. It was suggested that perhaps the high school is at fault in failing to nurture the prayer life of the student.

Instructor, faculty of education :

> At the elementary school level I get reports back from student-teachers that in many of the schools they are in, kids can put together prayer services, intercessions, petitions and compose their own stations of the cross. Something seems to happen when they reach adolescence! Maybe it's part of the rejection thing — they say : "That's kids' stuff!" Or, they aren't given the opportunity to do it : I would suspect that that's it! The prayer thing doesn't seem to be nurtured as it was in elementary years.

It was the general consensus, though, that students pray. The very nature of adolescence — the pressures and the insecurities, the highs and lows — would see prayer as a coping response, a means of getting through it and making some sort of sense out of it all.

Head, guidance department :

> The teen years are so tumultuous. These years are devastating to most kids, even if they don't let a lot of it show. There must be a lot of prayer! More formalized prayer, no! But I think there is a lot of reflection and attempts at interiority, more than we think, but not necessarily in the way we did it.

* * * * * * * * *

Question : As Church, how do we fail our young people ?

There is always the tendency for any teacher in the Catholic high school to see Church as something apart: the Church is the parish or the priest, the institution or the Pope! This is especially true when it comes to any critical evaluation of the Church's effectiveness in evangelizing and in becoming the community we are called to be. In their reflections on "how we as Church fail our young people today," the teachers correctly avoided this tendency. Their premise was clearly: "*We are* the Church. In the school *we are* the teaching Church! The Church's failures in many ways are our own!"

We began this consideration on "youth as the beneficiaries of evangelization" in Chapter 8 by acknowledging that the most effective instrument for the evangelization of students is the evangelization of teachers. Failure to see to personal renewal in the faith is surely a failure to tend to the faith education of our students.

Religion teacher:

> We really fail them because we probably haven't challenged ourselves to develop our faith as we should have. If we are going to do the students a service, we have to do ourselves a service first. We really do need renewal — as teachers, as parish. The responsibility here is the person's, the invididual's, and the school's.

In Chapter 8 we also developed in some detail the importance of "adaptation" and "participation" for our evangelizing strategies, for an evangelization that is both healthy and relevant. It is not at all surprising then that the teachers would conclude that we fail most as Church when we ignore these qualities of adaptation and participation.

On failing to adapt

Head, guidance department:

> And I think that that's where the Church has really failed. We have said: "Fit into our structure." We don't ask the kids: "Where are you at?" We say: "Fit in with us." We don't really have community. We talk about it, but we don't have it. Kids see the hypocrisy of this. Kids look at many of our parishes and say: "Give me a break! This is community?" I think they see it as really phoney.

English teacher:

> The Church fails to present kids with a means to give life meaning. Many kids see Church as pews in a building. It's not a way of life. Somehow we are not getting the message

across that our faith is a lived-daily thing — not just a Sunday, 60-minute thing.

On failing to invite adolescents to participate

English teacher:

> Look at retreat experiences where they are involved: their attention is marvellous. It means something! Look at a parish: there is one in the city in particular that has a dynamic sense of community. Kids are present in droves and are active there. But most of our students' experiences of Church, of parish, are very sterile. They just don't feel involved.

Chairperson, English department:

> We don't invite them to participate. They are not part of Sunday liturgies. And even at school, they are handed what to say: they are not involved in creating it. Church bulletins: nothing there to speak to kids! We don't make the links: their world and the gospel; the parish and the community; the school and society; the faith connection is not made.

And there are other failures as well!

On failing to challenge with the "hard word"

Guidance teacher:

> For a small minority of kids the retreat movement is wonderful. Students are nourished and challenged. But by and large today, our program for being Catholic today is pretty mediocre — for adults and adolescents. Looking at our practice, the thing expected is to check into the Church on Sunday. The content of Sunday preaching most of the time leaves me empty. There is no real challenge as to what Sunday should mean for the next week! We lack the radical commitment of, for example, the Mormons! Our faith: we fail to teach the social gospel. What is articulated is still pretty much a very private faith.

On failing to become a servant Church

Head, guidance department:

> We have to bring to the building, the structure, the parish organization that kind of humanness and caring, not an

aloof pomposity that we sometimes run into. We have to work really hard at all levels of Church to dispel that image. We have to get back to the Christ image of foot washing — the servant Church. We hear that gospel Holy Thursday, but if we analyse the way we operate as Church throughout the year, foot washing is hard to notice.

On failing to forgive

Physical education teacher:

This morning we heard the prodigal son gospel. The emphasis was on the Father going out to the son to offer forgiveness. I don't think we say this enough as Church. We don't communicate this acceptance and forgiveness as well as we seem to present the law and rules.

On failing to empower

Religion teacher:

A lot of what we are talking about is empowerment. We haven't evangelized adults or adolescents to let them do it! To empower them! The kids lack power in the Church. Maybe the best thing the priest could do in the parish is to disempower himself and get people involved.

* * * * * * * * *

The most appropriate conclusion to these reflections on the failure of the Church to evangelize effectively is to remember the introductory statement: "We are the Church!" The Church is not something or someone apart! To be sure, the Church is the priest in the parish who gives boring homilies, and the Church is the liturgy committee so enamoured with "high church" liturgy that it ignores the symbols and music that speak to young people today. But the Church is also the director of education of a Catholic school board or superintendent or principal who acts autocratically, failing to empower, failing to invite participation; and the Church is the religion department or chaplaincy team that can't be bothered or is afraid to risk in providing an environment for faith education that would allow for more personal participation and responsibility on the part of the students. And finally, the Church is each of us: in our selfishness and pride, in our reluctance to grow in our understanding of our own faith, in our refusal to "wash feet" and extend forgiveness.

212

Again, words of Pope Paul VI that we meditated on in Chapter 2 come to mind:

> She [the Church] is the People of God immersed in the world, and often tempted by idols, and she always needs to hear the proclamation of the "mighty works of God" which converted her to the Lord.

[E.N., #15]

Indeed, it is this humble perspective that should inspire and direct all of our evangelizing efforts on behalf of youth, the students in our Catholic high schools. And it is especially this perspective that should permeate and give shape to an agenda for evangelization for the 1990s that we shall now consider in Part Four.

NOTES

Chapter 10

1 Reginald W. Bibby and Donald C. Posterski, *The Emerging Generation* (Toronto: Irwin Publishing, 1985), p. 66.

2 See Chapter 6.

3 Synod of Bishops Second General Assembly, November 30, 1971, *Justice in the World*. The second section of Part III — "The Practice of Justice" — is entitled "Educating for Justice." The quote is found in paragraphs 2 and 3 of that section. The English version of the document is available as an individual booklet published by Polyglot Press in Rome, and in a number of collections of documents which articulate Catholic social teaching. The translation used here is found in: Michael Warren, *Youth, Gospel, Liberation* (San Francisco: Harper & Row, 1987), pp. 113-114.

PART FOUR

Evangelization — An Agenda for the 1990s

A CATHOLIC HIGH SCHOOL EDUCATION AND THE HOUR FOR RE-EVANGELIZATION

There is a paragraph in *This Moment of Promise*, the recent pastoral letter on Catholic Education in Ontario, that clearly and concisely sets the agenda for Catholic education in the 1990s:

> . . . .the lessening of the financial burden of Catholic education must be seen as freeing us to make the collective and personal choices and sacrifices necessary to enhance our educational communities of faith. As Pope John Paul II said to us during our visit with him in April, 1988, "Even though the financial viability of Catholic schools has been guaranteed, the task remains of ensuring their Catholic character." The great privilege of this new freedom cannot help but remind us that much is expected of those to whom much has been given. [Luke 12:48][1]

The mandate "to ensure the Catholic character" of the Catholic high school: for the Catholic high school community, this, in a word, is **our agenda** for the 1990s. While this book about evangelization in the Catholic high school hopes to help clarify what "the Catholic character" means, a book on evangelization in the Catholic high school is at best a resource. Essentially, "ensuring the Catholic character" has to do with process, with experience, with listening, with collaborative action. What I have elaborated so far in these pages is a written record of such a process:

- listening to the teaching Church meditate on the meaning of evangelization and Catholic education in our time and place;

- listening to and attempting to decipher the voices and movements of our social and cultural context that either promote or impede evangelization;

- listening to young people, our students, reflect on the gospel and on the possibilities and potential for a Catholic high school education;

- and listening to teachers as they share with one another their successes and failures, ideas and ideals, and hopes and fears for evangelization in the Catholic high school.

I am convinced that it is this type of reflective process that can prove to be invaluable in understanding and ensuring the Catholic character of the high school in the next decade. I suppose it is the preacher in me that makes me moralistically claim that similar reflection on evangelization ought to be a task for every Catholic high school educator and for every Catholic high school staff! It is in sharing our common experience as Catholic educators that our experience is deepened. Unless we reflect and plan together collaboratively, our strategies will not take root. Without the enormous anxiety of finances, our freedom is indeed incredible. But it is a freedom charged with the responsibility of ensuring Catholicity, a responsibility that calls for renewed commitment, imagination and collaboration.

Ensuring the Catholic character has much to do with the content of the education we propose as "Catholic high school education." This chapter synthesizes the central elements of evangelization in the Catholic high school that have been considered at some length. But ensuring the Catholic character also involves in a most significant way the person of the Catholic educator. Chapter 12, then, describes the exigencies at play in evangelizing the evangelizers in the Catholic high school as we enter the 1990s — the question of leadership.

* * * * * * * * *

In Chapter 8, I proposed the text, "We give our children roots and wings," as a helpful way of looking at our evangelization efforts in the Catholic high school.[2] In talking about the content of a Catholic high school education, we are very much talking about our roots, the fact that we want to pass on to our students everything that "roots" us as Roman Catholics, that nourishes us, that gives meaning and direction to our life and world. We want to tell and retell our Catholic story.

But what is our Catholic story, and how do we tell it today to our students? This is the central question in any discussion on the content of a Catholic high school education. The Vatican document, *The Religious Dimension of Education in a Catholic School*, presents a detailed and very useful outline of the critical elements of the Catholic story.[3] This should be must reading for every educator in the Catholic high school. But in addition to an intimate familiarity with our Catholic story narrative, as Catholic educators we should frequently ask ourselves how our curriculum differs from that of the public high school. An ongoing reflection on the curriculum question is also essential to ensure the Catholic character of our high schools.

In this chapter, however, I would like to look in two different ways at the roots we are mandated to hand on to our students. In the first place, faithful to the methodology employed throughout this text, I propose that we once more listen to the teachers as they reflect on the challenge of re-evangelization in our Catholic high schools. Here we look in a very realistic manner at the elements and dynamics necessary for a re-evangelization. Secondly, pulling together the significant dimensions of evangelization which have surfaced so far in our reflection, I present four salient characteristics of a Catholic high school education that takes seriously the challenge "to re-evangelize" in the 1990s.

1. A REFLECTION ON EXPERIENCE: THE CHALLENGE TO RE-EVANGELIZE THE CATHOLIC HIGH SCHOOL

On Re-evangelization: A Commentary

Our four groups of teachers began their final reflection on evangelization in the Catholic high school by considering Pope John Paul II's meditation, "The Hour Has Come for a Re-Evangelization," paragraph 34 of the apostolic exhortation on the *Vocation and Mission of the Lay Faithful*. After spending six hours in reflection groups discussing the formidable task of evangelizing in the Catholic high school in our time and place, the teachers found that Pope John Paul II's "hour for a re-evangelization" provided valuable theological and pastoral perspective for them as they met the final time to reflect on their notions of the challenge of evangelization facing us in the 1990s. As background to this reflection, I would like first to offer a commentary on excerpts of Pope John Paul II's "The Hour Has Come for a Re-Evangelization."

The Hour Has Come for a Re-Evangelization

[Emphasis added.]

* **The hour for re-evangelization in a society marked by indifference and secularization.**

34. Whole countries and nations where religion and the Christian life were formerly flourishing and capable of fostering a viable and working community of faith, are now put to a hard test, and in some cases, are even undergoing a radical transformation, as a result of a constant spreading of an indifference to religion, of secularism and atheism. *This particularly concerns countries and nations of the so-called First World*, in which economic well-being and consumerism, even if coexistent with a tragic situation of poverty and misery, inspires and sustains a life lived "as if God did not exist." This indifference to religion and the practice of religion devoid of true meaning in the face of life's very serious problems, are not less worrying and upsetting when compared with declared atheism. Sometimes the Christian faith as well, while maintaining some of the externals of its tradition and rituals, tends to be separated from those moments of human existence which have the most significance, such as, birth, suffering and death. In such cases, the questions and formidable enigmas posed by these situations, if remaining without responses, expose contemporary people to an inconsolable delusion or to the temptation of eliminating the truly humanizing dimension of life implicit in these problems.

Only a re-evangelization can assure the growth of a clear and deep faith, and serve to make these traditions a force for authentic freedom.

The "hour for re-evangelization" is indeed a felicitous expression for the evangelization project in the Catholic high school: it underscores dramatically the need to ensure the Catholic character of our schools;

220

it confirms the urgency of the hour, or, as the Ontario bishops write, the moment (*This Moment of Promise*) ; and it recognizes in a most realistic way that some Catholic externals have lost their bite and meaning due to the overwhelming forces of secularization and indifference so prevalent in our society.

* **Re-evangelization begins in the renewal of the ecclesial community.**

Without doubt a mending of the Christian fabric of society is urgently needed in all parts of the world. But for this to come about what is needed is to *first remake the Christian fabric of the ecclesial community itself* present in these countries and nations.

Like Pope Paul VI in *On Evangelization in the Modern World*, #15 — *"The Church is an evangelizer, but she begins by being evangelized herself"* — Pope John Paul II admits the needs to *"first remake the Christian fabric of the ecclesial community itself."* Note the emphasis on the crucial importance of the Christian community for evangelization. It is obvious, then, that we as Catholic educators must constantly tend to the quality of Christian community in our schools. Time and time again we must be ready and willing, in the words of John Paul II, "to remake the Christian fabric" of the school community if we are to take seriously our mandate to re-evangelize.

* **Integrating the gospel and the stuff of everyday life is essential for re-evangelization.**

At this moment the lay faithful, in virtue of their participation in the prophetic mission of Christ, are fully part of this work of the Church. Their responsibility, in particular, is to testify how the Christian faith constitutes the only fully valid response — consciously perceived and stated by all in varying degrees — to the problems and hopes that life poses to every person and society. This will be possible if the lay faithful will know how to overcome in themselves the separation of the Gospel from life, to again take up in their daily activities in family, work and society, *an integrated approach to life* that is fully brought about by the inspiration and strength of the Gospel.

This vital synthesis will be achieved when the lay faithful know how to put the gospel and their daily duties of life into a most shining and convincing testimony, where, not fear but the loving pursuit of Christ and adherence to him will be the factors determining how a person is to live and grow, and these will lead to new ways of living more in conformity with human dignity.

Pope John Paul II's *Vocation and Mission of the Lay Faithful* is a clear recognition and endorsement of the ministerial and vocational gifts of the laity — " ... they participate in the prophetic mission of Christ and are fully part of this work of the Church." This remarkable document is a powerful invitation to the laity to use their unlimited gifts for the purpose of re-evangelization. And how important and necessary this invitation is in our time and place, especially with decreasing numbers of religious and a shortage of clergy. Surely the 1990s is the time of the laity! But for re-evangelization to be effective, the laity must overcome and leave behind the dualistic approach to faith and society so prevalent among many contemporary Roman Catholics: the separation of faith from the matters and stuff of everyday life; the idea that faith is a private, individualistic attitude with little social or communal importance or meaning. This hour of re-evangelization calls for a new integration of faith and life. It is manifestly evident then that re-evangelization in the Catholic high school must privilege "this integrated approach of life," "this vital synthesis" in our total education project. Catholicity across the curriculum and teachers convinced and comfortable enough in sharing their own faith stories are two very excellent ways of promoting "this vital synthesis."

* Proclaiming: Humanity is loved by God!

Humanity is loved by God! This very simple yet profound proclamation is owed to humanity by the Church. Each Christian's words and life must make this proclamation resound: God loves you, Christ came for you, Christ is for you "the Way, the Truth and the Life!" [John 14:6]

A re-evangelization begins at the beginning! Humanity is loved by God! It is this reality, this saving deed, that we must proclaim above all else!

222

· Re-evangelizing the individual person, the situation and surroundings, the coming generations.

This re-evangelization is directed not only to individual persons but also to entire portions of populations in the variety of their situation, surroundings and cultures. Its purpose is the *formation of mature ecclesial communities,* in which the faith might radiate and fulfill the basic meaning of adherence to the person of Christ and his Gospel, of an encounter and sacramental communion with him, and of an existence lived in charity and in service.

In the case of coming generations, the lay faithful must offer the very valuable contribution, more necessary than ever, of a systematic work in catechesis. The Synod Fathers have gratefully taken note of the work of cathechists, acknowledging that they "have a task that carries great importance in animating ecclesial communities."

Re-evangelization is directed to the invidual person, to peoples, situations, surroundings and culture. The Catholic high school is one such institution / community "whose hour has come for a re-evangelization." And given the fact that lay Catholics are for the most part the power and inspiration in our Catholic high schools today, the mandate to re-evangelize rests clearly with them. As catechists and religious educators, "they have a task that carries great importance in animating ecclesial communities."

* * * * * * * * *

Question: Propose three or four elements that should constitute an education founded on the gospel and our Catholic tradition!

With Pope John Paul II's theology of re-evangelization as backdrop, our discussion focussed on the content of a Catholic high school education. What should such content consist of as we enter the 1990s?

"We need knowing and doing" was the way one teacher phrased it, emphasizing the importance for a balance between the cognitive dimension and the experiential dimension of a Catholic high school education. Others underscored the importance of scripture and tradition and the need to prepare over four or five years a synthesis of faith for our students. But most insisted that as a companion to the understanding, the intellectual, our students must be involved in serving, in doing for others.

Instructor, faculty of education:

> We need... knowing and doing! I see a three-pronged process! *The Word* — the study of scriptures and Church documents, but from a literary-critical point of view, not literalism! Then *Sacrament:* celebrate liturgy, even in some classes like environmental studies — a prayer that celebrates the environment! And finally, *Outreach:* get involved personally in service, in causes for justice; study and act! This has to be present in our education: Word-Sacrament-Outreach.

Principal:

> ... areas of co-operative education! This illustrates hands-on type of experience for kids. Our academic religion can be — I say can be — not always the case — stifling! A service or experiential component can be refreshing and really will address the kids more in their own needs.

A sensitivity to the needs of the students was deemed important and considered essential to our content. Such sensitivity pertains to all students in our schools, no matter what their academic abilities or propensities. Such sensitivity needs particular consideration with the academically-oriented students, whose classes have a greater tendency toward intellectualizing and consequently away from affectivity and experience.

Chaplain:

> Evangelization, even for the brighter kids, will not engage them if it ignores their needs, and most of it doesn't happen in the classroom. It will happen in an environment that personalizes, that allows the gospel to speak to the kids in their needs.

Special education teacher:

> What about a preferential option for the educationally poor? Kids with troubles, behaviour problems, handicaps! We need to look at this in a wider way. The board's psychologists and social workers are essential. We need this commitment to the "problem-ed" and handicapped kids. An

elitist education is not founded on the gospel.

Over the course of 40 hours of discussions it was often admitted that it is not easy to be a follower of Jesus in our very confusing world. The vocation to follow Jesus demands much of us, but perhaps more than anything else it demands "an integrated approach to life" and "the vital synthesis" as Pope John Paul II reflects in "The Hour for a Re-Evangelization." Our students need assistance. They need a sense of prayer, they need especially an appreciation of their vocation as followers of Jesus, and they need help in interpreting and making the connection between faith and the world.

Religion teacher:

> Another thing: we really need to give the kids a chance to develop their personal relationship with God. A lot of the kids have missed out on a sense of prayer, a sense of belonging to God, because of what hasn't happened in the home.

Guidance teacher:

> A sense of the sacred should mark our education: prayer, worship, the sacredness of the person. Also, emphasize the vocation of the Christian: to love, to serve, to be stewards of creation. And get across the idea of a person's responsibility to develop his/her talents and to employ those talents for transforming our society. Next, I see a vision of the world as important: North/South, rich and poor. The last thing: the Christian aspect of the subjects we teach. Make the connection between our faith and our world.

Religion teacher:

> In a way we have to mediate our culture for our students. The kids in a sense know *who they are* in North American culture, 1989. They have gotten that message from the media! I think our task is to bring the gospel into this mix; at least to help the students understand what the gospel has to say about what and *who they could be* in North American culture.

It was unanimous that education in the Catholic high school today in our time and place must have a definite counter-cultural dimension to it. We cannot accept the dominant values of our culture because so much of it is contrary to Jesus' teaching. As well, there must be "the upsetting," the critical edge to our education — a pedagogy that looks at situations and events not from the viewpoint of the rich and power-ful but from the perspective of the voiceless poor.

Religion teacher:

> In the world of the village you didn't have to be critical to be a Christian, but in our world you have to be able to analyse things socially. The game is changed for being a Christian.

Priest-teacher, English and religion:

> Our education has to be an education of social responsibil-ity. First of all, the students should know what's going on in the world and then give them some tools to look at the world critically and responsibly. Lately with the kids I detect a terrible inward-turning, a new kind of selfishness. Some-how we have to try to reverse this trend.

Chaplain:

> Our education today has to be counter-cultural. Our con-tent is important, but it has to touch the heart. In class you can present the beatitudes, show how they are a real cri-tique of our society's priorities, but they have to touch the heart. To do that we have to put ourselves in other people's shoes, walk around in their skin — the Gospel of Matthew, chapter 25, verses 31-46! Be compassionate. Suffer with. Be sympathetic! That is important. That changes a person's view or perspective.

The teachers were very much aware that this particular question on content had to do with the totality of a Catholic high school educa-tion, not just the religious education component. They insisted that there be a definite cross-curricular thrust to any Catholic education seri-ous about re-evangelization. Again, it is "an integrated approach to life." And realizing or activating this total approach to a Catholic high school education is the responsibility of every Catholic educator. In this way, our education becomes a credible alternative education based on the gospel and our Catholic tradition.

Head, guidance department:

> Unfortunately, OS:IS is a very limiting model of education for us: prescribed time, curriculum, etc. Now the one thing we have to do then is interpret values, humanistic ideas, very much in terms of the gospel! So, economics for exam-ple. OS:IS is not going to refer to the Church's social teach-ing, but *we must* do that! Or, communication skills: so

much of it stays shallow. I think we have to risk going deeper, sharing our feelings, especially about Jesus and faith. We have to risk sharing, communicating at that level.

Principal:

One fundamental element: a continuing type of social analysis, a critique of societal values! Our whole education system is reflective of the predominant values of society. An alternative education based on the gospel has to take a profound look at those values: "Where is the conflict with the gospel?" And to have impact, it has to be integrated in every dimension of our education . . . and in every school activity. For example, if business and economics classes don't opt for this and religion and social sciences do, our whole project is neutralized. This is very difficult to do. It assumes a depth, a social consciousness on the part of teachers. It's hard to get! But we have to work at this!

And finally, there is community, the context in which our education takes place. Community is very much a constitutive element for a Catholic education. Community, too, as Pope John Paul II writes, is the starting point for a re-evangelization: "What is first needed is to remake the Christian fabric of the ecclesial community itself."

Religion teacher:

While it's not academic, kids do experience the gospel, the Good News, by being influenced by a community of faith. I think kids can do this by seeing people around them, especially teachers, as belonging to the community of faith and happy in it. In this morning's gospel [Third Sunday of Easter "C"], the apostles at first don't even recognize Christ. And that's how it is for many of the students. They don't know how to recognize Jesus. But they will find Christ in the community, in the people around them. They need the tools: "How do you recognize Jesus?" After time and reflection, the kids will see Jesus in the quality of the community.

* * * * * * * * *

Question: Propose three or four steps to take (adjustments or adaptations) to implement this "process of evangelization."

The moment of implementation is always the point where the ideal meets the real. Upon reaching this juncture, inevitably it seems, there comes into play some healthy skepticism which keeps the planning grounded in the practical, and some very imaginative thinking which assures that the ideal will be factored into the elaboration of the ultimate strategy. Implementing the process of re-evangelization in our Catholic high schools proved to be no exception to this tension between the ideal and the real. There were the sincere skeptics:

> Practically speaking can it be done? A lot of the teachers are not really into the gospel!

> A very practical thing: what do you do when there are not only people who don't go along, but actually fight it?

> In talking about an alternative Catholic education, we are talking about really a radical Catholic Christianity. This can be very upsetting. Is it too much really to expect that Catholic education can be different?

And there were the creative, comprehensive theorists, convinced that our ideals — the Catholic character — are indeed workable.

French teacher:

> A couple of years ago there was an ICE [Institute for Catholic Education] symposium on partners in Catholic education: parents, teachers, boards, parishes. A good thought, that, but it was not implemented around here to my knowledge. For our Catholic system we *have* to look at partnership: is it real or fictional! Three or four of our board members seem to have profound convictions about "partnership": they relate, they consult and they include school staffs in some of their decision-making. But they are not the norm on our board, and there isn't any indication yet that they are the norm in the province.

> Also, at our individual schools, some on-going small reflection groups like this one would be great. This is a way for us to be evangelized.

> And then, service components are critical, especially for our religious education classes.

> Finally, I would emphasize the transcendent or integrating dimension of our Catholic education. Education should be more than a four-subject-a-day experience. How do we integrate the gospel? How do we allow kids the chance to

228

see how it all fits together?

In the final analysis, the three or four steps consistently suggested were reduced to two very critical areas for implementation of the process of re-evangelization:

- the re-evangelization of staff;
- the pressing need to integrate faith and the gospel into the total education project offered in the Catholic high school.

On re-evangelizing teachers

One teacher began a reflection on re-evangelization with a very Catholic confession: "We have to acknowledge and accept our faults and imperfections; that is, teachers, students, processes and structures — all of this [and us] is in need of redemption and forgiveness."

I was pleased with this very theological bit of candour, for it certainly placed our entire discussion on the re-evangelization of staff in a healing, optimistic perspective. While this theme will be examined in more detail in Chapter 12 it is informative here to listen to the following testimonies that focus on the re-evangelization of the teacher as essential to the content of the process of re-evangelization.

1. On ownership of the Christian stance

Religion teacher:

> I think that re-evangelization is the key. As a staff community we need a clear understanding of what we are about, where we are going, what we want to do. And then we have to convey this to the students. In my classes, every student has an opinion, and they get upset if you don't accept their opinion. But our education is more than just opinions. It is learning and applying the Christian stance. Critical awareness must be based on the Christian stance. As a staff this is what we have to convey. But we have to work hard personally appropriating the Christian stance.

2. On formation in prayer

Chaplain:

> For implementation, the teachers are the most crucial element. We absolutely must have a formation program for the teachers. I'm talking about sessions for prayer, for formation as evangelizers, for experience in community.

3. On the commitment of a separate school board

Principal:

> The process of re-evangelization could falter on the rock of
> teacher resistance to their vocation of bringing the *good
> news* to the kids. Are Catholic boards prepared to ade-
> quately evangelize Catholic teachers? Are there any serious
> efforts made to withdraw teachers from the classroom: to
> give them an opportunity to explore their values together,
> to experience a faith community? I don't know of any
> board in Ontario doing this! The overall priority has to be
> the evangelization of teachers.

4. On the evangelization of time

Vice-principal:

> The other thing is personal conversion. This is the begin-
> ning point! Also time! "I don't have time!" Time overload!
> As individual teachers, as a staff, I think we should look at
> *time*. It has to do with what we prioritize.

5. On the need for collaborative structures

Vice-principal:

> Our schools are organized on an isolationist principle, espe-
> cially secondary schools. I can't walk into your classroom:
> that would be an intrusion! Teachers are left very much
> alone. I close the door. I'm in charge! Which is okay, but I'm
> very much alone, and we're finding out that this "alone-
> ness" is hurting a lot of teachers. We don't have collabora-
> tive structures.

* * * * * * * * *

On integrating faith and the gospel into the total education project of the Catholic high school

The theme of integration — an integral Catholic education — was
prominent in all of the reflection groups. Again we have convergence
— an instance of the "theology" of the teachers being very much in
harmony with the "theology" of the teaching Church: John Paul II's
"an integrated approach" and "vital synthesis" that have already been
considered. One teacher remarked: "Teachers need skills and tools to
make connections." Indeed they do, but even prior to that is the need
for the theological understanding that our faith touches every aspect of

our life and that a Catholic education must promote the Catholic world view, which is very much a world view steeped in gospel values and in our tradition, and quite at odds with so much that is accepted and valued by our culture. The skills of "interpretation" and "making connections" flow from such an understanding. The following testimonies flesh out different aspects of an integral Catholic education. As such they are valuable in advancing possibilities for the implementation of faith and gospel values across the total curriculum.

Religion teacher:

> It's even more critical now that as teachers we have our act together as to who we are and what kind of an education we want to give at our school. There has to be very evident coherence: the gospel values have got to be present throughout that education.

Chairperson, English department:

> Well, it is pretty clear: we need staff evangelization — or re-evangelization. Teachers, the adults in the school, are key. Also, look at our tools and skills for linking faith with reality, with the world, with English or chemistry or the stock market or the world of VCRs. I think we have to take a hard look at how we can transmit gospel values! And in writing curriculum, we can adapt; we can inject or infuse Christian tradition and gospel values. Really, the leadership at the school has to ask these questions!

English teacher:

> Teachers need skills, tools to make connections. Act Three of *King Lear* — a storm: Lear is out on a heath; he has this insight: I'm the King of this country and I don't know where the poor people are living! Then you pick up the *Star* this morning and read about the protest at Queen's Park: a couple of thousand people wanting the SARC [Social Assistance Reform Commission] recommendations implemented! Here are the poor! So, an independent study project could be, for example, the poor of Dickens' time and the poor of today. Compare Dickens' protest with the protest today. Teachers need some connecting skills, but I think so much can be done.

* * * * * * * * *

Question: Identify elements of understanding or attitudes or values that you would like our students to have made their own on leaving the Catholic high school.

This question proved to be an excellent means of pulling together the different strands that when woven together became the fabric, the content of the education we offer as a Catholic high school education. And what a marvellous tapestry it is — at least in the desired ideals! Yet, these are essentially "the roots" we want to give to our students: and this is very much the Catholic character that we must work to ensure. I have synthesized these "elements of understanding or attitudes or values" into six broad but equally important categories.

1. The Sense that Humanity Is Loved by God

All people are worthy of love and in need of love, and love is possible because God first loved us! The sense of love, the sense of the goodness and sacredness of the person, a profound respect for life — this is of capital importance and is at the very heart of an education we call "Catholic"! It is as well, according to Pope John Paul II, the core of our proclamation in whatever re-evangelization we set out to accomplish!

Physical education teacher:

> That they appreciate that humanity is loved by God . . . and that we discover this love . . . through the love, forgiveness, affirmation and compassion of other people. Also, that differences are blessed; they are not bad; that is, races, opinions, approaches, and so forth.

Chairperson, English department:

> That the students appreciate the primacy, the importance of the human person. In our society now, this is a tough primacy to bestow!

2. A Knowledge of the Gospel: A Love for Jesus Christ

To facilitate a young person's love for Jesus: this is such an easy idea to play with and articulate; but given our culture, the secularism and indifference and competing idols prevalent in our society, it is a terribly difficult thing to achieve.

Chaplain:

> I would like to see the kids leave with a knowledge of the gospel: who Jesus is; what Jesus teaches. And then — that they have an option for compassion and forgiveness,

that they are confirmed in their faith. Thirdly, that they have a critical awareness of the culture in which they live, but tempered with a sense of hope . . . that they see the world through Jesus' eyes.

3. Owning and Personalizing One's Faith

Assisting in the process of "Christian emergence" is also vital to evangelization in the Catholic high school. That the students have new insight into their own uniqueness and self-worth; that they take responsibility for their relationship with God; that they come to appreciate prayer, to appreciate what a gift it is to be a follower of Jesus; in a word, that they grow in the knowledge and acceptance of their own vocations. This, too, constitutes our roots and is central to our evangelizing mission.

Priest-teacher, English and religion:

> Self-worth is so important, but not selfishness! It has to be an authentic self-worth. They are good, unique, with lots of potential, but also with responsibility attached! And also faith — that there is meaning beyond the here and now. And generosity — to give of themselves.

Chaplain:

> I would like students to assume personal responsibility for their relationship with God. I would like them to automatically look to Jesus' values as a means of critiquing non-gospel values, and I would like them to appreciate what a privilege it is to be a Christian and what a sacred challenge it is. Finally I would like them to see that prayer is important in the life of a priest, but it is just as important in the life of a banker or nurse, businessman or scientist, worker or farmer.

Chemistry teacher:

> A sense of faith — that the person is not alone and will not be abandoned if he/she makes a mistake. They can begin again.

Guidance teacher:

> I'd like the kids to own their faith; to know that God has created them unique and irreplaceable; that they have a relationship with this personal God. Secondly, the realization that each person has a "vocation." God who calls

them into being intends for them to accomplish his Word and will. [To know] that if they don't do it, it won't get done.

4. A Love for, and Understanding of, the Church

Membership in the Church, the community of believers, and an active participation in the Church, indicating that one assumes one's share of the responsibility for the evangelizing mission of the Church, is very much a value that teachers would love to hand on to our students. And given the fragility of the family, especially when it comes to handing on the faith, this becomes an evermore important value as we make our way into the 1990s.

Chaplain :

> That our students might be real Church people, faithful to the Word, the Eucharist, and service to others. And that as Church they may be critical of so much of the anti-gospel spirit in the world. More and more the Church is becoming "critical" in that sense.

Guidance teacher :

> I would like to see our students grow in love for, and service in, the Church. We got it from our parents and parishes. I'm not sure that happens today. School perhaps is the only place they will meet the Church and learn to become part of if.

5. Empowerment

"Even one person can make a difference" — this thought surfaced several times. A Catholic education must be an empowering education, an education that stresses stewardhip — that we are responsible for this planet of ours and for one another. As such, a Catholic education promotes a vision of the world that is understood in terms of interdependence and solidarity. The upsetting evangelization or critical education that has been mentioned time and time again has as its purpose service and the transformation of our world. Increasingly, the re-evangelization of the Catholic high school means that more emphasis must be placed on an education that empowers; that cultivates a leadership, in turn founded on stewardship, solidarity, interdependence and service — all very much constitutive elements of our Catholic character.

Chairperson, English department :

> I would like our students to have the sense that the per-

son... that as people... we are here for a while on this earth. So, how can we best use this time? We have power to change things that are not right. That's our task during our time here and now. To do this the students must have the ability to question: they must have those skills.

English teacher:

If you look at the Catholic system and judge it from the yardstick of the gospel, we are really called to a radical conversion. We should educate to produce leaders in today's world.

Principal:

That students will be able to critique — from the point of view of the gospel and our Catholic tradition — the society, the structures, all the movements that deny life in our world, and offer alternatives based on the gospel... and movements that foster life.

Religion teacher:

I would love to see our students develop a strong social conscience — an understanding of injustice that's out there — and the fundamental courage to come to grips with it, to change things, to transform them. To know that any effort they make will move us one step ahead.

Chemistry teacher:

I feel that we can't talk enough about social responsibility. I want the students to feel that we are all part of a connected world. There is interdependence; therefore, we have a responsibility for others, for the poor, to bring about justice and peace. And that we are called to serve, to wash feet.

6. The Sense of the Sacred

We began this chapter by listening to Pope John Paul II reflect on the meaning of re-evangelization for our time and place. John Paul II notes that re-evangelization is imperative, because, in a country like ours, secularism has taken deep roots and consequently there is widespread indifference to religion. People in our society have lost the sense of the sacred. The striking testimony which follows gives added meaning to Pope John Paul's words, adapting them to the evangelization project in the Catholic high school. The hoped-for ideal: that students might develop a religious sense, a religious understanding of life, a religious sense of the world.

Principal:

> First of all, that they have a genuinely religious sense. We seem to have anesthetized kids to true religion. I would love for them to have a real sense of awe — an understanding of God as mystery, source, ultimate good. Next, a religious understanding of life — as joy, beauty, gift and service. Life especially as a call to service: to serve the needs of others. And I would like them to have a religious sense of the world: that the world is sacred; that there is no dualism [faith / secular, spirit / matter], but that faith and our sense of God penetrate everything and belong everywhere. There is interdependence and interconnectedness.

* * * * * * * * *

Such is the picture that comes into focus when a number of committed Catholic educators get together to talk about the type of Catholic education we could be offering in our high schools. It can be said, as well, that this is the Catholic character we must work to ensure in the coming decade. Such a Catholic education:

- respects the balance between intellectual content and experiential involvement;
- is sensitive to the particular needs of the students;
- cultivates the sense of personal vocation and helps students interpret the demands of the gospel and how faith must connect with, penetrate, and give meaning to, our culture and social context.
- And so, it is a Catholic education that is often counter-cultural and whose purpose is to transform society;
- and consequently, it must be an integral Catholic education, not just a religious education component or chapel-time experience.

To re-evangelize the Catholic high school, then, is to work to implement such a Catholic education. This is really our agenda for the 1990s. And it is the best way possible to ensure the Catholic character of our schools and of our education.

236

Such re-evangelization must begin with ourselves: the evangelizers must be re-evangelized. Energy is called for, along with unlimited creativity and large doses of boldness, to elaborate an integral Catholic education in which our faith and gospel values penetrate every aspect of our total education package. Only then can we really speak of a credible Catholic alternative education to that of the public high school.

And our students? If we take to heart the urgency of this hour for re-evangelization, our students, indeed, would be the real beneficiaries. After four or five years in our Catholic high schools, we would hope they would be well on their way:

- to having a deep sense that humanity is loved by God;
- to knowing the teaching of the gospel and growing in their love for Jesus Christ;
- to owning their faith in a unique and personal way;
- to participating in the Church as a life-giving community that becomes the channel for service rendered to the world;
- to having an invincible conviction about the value of their own worth and the dignity and worth of every person from womb to tomb; to being empowered with a sense of their own gifts and their own responsibility for the transformation of society with a preferential love for the poor and marginalized in our world;
- to developing a sense of the sacred which leads to love, to service and to prayer.

Such are our ideals as educators in the Catholic high school! Such is the challenge of re-evangelization for the 1990s!

* * * * * * * * *

2. EVANGELIZATION IN THE CATHOLIC HIGH SCHOOL: AN AGENDA FOR THE 1990s

My purpose now is to pull together what I believe to be the salient characteristics of evangelization in the Catholic high school. From the outset I have used the term "evangelization" in the broad sense. By reviewing some significant Church teaching on Catholic education and by listening to some profoundly vital and insightful testimony of Catholic educators, we have been able to mine some of the richness of evangelization. We have been able to appreciate the why and the how of evangelization as it can be realized in the Catholic high school.

There are, however, the preliminary observations to make before any synthesis of the fundamental characteristics of evangelization is possible.

I began this account on evangelization in the Catholic high school by presenting a critique of what a contemporary Catholic high school education in Ontario is all about. Martin Royackers objected that we are failing to provide a credible Catholic alternative education. Our graduates are really no different than public school graduates; our Catholic system gives the impression of completely subscribing to the values of the dominant ideology of liberal capitalism — many of these values counter to the gospel. Where is the upsetting quality, the transforming dimension to our Catholic education, Royackers wonders.

Kenneth Westhues, in his critique, sees our schools as "a curious inheritance." Catholic schools and public schools share the same hyper-secularized culture. There is an inexorable standardization of cultural values happening as well that often renders "Catholics" indistinguishable from their secularized North American compatriots. Also, according to Westhues, research shows little difference in moral values or social involvement between graduates of both systems, so why the duplication of systems?

But there is more. The Royackers-Westhues assessment is invaluable and indeed necessary insofar as it makes us look hard at the content of our education: is it a critical, transforming education, an authentic alternative to that of the public high school? But as we enter the 1990s, there is another essential dimension to a Catholic high school education that also demands our attention. Given the theology of evangelization we have considered, their critique should have no basis at all! We have listened to the teaching Church, to some very committed Catholic educators and students. The evidence is clear that even now there are instances where our education is already a credible alternative. But it would be wrong to make too much of "instances." Perhaps these teachers are only voices in the wilderness. But, they are very definitely voices of hope and a sign and confirmation that authentic evangelization is possible. And if, as Catholic high school educators, we accept that "the hour for a re-evangelization" is now upon us, then our Catholic education could indeed become a transforming education; our schools could become "conduits for Catholic social thought."

But there is still more. The investigation we have made into our social and cultural context and the testimony we have heard from many of the teachers point to a new social and ecclesial reality: there is an increasing failure on the part of the family to pass on and nurture the faith, and there is much brokenness in our society. The Catholic high school now, as an ecclesial community, is very much in the front lines. The school community and individual teachers are increasingly assuming a more profound healing and spiritual ministry. In *This Moment of Promise*, the Bishops acknowledge this new role for Catholic educators:

> Within a society which is increasingly secular, there is more need than ever before for an educational community which stakes its existence on the infinite promise which Jesus Christ has offered through his death and resurrection. He came that we may have life and have it more abundantly.

> Given the increasing fragility of families and the overextension of parishes, it is becoming more obvious that the school, for some, is often the primary place where young people experience the Church as an alternative community which is shaped more by faith, hope and love than by values of our common culture.

[p. 16]

This is another dimension of the importance and the possibilities for a Catholic high school education. To exploit these evangelizing possibilities to the fullest, it is imperative that we take seriously "the hour for re-evangelization."

The final observation concerns the strategies we adopt for evangelization. As we have seen in Chapter 8, unless we are sensitive to the faith development of the adolescent and pay attention both to the different psychological stages of growth the young person must negotiate and to the ever-evolving social context, then our evangelization will be ineffective and our evangelizing efforts frustrating. We must adapt evangelization. We must propose an evangelization that empowers, that is participative. And our evangelization must be particularly sensitive to emergence — the primary task in adolescent development. Incorporating these principles in our various evangelizing strategies is a clear indication that we accept "the hour for re-evangelization."

To conclude, I believe that there are four dimensions to evangelization that must be tended to and privileged in the Catholic high school through the 1990s. Undoubtedly, there are more than four. Or perhaps one might choose a different emphasis or opt for different phrasing. But in reviewing the teaching of the Church on Catholic education and listening to some very sincere and dedicated Catholic educators, there are four dimensions of evangelization that strike me as most significant.

I see these four dimensions of evangelization as essential elements to the total evangelization effort in the Catholic high school. Together they give coherence and force to evangelization. With one or other of these elements missing or de-emphasized, the evangelization project is quite incomplete. I present them now in outline form.

An Evangelization Faithful to the Catholic Tradition

Constitutive Elements

1. **Telling the Catholic Story.** Refer to *The Religious Dimension in a Catholic school*, Part Four — Religious Instruction in the Classroom and the Religious Dimension of Formation:
   - Chapter 3 — An outline for an organic presentation of the Christian event and message (paragraphs 74-81);
   - Chapter 4 — An outline for a systematic presention of the Christian life (paragraphs 82-95).

2. **Recognizing the new reality: faith, the family, the Church in Ontario in the 1990s.**
   - Headline — *Globe and Mail*, March 13, 1989, p. A8: "Schools providing first contact with Catholicism, bishops warn."
   - Refer to: the Ontario bishops, *This Moment of Promise*.
   - Note the urgency of teaching a moral and religious education today, *even* in public schools:
     Headline — *Globe and Mail*, May 2, 1989: "New curriculum urged to teach young people moral responsibility."

3. **Giving primacy to the nurturing of Christian vocation.** Refer to: Pope John Paul II, *Vocation and Mission of the Lay Faithful*.

4. **"Ensuring the Catholic character."**
   - How is this to be done: in the wake of full funding and in the hour for re-evangelization?
   - Refer to the teacher reflections in the first part of this chapter.

5. **Sharing one's own faith journey** — one's experience of Jesus and his forgiveness. This is the type of witness that helps students interpret the gospel and the world and make the connection between faith and culture.

An Upsetting Evangelization

Constitutive Elements

1. Refer to the discussion in Part Two — **The Context for Evangelization in the Catholic High School**:
   - the obstacles to evangelization: consumerism, greed, competition and violence, exaggerated individualism, relativism, hopelessness;
   - the mandate to bring the gospel to bear on our culture;
   - signs of hope in our society today: prophetic defence and promotion of life.

2. Refer to the Church's **"upsetting social teaching"**:
   - Pope Paul VI — *On Evangelization in the Modern World* — "upsetting through the power of the Gospel, humankind's criteria of judgment";
   - Pope John Paul II — *Concern for the Social Order* — themes of interdependence, solidarity, underdevelopment and super-development;
   - The Synod of Bishops — *Justice in the World* (1971) — "Education must awaken the capacity of critical reflection on our society and on its current values";
   - Ontario bishops — *This Moment of Promise* (1989) — "Catholic education... must also be critical of those aspects of our culture which are contrary to the values of our faith tradition."

3. **Choose between two models of Catholic education:**

   The Upsetting Model: An upsetting, critical education based on the power of the gospel to critique everything in society that dehumanizes and oppresses. The framework for such a Catholic education is found in #2 above.

   Or

   The Accommodating Model: Item from *Newsweek*, April 17, 1989, p. 63, celebrating so many of the cultural values at odds with the gospel. A Catholic education that finds its meaning: in the trivial, wanting to be number one, competition, excessively catering to rather than trying to stretch juvenile adolescent interest.

A 17-year-old is not interested in whether or not a professor is fusing an atom, says Msgr. John Petillo — chancellor of Seton Hall University (a Catholic University), explaining his school's interest in high-profile sports. "What they want is something that gives them recognition and an identity. A championship basketball team does that."

4. **Privilege media education**, an integral component of an upsetting evangelization.

Michael Warren, respected authority on youth ministry:

... we can lead our young people to become more aware of our social world. If I had two days with a group of young people, the first thing I might do is teach them how to read the newspaper for real news of the events and decisions that will affect them and their children.[4]

5. **Let the experiential and hands-on education of involvement** accompany the critical and analytical.

6. In the context of the Catholic high school, **strive for a counter-cultural education** that leads to the empowerment of the student for the transformation of society — as articulated in the first part of this chapter (teacher reflections).

7. **Apply the Church's preferential love for and option for the poor to our Catholic high schools:**

As a directing principle, *the preferential option should touch all facets of school life.* It suggests that our *developmentally handicapped students* be integrated. They should not be on the periphery of the school, isolated in their own class. *Handicapped students* and those in the regular stream can learn a great deal from each other. It suggests that our time and energy in athletics should focus on the entire school, rather than on a few select teams. Let the outside community produce the elite athlete. Schools should concentrate on fitness and intramurals.

It suggests we drop our school populations to a level where we can still offer a variety of programs, yet be small enough that the numbers are not automatically dehumanizing. It suggests that the arts and science subject look at their material from the perspective of the world's poor. It suggests that we examine school structures; e.g., uniforms, lack of shops, etc., to see if they screen out *a priori* the poor. It suggests that we examine to see if schools in richer areas with strong and vocal parents' associations are getting better teachers, equipment and class sizes. It suggests that decisions be made according to the question: "At whose service are we putting our resources? What powers do we serve?"[5]

* * * * * * * * *

An Evangelization to Brokenness

Constitutive Elements

1. Brokenness is a sign of the times for teenagers.

*Item — an editorial, *Globe and Mail*, May 22, 1989:

"A Friend on the Line":

A great many things can push the world of the teenager askew — loneliness, school problems, abuse or neglect, the domestic trauma of divorce, drugs, depression, differences of opinion with parents. Sometimes the remedy of first choice, a face-to-face chat with a parent or school counsellor, is just not practical.

For Canadian children in urgent need of a sympathetic adult ear, but unwilling to risk the additional bruising of being made to feel self-conscious, the Canadian Children's Foundation recently installed the Kid's Help Phone. From anywhere in the country, a call to 1-800-668-6868 will put a troubled youngster in touch with someone ready and willing to help. And not just by lending a suitably distant ear;

counsellors have access to a computer data-base of 20,000 children's services across the country.

It is an impressive resource and, sadly, one that seems to have become more urgently needed with each year that passes. This may be the first time that teenagers have actually been urged to get **on** the phone, but the reasons could hardly be better.

- Refer to the teacher reflections in Chapter 6 on family brokenness.

2. Refer to Pope John Paul II, *Vocation and Mission of the Lay Faithful*, #34:

> **Humanity is loved by God!** This very simple yet profound proclamation is owed to humanity by the Church. Each Christian's words and life must make this proclamation resound: God loves you, Christ came for you, Christ is for you "the Way, the Truth and the Life!" [John 14:6]

3. The proclamation that "humanity is loved by God" must colour, inspire and inject meaning and purpose into every aspect of a Catholic high school education. Given the reality of so much affective and spiritual poverty in contemporary family experience, the school as an ecclesial community becomes the primary locus of socialization into our Catholic tradition for many students.

4. An evangelization to brokenness is manifest in a school or ecclesial community that deems it a priority to provide:

- presence — being with, listening to . . . ;
- affirmation — rendering value and self-worth;
- compassion — channelling forgiveness;
- ministering to young people during inevitable moments of crisis.

5. An evangelization to brokenness is intrinsic to the meaning of the Good News of Christianity.

- It is an evangelization that *offers hope* and a plan of action based on the gospel as the alternative to so much hopelessness and helplessness.

- It is an evangelization that *proposes "an integrated approach to life"* as the way to make sense out of so much fragmentation and conflicting values.

* * * * * * * * *

An Evangelization into Prayer

Constitutive Elements

1. As background, refer again to the **Bibby-Posterski assessment** in Chapter 8:

> Thus, some 70 % of teenagers seemingly have clear religious and spiritual interests. To the extent that religious groups fail to captivate young people, it is not because "the religion market" is not an appreciable one.

2. The goal of evangelization is interior change — conversion. Testimony of the students in Chapter 9 and the teachers in Chapter 10 confirm both the vital importance and the efficacy of *"a spiritual experience"* for students: retreat days, SEARCH, COR, etc. The *experiential and relational are constitutive of such experience: "The heart can be touched!"* Such experiences must be privileged and seen as an integral part of a Catholic high school education.

3. Adaptation, participation and a **respect for emergence** are the principles that must shape any evangelization into prayer.

4. The pressing challenge in the 1990s is to overcome dualism — the compartmentalization and isolation of faith and prayer from the rest of life's questions and interests.

- Refer to Pope John Paul II's *Vocation and Mission of the Lay Faithful*, #34 (emphasis added):

> The lay faithful must know how to overcome in themselves the separation of the Gospel from life, to again take up in their daily activities in family, work and society, **an integrated approach of life** that is fully brought about by the inspiration and strength of the Gospel.

- Refer to a chaplain's testimony in Chapter 10 on "holiness":

> Their [the kids'] sense of holy is a woman dressed in black, carrying a Bible and going to Mass on Sunday. That's

"holy" to kids. They don't see holy as someone working for the homeless or caring for AIDS patients or lobbying for the peace movement. They don't see that as holy. We have to get Matthew 25:31-46 across to the students.

- Refer to a principal's hoped-for ideals for our students found at the end of part one of this chapter:

> I would love for them to have a real sense of awe — an understanding of God as mystery, source, ultimate good. Next, a religious understanding of life — as joy, beauty, gift and service... And I would like them to have a religious sense of the world: that the world is sacred; that there is no dualism [faith/secular; spirit/matter], but that faith and our sense of God penetrate everything and belong everywhere. There is interdependence and interconnectedness.

5. **Evangelizing into prayer is to preach and teach a hard Word — the Word of sacrifice and the cross.** And the cross, which is so central to the gospel, is a hard lesson to teach in our time and place. Following Jesus must cost.

* * * * * * * * *

I believe that this agenda for evangelization meets the spirit and demands for the hour of re-evangelization now upon us in the Catholic high school. It is to be sure a lofty agenda in its intent: to understand the Catholic character of our high schools, to read the signs of our time and place, to let God's Word challenge and inspire us as evangelizers. But at the same time it is a practical agenda because so much of it comes from the lived experience of some dedicated Catholic educators. The real challenge, however, as always, is the implementation of this agenda for evangelization. And as is the case with all evangelizing activity, it must begin with *the evangelization of the evangelizers*. It is to this critical question that we now turn.

NOTES
Chapter 11

1 The Ontario Conference of Catholic Bishops, *This Moment of Promise*. A Pastoral Letter On Catholic Education in Ontario (Toronto, 1989), p. 11.

2 Chapter 8, p. 160.

3 Congregation for Catholic Education, *The Religious Dimension of Education in a Catholic School* (1988), Part Four: "Religious Instruction in the Classroom and the Religious Dimension of Formation."

4 Michael Warren, *Youth, Gospel, Liberation* (San Francisco: Harper & Row, 1987), p. 70.

5 "Catholic Education in Exile: Retrieving the Religious Dimension," an unpublished paper by Bernard Smyth, religion teacher at Cardinal Newman High School, Toronto (Metropolitan Separate School Board), April 1989, p. 12 (emphasis added).

CHAPTER 12

EVANGELIZING THE EVANGELIZERS — THE CHALLENGE OF LEADERSHIP

To ensure the Catholic character of our high schools: this is the agenda for the 1990s! Elaborating the content for a Catholic high school education that takes seriously the mandate to evangelize is one important starting point. But ultimately, hearkening again to Pope Paul VI's words:

> Modern men and women listen more willingly to witness-
> es than to teachers, and if they do listen to teachers, it is be-
> cause they are witnesses.
>
> [*E.N.*, #41]

— it is the person of the evangelizer, the teacher in the Catholic high school, who is the main protagonist in the drama of evangelizing the Catholic high school. And as we have seen, this is a drama of enormous import for the future of Catholic education in Ontario. We are either going to offer an authentic Catholic education, an alternative to that of the public system, or we are going to settle for duplication, with a smattering of Catholic "cosmetics," and try to deceive ouselves and the public school taxpayers that we are different. A committed, bold and imaginative leadership must be the order of the day!

Happily, these final months of the 1980s have produced several intelligent and very practical articulations of the challenges that confront us in Catholic education in Ontario. In their 1989 pastoral letter, *This Moment of Promise*, the Ontario bishops propose in practical, theological language 11 challenges, that, when taken together, become the global challenge for us "in this moment of promise."[1] And the recent *Partners in Catholic Education Symposium II*, sponsored by the Institute for Catholic Education, was the occasion for three excellent reflections on leadership in Catholic education that should give meaning and

248

direction to whatever visioning we may engage in at the school level or board level for the 1990s.[2]

In reflecting on the renewal of leadership, the question that inevitably surfaces is: "Where to begin — at the top or the bottom?" Spending many hours with teachers on this question, there was a feeling that one must begin at the top. Among their questions about the top are the following:

- Do trustees really comprehend the scope and urgency of evangelization in the schools and for the system?
- What sort of a theological vision is it that governs the important decisions taken at the board level?
- What weight does a board give to being "an evangelizing leader" in its hiring policy for directors, superintendents and principals?
- In the layers upon layers of impersonal bureaucracy we have established, how are we any different from public school boards?
- And how, at the local or provincial level, is the *modus operandi* of OECTA different from OSSTF?
- What does the "servant leader" descriptive that appears so often in *Globe and Mail* adverts for separate school positions mean in practice?
- Where is the formation program for "a theological vision of Catholic education" for our principals, superintendents and directors of education?
- And resonating with teachers' concerns about a present and future leadership vacuum in Catholic education is this reflection of the Ontario bishops in *This Moment of Promise* (emphasis added):

Leadership Selection

In a country in which appointments are often made for political reasons alone, we ask you [trustees] to make decisions about future leadership *with a view to what will ultimately further the process of Catholic education.* A number of significant decisions are fast approaching. Many directors of education, supervisory officers and principals will soon be retiring, and it is you [trustees] who must appoint their successors. We ask that you make these decisions *prayerfully* and *with a profound grasp of the vision of Catholic education and of the justice which it demands.*

[pp. 29-30]

These are some of the preoccupations with leadership in Catholic education analysed from the top-down perspective. I am convinced that these are crucial preoccupations, that the teachers' critique here is accurate, and that these are the key questions that must be discussed openly and frankly by the different partners in Catholic education over the months and years to come.

But the renewal of leadership question also has a bottom-up perspective, and it is this perspective that I propose to focus on in this chapter. For me as one teacher in a Catholic high school, or even for a community of teachers in any Catholic high school, the election of trustees and selection of administrators is pretty well beyond our sphere of influence. But the fabric of the community we form in the school, the impact of our witness, the faith content of my life, my teaching and yours — all of this we can create and recreate. This is the witness that directly touches the minds and hearts of students, and it is this personal witness, in the final analysis, that is the foundation for the evangelization project in the Catholic high school. Evangelizing the evangelizers is the necessary point of departure for evangelizing in the Catholic high school. In this sense, then, it is the primary leadership question.

A few weeks ago, I reached a point in my research and writing where some people began to ask me: "What are you going to prescribe? How must we go about it? What are the steps? When do you identify the skills and strategies for us to put this 'evangelization package' together and implement it?"

But there is no package! Guidelines, yes! Resources, yes! Inspiration, tons of it! But no package! Evangelization is a process! It has to do with faith in Jesus Christ and my readiness to share my experience of Jesus Christ with the people who constitute my life and work: the students and colleagues in the Catholic high school. It is for this reason that the Catholic high school exists! This is not a package! Deepening my understanding of my vocation, my baptismal call to follow Jesus; hearkening to the invitation to change my life, to conversion — this is the beginning of evangelization.

And how does this happen? It happens through self-awareness and prayer, reading and study, a mutual sharing and reflection with my co-workers in the Catholic high school. But this is not a package! My hope is that somehow these pages can help teachers look again at our vocation as Catholic educators. Perhaps in this sense, too, these reflections can become an invitation to conversion — to a deepening of one's commitment to the mandate to evangelize in the Catholic high school.

250

Yet there is always the *realpolitik* of the school: the practical, very concrete, everyday situation in which we find ourselves as Catholic educators, both evangelizing and being evangelized! The sincere skeptic in Chapter 11 remarked:

> Practically speaking can it be done? A lot of teachers are not really into the gospel.

And the student, Bill, 18, in Chapter 9 posed the same problem even more insightfully:

> I really think a lot of teachers are just too busy leading their own lives, and if Jesus or the gospel isn't part of their lives, there is no way it will come out in school, classes, or wherever. There are some teachers like this. They stand out in contrast to the dedicated ones.

This is the real conundrum, the ongoing challenge for every staff. But we cannot be apologetic to such teachers! Catholic education does not exist to give such teachers employment. That is not its mission. The mission is to evangelize, and evangelization is both gentle and upsetting. It is gentle in its invitational quality. Here, then, we must respect colleagues "who are not really into the gospel," allowing time, mindful that the Holy Spirit touches hearts in different ways and at different times. But inevitably there must also be a time for the critical upsetting word of evangelization — a prophetic word to challenge these teachers, especially at decisive moments when indifference and mediocrity threaten to smother enthusiasm and gospel ideals.

The *realpolitik* must also take into consideration the community dimension of evangelization. The individual evangelizer needs others. One may have an abundance of good will and rock-solid commitment, but ultimately to survive, to be effective and to be renewed, we need the support of one another. Teachers who share evangelizing values and vision should meet often to affirm one another, critique one another, and reflect together on the nature of the evangelization project in the Catholic high school (for example, the agenda presented in Chapter 11). The evangelizers can only be evangelized in the context of community.

Throughout this book I have opted for a "listening methodology" — listening to teachers, listening to students, listening to the teaching Church, listening to our social context. The 1990s are a moment of promise for Catholic education in Ontario. They are the hour for a re-evangelization. My hope throughout these pages is that the testimony of some committed teachers does provide some of the *what to* and *how to* data for the evangelization project. My own conviction is that there is much happening already, and we can learn from one another. So let us now turn our attention one last time to the teachers' reflections on what it means to evangelize evangelizers.

I will then conclude by outlining the four critically important sources for renewal that we must return to continually in our own re-evangelization which is always the necessary starting point for evangelizing in the Catholic high school.

1. A REFLECTION ON EXPERIENCE: EVANGELIZING THE EVANGELIZERS

Question: What values and attitudes are most desired for a principal (vice-principal) of a Catholic high school? And what are the least desired aspects of leadership for the principal?

We arrive at the core of the leadership discussion in the Catholic high school. The teachers insisted that their reflections on the desired values and attitudes for principals are just as applicable to every member of the staff. And yet, it was my sense that they would not push that idea too far. Not every teacher has the gifts to be principal. And in the Catholic high school, gifts must be understood very much in terms of leadership of a Christian community.

What does one look for, then, in a principal?

A dynamic, relevant vision of Catholic education and a profound grasp of the mission of the Catholic high school — more than anything else, this is what the teachers look for in the principal of a Catholic high school. It is obvious that a very deep faith commitment must be the foundation, the grounding for both vision and mission.

Guidance teacher:

> ... a deep faith commitment and the sense of vision of the uniqueness of a Catholic high school education... and one who will work hard at creating the environment to make this possible. Also, a person who respects, who sees the sacredness of each person. And then, an enabler: the job is one of stewardship; therefore, service, calling forth gifts, delegating responsibility and authority.... The enabler invites people to grow by contributing.

Inherent in this vision of a Catholic high school education is the imperative to care for the community life of the school. Skills in initiat-

252

ing, sustaining and animating the school as Christian community are called for.

Physical education teacher:

> ... should see the role as one of leading and affirming the Christian community; and then to nurture the vision, making clear to everyone the idea and ideal of the school and promoting that vision. Finally, service: leadership in the gospel sense, stewardship.

It is recognized, too, that leadership today is collegial and collaborative. Other gifts must be affirmed and called forth. Teachers and students must be empowered.

Chairperson, English department:

> The first thing: a vision of what Catholic education is all about. Leading is a vocation of service. And then, to empower, to lead a team.... Will find talent and gifts and call that forth. Collaborative!

English teacher:

> Number one in my mind: a genuine love for students. Secondly, a strong faith commitment! Finally, energy: an unending supply of energy and a willingness to infuse that energy in the staff.

In the gospels, authority is understood as service — foot washing! To talk about authority and power to most people of our time, however, is to talk about power, ambition and prestige. And yet, in terms of the Christian community, ambition can be an important and necessary gift when it is for the purpose of the gospel.

English teacher:

> Ambition is good when it is the recognition of a talent one has or a gift that can help further the purpose of the gospel. In this sense, one feels one's obligation to lead as a vocation! And such a principal will collaborate, will delegate, will recognize gifts in others. And he / she will have a sense of the whole picture, not be hung up on legalism.

Vice-principal:

> We're talking Catholic education. We have to emphasize gospel leadership as much as we do OISE management styles! Service is humble and collaborative! Also courage:

our faith and the gospel are radical. They demand courage to implement. And I see the principal as healer — compassion, reconciliation.

It is fitting that a principal have the summary word on this question of attitudes and values:

The vision of a Catholic high school education is enormously important — the vision that sees the school as a community itself — and so our values have to be integrated in the entire operation of the school. Grade 9s have to be treated as though they are every bit as important as anyone else. Also, principals have to have the courage to take a stand. Their loyalties are to this community first: students, then teachers, parents, and then board. I really believe that it is summed up in servant leadership: Jesus as the model, not the IBM or General Motors model.

And the least desired attitudes?

Ambition in the "power-prestige" sense very much heads the least-desired list. Not only is the superficiality in terms of faith commitment and ecclesial consciousness decried, but the consensus is that much counter-testimony is rendered by men and women educators aspiring to leadership in Catholic high schools who have no sense of the vocation of the Catholic teacher and the mission of the Catholic high school.

English teacher:

What I don't want is someone who is in it for anything other than the vocation of Catholic education. I don't want someone who is in it because it's a scramble to the top or for power.

Head, guidance deparment:

I hate to see a principal in a position of power but who is sort of an "on-the-surface Catholic" — a phoniness — because not only is he / she not doing the job; they are being totally counter-productive because kids will see right through them. It just adds to the idea that it's a sham. It really presents a huge obstacle to what we are about as evangelizers.

Religion teacher:

The least desired aspect, which is just deadly in a Catholic high school because it just flies in the face of our mission and the idea of service we want to get across, is the person — the teacher, department head, vice-principal or principal who has a career agenda: to hop, skip and jump their way to the top as quickly as possible.

These people are death, because they really don't see their lives as vocation, but rather as a means to an end.

* * * * * * * * *

The Bishops Address Principals and Vice-principals — A Commentary

From This Moment of Promise

As no one else, you who are principals and vice-principals have a unique opportunity to create the character of your school. Your reach extends both into the classroom and into the community. The life, the values, and the feeling of each school derive in large part from your commitment to your staff, to your students, and to the gospel.[3]

Listening to the testimony of the teachers on the subject of leadership in the Catholic high school, and considering the above pastoral reflection of the bishops on the principals and vice-principals, several thoughts on Catholic educational leadership come to the fore.

• *Vocation.* To ensure the Catholic character of the school in the 1990s, to meet the challenge of "this moment of promise," it is imperative to understand the vocation of the Catholic teacher. Obviously, teaching is a profession that calls for talent, skills, a philosophy of what education is all about, and technical competence. But in our time and place, it becomes even more obvious that teaching in the Catholic high school is more than that: it is a vocation — a call to be the teaching Church in the context of the high school, to proclaim the Good News of Jesus Christ, and to be what we proclaim for the students in our care. The past history of Catholic education in Ontario, with its emphasis on the politics and economics of the enterprise, is prologue to what confronts us now: to become an alternative school system, an alternative forged by gospel values and our Catholic experience. The need now is a theology of the laity, a theology and spirituality of the Catholic teacher, a vision of a Catholic education that is authentic evangelization. Catholic teachers engage in a most valuable and necessary ministry of the Church — the *traditio fidei* — the handing down of the faith.

Fidelity to the mandate and mission of Catholic education in the 1990s demands a renewed appreciation of the vocation of the Catholic teacher and the ministry of the Catholic educator. It is the built-in cost of Christian leadership that makes this even more the case for the principal of the Catholic high school. The bishops recognize the truly pivotal role of principal. Principals are the leaders of the school community, and whether or not that school community becomes as well a faith community or an ecclesial community depends on the principal's "commitment to the gospel." Indeed, so much depends on the principal's commitment to the gospel: "the life, the values and the feeling of each school"! What an awesome privilege and responsibility! There is so much involved and so much at stake when we look at the vocation of the principal. To approach this vocation merely as a "Catholic cosmetic" applied with a letter from the pastor and an OECTA / OSSTA religion course or two would be the ultimate failure of leadership in Catholic education — for the person and for the board.

- *A Vacuum in Leadership.* At the present time there is cause for concern. There seems to be no lack of candidates for positions of leadership possessing Ministry (Ontario Ministry of Education) qualifications. The concern is how many of these qualified applicants for leadership responsibility in the Catholic high schools have both lived experience in the Catholic high school and a theologically grounded, dynamic vision of what Catholic education ought to be. The leadership agenda for the Catholic high school in the 1990s demands both the Ministry qualifications and the theological grounding. We noted earlier the Bishops' appeal to trustees "to make decisions about future leadership with a view to what will ultimately further the process of Catholic education." But in Ontario's Catholic high schools those decisive leadership decisions are already upon us: they arrived shortly after Mr. Davis' announcement of full funding in 1984. Since full funding, such doubly qualified candidates have not always been chosen for all the positions that have needed to be filled. As Ministry qualifications are a given, only those who have made the selections know how serious is the problem of availability or how much of a failure there has been to give competence and formation for faith leadership the priority they must have. It is regrettable that the prioritizing of the vocation of the principal and the formation of Catholic educational leaders has not kept pace with the expansion of the Catholic system and the launching of new Catholic high schools across the province. It is doubly regrettable that we lack ongoing formation programs to assist new Catholic high school leaders who, though lacking professional experience in a

Catholic high school, have joined the Catholic system out of a sense of genuine enthusiasm and commitment.

In a timely and very thoughtful paper on leadership in Ontario's Catholic schools, Larry Trafford elaborates on the present vacuum of leadership.[4] There are leaders who are "mentors" and leaders who are "facilitators and enablers." There is, however, a paucity of "visionaries," leaders with a profound understanding of their vocation as animators of the faith community of the Catholic high school. This is the present reality, and it is critical that this present reality be understood by trustees, administrators and teachers in the Catholic high school.

• *Selection of Leaders.* The problem here is double-edged. Approached from the top-down perspective, it is really a question of identifying, calling forth and affirming leaders. The following example illustrates this need. Friends teaching in a very challenging inner-city Catholic high school where the "daily pressures and heat of the day" are more intense than in most schools, talk of three competent and dedicated teachers now looking to transfer to other schools. There are headship and assistant headship openings. Yet, they very much enjoy their present school, and they love the kids who have greater educational and emotional needs than most. And indeed, they would stay, foregoing personal advancement, if they received from the board any appreciation at all for their contribution. But the recognition and affirmation are lacking.

Administrators and trustees must become more sensitive to the explicit emphasis the gospel bestows on ambition : it is zeal for the purpose of the gospel! There is an abundance of gifted and committed Catholic teachers with proven leadership skills, recognized especially by their peers. These teachers are not into self-promotion and, for any number of reasons, many of them have not acquired the Ministry credentials for leadership positions. Unfortunately, this "gospel reluctance" is too often interpreted as "lacking the tough, aggressive stuff" part and parcel of the corporate definition of management. Yet, more than a few of these same teachers would certainly respond to the invitation to lead — to come forth and accept more responsibility for the Catholic education project — and if asked, would get qualified. The challenge for boards is to cultivate a new gospel understanding of leadership — to identify, call forth and affirm teachers with this leadership potential. A further challenge for boards is to recognize that leadership talent is best identified by the colleagues of leadership candidates, by their co-workers in the schools, **not** by central office administrators who use primarily the criteria of paper qualifications. It could be very prophetic for a board to experiment with the process of enlisting principals, vice-principals and teachers to identify the most promising leadership candidates and then directing superintendents to invite these nominees to apply for positions, provide them with on-the-job training, and allow time to take the Ministry courses.

The other edge of this problem concerns the bottom-up perspective on leadership. There is a malaise on the part of many teachers that finds its origin in the frustrations emanating from the bureaucratization of Catholic education and its fruits, centralization and impersonalization! In any staff room stories abound of the hassles, intrusions, unreal expectations, and lack of comprehension on the part of the trustees, directors and superintendents. Such frustration soon gives way to cynicism, and this cynicism is anything but helpful for the promotion of Catholic education in the 1990s. Indeed, this cynicism becomes as much an obstacle to what we are about as Catholic educators as the bureaucratization it is meant to protest!

As human as it might be, such cynicism is not, however, above scrutiny. There is a certain arrogance inherent in such a cynical attitude that seriously compromises the vocation of the Catholic teacher. There are many excellent and very committed trustees and administrators spending enormous energy to Christianize the institution, the board ; this is a fact! And at the same time, at the base, in the ranks of Catholic teachers, there are committed women and men with a dynamic vision of what Catholic education could be, but who are reluctant to come forward — reluctant in a gospel sort of way! If our agenda for the 1990s is to ensure the Catholic character of our schools, this "gospel reluctance" must be translated into "gospel ambition" — zeal for the purpose of Catholic education. Much as we look for affirmation and invitation from the top, we should be affirming and encouraging our colleagues at the base, calling one another forth to accept the challenge of leadership in our Catholic high schools for the 1990s.

Inherent in the vocation of the Catholic teacher is a love for and a responsibility for the global Catholic education project. It is clear that the 1990s demand visionary leadership. Teachers, convinced of and committed to their vocation as Catholic educators, must respond to the invitation to lead.

* *Formation of Leaders.* Finally, to ensure the Catholic character of our schools, reflection on one's vocation as a Catholic teacher and the ongoing elaboration of a vision of Catholic education will have to become as essential as Ministry of Education requirements and business management skills. But how and where does this formation take place? Larry Trafford of the Metropolitan Toronto Separate School Board

makes this assessment of leadership formation possibilities:

> What is not in place, however, are opportunities for prospective leaders to reflect, study, and discern the meaning of the Christian Story and Vision for Catholic Schools. Similarly, the time and energy necessary to develop educational goals and objectives that allow staffs to shape a vision for their school communities and to integrate gospel values across the curriculum have not been viewed as essential to the professional development of Catholic teachers. Both of these concerns need to be given greater priority by those who presently hold leadership positions in Catholic education.[5]

It is incumbent upon the leadership of Catholic education to do much more. The politics and economics of Catholic education must now cede priority of place to the theology of Catholic education and the spirituality and ministry of the Catholic teacher. This must become the priority for the 1990s.

And it is incumbent upon teachers to work continually at their own evangelization, to challenge and affirm one another, indeed, to be resources for each other as evangelizers in the Catholic high school!

* * * * * * * * *

The Bishops Address Teachers — A Commentary

As we near the end of this reflection on evangelization in the Catholic high school, I feel that it is important to touch again on the theology elaborated in the meditation in Chapter 2 — to teach in a Catholic school is really to participate in the evangelizing mission of the Church! I feel that if as Catholic educators we can better understand how we are representatives of the teaching Church — the Church's privileged instruments of handing down the faith — we will more easily appreciate the urgent need to be evangelized ourselves. Recall Pope Paul VI's words: "The Church is an evangelizer, but she begins by being evangelized herself"! As evangelizers, we participate in the teaching office of the bishop, the first teacher in the diocese. Is it any wonder the bishops refer to our teaching as "an awesome privilege and responsibility"! It is good, then, to listen to the bishops speak directly to us, as they do in their recent pastoral letter on Catholic education, *This*

Moment of Promise. We are their co-workers. They have a grateful, supportive, encouraging and challenging word for us.[6]

* A grateful word!   Parents entrust their sons and daughters to you for a large part of the day. Society confides its future citizens to you. The Church entrusts members of the Body of Christ to your care. Perhaps this is why we expect so much of you — not only professional competence and care but also the integrity of a Christian life. It is also why we have such a debt of gratitude to you.

Nothing can kill a relationship like taken-for-grantedness! The bishops know this. We are their co-workers; they thank us. And they underscore, too, that it is witness — "the integrity of the Christian life" — that is most effective when it comes to initiating our students into a full and active membership in the Church.

* A supportive word!   There is no doubt that it is you who bear the heat of the day in Catholic education. The daily pressures you face are enormous, and the rewards of teaching are sometimes long in coming. You deserve the support and understanding of all those involved in Catholic education.

More affirmation! And it is important! There is recognition of the cost and suffering inherent in discipleship lived out through teaching in the Catholic high school.

* An encouraging word!   It is not necessary to be free of faults and failures to be faithful to the integrity of the process of Catholic education. Otherwise, none of us would dare to be involved. However, your example is the one that will have the greatest direct impact on students. We wish to do all we can to sustain you as you carry this great responsibility.

This reflection I find most refreshing, for it acknowledges our failures and incompleteness as something quite ordinary — to be expected — as part and parcel of the evangelizing experience. The important thing the bishops emphasize is the struggle: "to be faithful to the process of Catholic education." Faults and failures are happy developments in a way, for they occasion forgiveness and underline the

260

ongoing need for interior change — both for the person and the institution. But be faithful to the struggle!

*** A challenging
word!**

As your Catholic professional associations
have recognized, *it is only through ongoing faith development that teachers can
hope to meet the challenge of this moment — the challenge of forming educational communities of faith.* Courses in
religious education, family life education,
spirituality and theology are already
offered. To these courses must be added
others in areas such as the history and
philosophy of Catholic education. We
support your desire to be involved in these
experiences. It is your ongoing education
and your own deepening experience in
the Catholic tradition which will expand
your capacity to help students to become
more constructive, creative and critical
within our society. [Emphasis added.]

"Only through ongoing faith development" — this indeed is the
heart of the bishops' words to teachers in Catholic education. If the
Catholic character of our schools is to be ensured, it will surely be because teachers are serious about deepening their own experience in
and understanding of the Catholic tradition. Again here, the evangelizers must be evangelized. It is the question of ongoing formation.

Remark, too, how the bishops stress "a constructive, creative and
critical" evangelization. As evangelizers, we are to interpret the Good
News and the richness of our Catholic tradition to our students. But at
the same time, we must also interpret our young people — their struggles, hopes, disappointments and dreams — to the teaching Church.
An evangelization that invites participation, respects emergence, and
adapts itself to culture, language and circumstance is a sign that the
teaching Church is listening to youth.

* * * * * * * * *

Question: How would you describe the spirit of evangelization?

So, what do you think it looks like — this evangelization? What
are the signs that it is happening? From the teachers' reflections on this

261

question there are especially two elements that must be present for an authentic evangelization. The first: openness to and trust in the voice of God and in the presence and dynamic working of the Holy Spirit. Here, evangelization was described first and foremost as listening: a desire to recognize the Lord in personal prayer, in the needs and the gifts of others, in places and situations that surprise us. There is an honesty involved too: that it is okay to admit the struggle of trying to follow Jesus; that we don't have all the answers all the time. And there is detachment: "evangelization happens in spite of me, not because of me."

Guidance teacher:

> One important element is an openness to Christ as the Way, the Truth, and the Life. And then, an openness to relationships: we are all called together. As well, courage: our evangelization should be marked by courage, for oftentimes it's easier to be quiet or passive.

Principal:

> An openness... an attitude always open to the voice of God, the movement of the Spirit from whatever source that voice comes. This can be from any direction, at any time, under any circumstances. Most often the source will be from watching, listening to other people.

Religion teacher:

> I think risk is the main element: knowing that there is a cost and a price in simplicity and humility. Also, the quality of detachment: evangelization happens in spite of me, not because of me.

And the second essential element that must characterize evangelization is the capacity for reflection and self-awareness. It was the consideration of Pope Paul VI's words on authenticity that triggered the discussion on the significance of personal reflection. Paul VI underscores authenticity as the pre-eminent quality for the evangelizer:

> Let us now consider the very persons of the evangelizers.

> It is often said nowadays that the present century thirsts for authenticity. Especially in regard to young people it is said that they have a horror of the artificial or false and that they are searching above all for truth and honesty.

These "signs of the times" should find us vigilant. Either tacitly or aloud — but always forcefully — we are being asked: Do you really believe what you are proclaiming? Do you live what you believe? Do you really preach what you live? The witness of life has become more than ever an essential condition for real effectiveness in preaching. Precisely because of this we are, to a certain extent, responsible for the progress of the Gospel that we proclaim.

[E.N., #76]

Do we really believe what we are proclaiming? Do we live what we believe? Do we really preach what we believe? These are the hard questions that demand authenticity, an authenticity that can only be achieved through an openness to question and reflect on the stuff of one's own life and work. One teacher noted: "You don't learn from experience but by reflecting on your experience."

Chaplain:

There is a reflective element, the ability to look at one's life, discern how God is present or absent in one's life. This needs time: thinking about what I am doing, about evangelization.

English teacher:

A desire to understand your own needs and an openness to yourself, to knowing yourself, to reflecting on your own life!

Other qualities as well were proposed as being significant for the spirit of evangelization. "Joy," "a message of hope, enthusiasm and humour," "generosity and sacrifice."

Chemistry teacher:

... wanting to serve and being happy doing it... not begrudgingly, but feeling fortunate in being able to serve.

English teacher:

I ask myself the question: "To evangelize me, what would I look for?" First of all, a message of hope. Secondly, an enthusiasm for life. Depressed people depress me! Thirdly, a sense of humour!"

Vice-principal:

Whenever people are nostalgic for the old-time Catholic

263

school and what we are afraid of losing with full funding, this really means afraid of losing that which we most associate with the Catholic school tradition: generosity, giving one's time and talent over and above what is expected, the whole idea of sacrifice.

*   *   *   *   *   *   *   *   *

Question: How are you personally evangelized as a Catholic educator?

Earlier we had occasion to listen to these teachers talk about the impact students have on them and how they are evangelized by the students. Here the question was more general: what is it that sustains and nourishes you in your ongoing faith development, "in your own deepening experience in the Catholic tradition," to use the words of the bishops. And the reflections were rich! I find that this particular reflection on the part of the teachers is of enormous help and can serve very much as a practical, workable model for evangelizing the evangelizers.

Repeatedly, colleagues on staff "interacting, sharing, dialoguing, listening" were mentioned as an invaluable source for evangelization. In this sense teachers affirmed, challenged, edified and supported one another.

Principal:

> I am evangelized by many of our teachers who have kept me honest. I'm evangelized by their integrity, their human values, and the way people are treated... explicitly or implicitly drawn from the gospel.

Chaplain:

> A group of our teachers formed a prayer group for Lent. They met in chapel for scripture reflection. The group started out of a discussion at lunch... no publicity... no boasting... very quietly. Also, I'm evangelized by so many teachers... who are really searching, trying to add more quality to their own lives.

Chairperson, English department:

> ... the adult environment at the school. There are enough people here. One can sit down, compare notes, think in a frame of mind that is gospel sometimes! This is enriching.

Personal prayer and study and the need to update and renew oneself are also deemed absolutely essential for ongoing faith development. Many remarked that they draw energy and meaning from Sunday Eucharist: a few spoke of shared prayer or small-group prayer; several commented on the importance of reading and study for interpretation and understanding of what is going on and how we are called to be Church today.

Religion teacher:

> I have been part of the RCIA team in my parish. This experience really has been an evangelizing thing for me. I have to ask: "What does this gospel... or this faith... mean to me? Do I really believe it?" I really have to personalize it, to own it.

Religion teacher:

> But maintaining my interior life means I have to find time and space for prayer and introspection. This is a central evangelizing experience for me because I tend to get swallowed up in doing and in action.

English teacher:

> I take time every year: a personal retreat... away from family and job. It keeps me in contact with me... and with God.

And finally there is the incredible impact of personal witness: the stories of others do so much to build us up, stretch us, give meaning and direction to what we are about. A central thread throughout these reflections has been the primacy of witness: the teacher "preaching" more effectively by who she is, or what he stands for, then by actually what he or she teaches. The testimony of these teachers more than confirms the validity of that proposition. We are evangelized constantly by others: by their stories, their struggles, their poverty, their resilience, their commitment. Indeed, just remembering such people becomes an evangelizing experience in itself.

English teacher:

> Very definitely certain individuals.... These have been models of faith commitment... their lifestyles! Just remembering some of these people is evangelizing. It tells me that the task of being a Christian is possible.

Priest-chaplain:

> The stories I hear from the people I work with; the faith that comes through. A 60-year-old woman janitor talking about escaping Naziism during the war; the struggle of a colleague to make sense out of life. So much faith, and it comes through in the story of a person.

Principal:

> I'm a hero worshipper. I have my own pantheon of saints who are a source of evangelization for me: the heroes who tackle the problems of the poor — whether it is here in Canada or in the Third World. They inspire me. They directly reflect the gospel for me. They are models. They always take me back to the gospel because what I see in their lives is a direct reflection of the gospel.

* * * * * * * * *

Question: If you were giving a mini-course to teachers preparing to teach in a Catholic high school, what would you emphasize?

Evangelizing the evangelizers begins with awakening in the person the sense of vocation. In opting to teach in a Catholic high school, one's baptismal call is charged with new meaning and added responsibility. The Catholic teacher represents the bishop. The Catholic teacher has "the awesome privilege and responsibility" of facilitating the young person's deeper understanding of Jesus and further participation in the Christian community. The essential starting point, according to teachers, must be a heightened awareness of one's own vocation as a Catholic teacher. As one teacher phrased it: "Respectfully but firmly, we must have the student-teachers look hard at their motivation: a job only — employment — over and against a vocation and the sense of mission that entails!"

Principal:

> Without being at all apologetic — people may not want to hear but it has to be said — teaching in the Catholic high school is a vocation. There is an element of divine call in it. Some people don't want to hear this. They don't want to carry this additional burden.... But that is our reality in the Catholic school: you're a teacher, but you have to go beyond that.

Indeed, the vocation of teaching impacts on the type of education we propose: an alternative, counter-cultural education. And the way I live, the way I teach, the witness I project, is itself content of evangelization in the Catholic high school.

French teacher:

> The real need is to get across the idea that it is a vocation, a ministry, not just a job. It has to do with the centre of meaning in our own lives. Secondly, our education should be intrinsically different. Therefore, this "difference thing" should have implications for most of the subjects we teach, for the way we teach them, and the way we do extra-curriculars, for our relationships. Thirdly, the understanding that kids can develop a sense of faith and worth from their relationship with us, from the way we model the gospel.

Once this sense of vocation is awakened, it must be tended to and nurtured. Consequently, ongoing faith development is seen as a priority for student-teachers.

English teacher:

> Make the point that our teaching is a vocation. Also, highlight the need for growth in this vocation part of our life: personal needs, reflection, prayer. And then, clarify their own beliefs, to become more authentic in their faith.

Vice-principal:

> Emphasize the need for further development. I have just finished Part Two of the religion course. It is frightening, some of the old, simplistic, elementary kinds of concepts that people are tied up in for so long. And if this is the basis of our faith, we're not really giving very much to our students, that's for sure!

Religion teacher:

> ...really to understand their own personal faith and what faith commitment means. But also, teachers have to know the process that teenagers are going through, the characteristics of adolescent psychological and faith development. Also, an appreciation of what and where the Church is now, 1989, and what my role is as a lay person in the Church.

And the *realpolitik* of the school is appreciated, too! One teacher noted:

> The problem is that we present ideals, and then they arrive at school: the poor student-teacher wouldn't recognize the place!

This very realistic point was picked up by a vice-principal who underlines the importance of a support group:

> I would emphasize the need to be discriminating, to be adaptable, flexible and open; to go into a system now where I think all is not what it should be in a Catholic high school. To encourage them [student-teachers] to search out the core group of teachers that I think can be found in every Catholic high school — to dialogue, share, learn from them. There is enough of a negative element to dampen any idealism they may have. And along with this, the old cliché: a lot more is caught than taught! And kids read us well — and read us quickly! If there is no depth in our faith, kids will know this.

Such a mini-course would contain other elements as well:

- the importance, of knowing, loving and respecting the students;
- the acceptance of failure — as Christians we should not be strangers to weakness and failure;
- the need to provide copious examples of integrating the gospel into the curriculum and school life;
- the ability to balance the academic and relational — subject matter is important, but we teach persons;
- the emphasis on teaching students how to learn — not just mastering information but learning how to be independent, how to critique.

* * * * * * * * *

Question: Given everything we have shared and discussed so far, how do we go about evangelizing or re-evangelizing the evangelizers in our Catholic high schools?

Not surprisingly, the top-down and bottom-up perspectives on the leadership question surfaced again in this discussion as the appropriate starting points. There was a focus on the board of trustees —

the mission and Catholicity statements it produces and the actual praxis!

Vice-principal:

> I really feel that at our board we have to start with the trustees. What our board says it is doing — in Catholicity and mission statements and so on — it just isn't doing. The reality is different. There is a pocket of trustees who are very serious, but most of them don't understand, or they don't care.

And the more fundamental, philosophical questions touching on leadership, formation and vocation were also posed.

French teacher:

> Full funding has called a lot of things into question. For example, what background do you need to be a leader in the Catholic high school? Those qualities we listed imply a pretty deep theology and commitment! Boards don't require that! OECTA and OSSTA have to do something about "principals' courses": the ministry course does not have "servant leader" or theology components. Where do principals or aspiring principals get these? And look at the social teaching of the Church. Counter-cultural as it is, where do our economics and business teachers get their formation? Do we mandate it? Vocation and ministry: that's how we define ourselves, but where is the formation?

One's own faith development as a Catholic teacher was especially felt to be a priority.

English teacher:

> My feeling is that we need to give teachers the opportunity to learn more about their faith. I don't know that professional development days actually are that effective. Perhaps, once a month, an optional session. I think a surprising number of us would participate. We are hungry. . . . There are texts — *Laity, Evangelization*, etc. — that are there, and we don't know about them. How do we find out about these resources?

The overwhelming consensus was, too, that *"reflection on evangelization"* groups have proven to be a rich resource and an occasion for both intellectual growth and a deepening of one's own vocation and commitment as a Catholic teacher.

The frustrations of the times and the stress occasioned by full funding were also recognized! But rather than submit passively to the vagaries of the new bureaucratization, it was felt that committed teachers must look to one another for affirmation and enlightenment. And trust profoundly in the Holy Spirit! The legacy we have to pass on is too precious by far for it to be lost in feelings of helplessness and defeatism.

English teacher:

> I think somehow that those of us who feel strongly a commitment to Catholic education — we have a legacy to hand down. And given the situation that some of us are in today where trustees and administrators don't appear to have that same vision and commitment, somehow, through it all, through the layers of impersonal bureaucracy, we have to hang on to our vision and try our best to make it a reality. We owe this to people — to the past and to the future. It's the legacy.

Head, guidance department:

> These first years of full funding are pretty negative now .... frustration level is high. I really think we need some "resistance cells," and we need patience and long suffering. We've gone through nine hours of this. It's been great! But looking at administrators and boards, a lot of our evangelization sharing is really like a foreign language. I think we really have to trust in the Holy Spirit, and do our best!

And finally, the unlimited potential for evangelization that the Catholic high school remains was appropriately celebrated!

Principal:

> I remain absolutely convinced that the Catholic high school system in Ontario is the last best hope for evangelization in the Church in Ontario. There is a dynamic core of very committed educators with a wonderful understanding of the Church and the gospel and society. The potential is there to do marvellous things. I am personally very excited about what we could do! I remain filled with hope.

* * * * * * * * *

After nine hours listening to each of the four groups of teachers, I concur with the principal above: "There is a dynamic core of very committed educators with a wonderful understanding of the Church and the gospel and society." My hunch in starting this research was that the lived experience of committed evangelizers, teachers in our Catholic high schools, both validates and breathes life and meaning into the theology of the teaching Church on what Catholic education "in our situation and circumstances" could be and should be. My hunch was correct. I am convinced now more than ever that there is indeed wonderful potential for evangelization in the Catholic high school.

I sincerely hope that I have recorded the teachers' reflections accurately. There is always the possibility of misinterpretation. If that has happened, the fault is mine. And I have been sensitive, too, throughout this writing to the possibility of manipulating reflections to serve my editorial purposes. This, too, I have tried very hard to avoid. It might make for a more coherent ordering of material, but it would prove to be a distinct disservice to the evangelization project in the Catholic high school. My intention from the outset has been to provide clarity — to help us see our way with much hope through the different obstacles to evangelization; not to place another hidden obstacle in the path.

This experience — being with the teachers as they reflected on their own evangelizing experience in the Catholic high school — has been for me a long moment of renewal and re-evangelization. In our Catholic high schools, we are already doing some marvellous things. To accept the challenge of the hour for re-evangelization will allow us to do even greater things for the gospel.

This experience has profoundly renewed my hope!

* * * * * * * * *

2. SOURCES FOR RENEWAL FOR THE HOUR OF RE-EVANGELIZATION

If the agenda for the 1990s is to ensure the Catholic character of the high school, then the priority agenda item is *renewal — the evangelizers must be evangelized*. This truth dominates the teachers' reflections on both leadership and re-evangelization. Ongoing faith development takes different forms and content. Some of the possibilities have been suggested earlier in this chapter.

271

I believe, however, that *there are four critically important sources for renewal* that should constitute any renewal or updating program for Catholic teachers. As Catholic teachers, both individually and in groups, we must continually return to these sources for re-evangelization. As I have already elaborated in some detail on these sources, I present them here simply in outline form. I include, however, some pertinent and very valuable texts, evidence of the relevance and urgency of Church teaching, with the hope that they may be helpful for your own personal hour of re-evangelization.

* To discover and live one's vocation and mission

From Pope John Paul II's
Vocation and Mission of the Lay Faithful

VOCATION

#58.   The fundamental objective of the formation of the lay faithful is an ever-clearer discovery of one's vocation and the ever-greater willingness to live it so as to fulfill one's mission.

God calls me and sends me forth as a labourer in his vineyard. He calls me and sends me forth to work for the coming of his kingdom in history. This personal vocation and mission defines the dignity and the responsibility of each member of the lay faithful and makes up the focal point of the whole work of formation, whose purpose is the joyous and grateful recognition of this dignity and the faithful and generous living-out of this responsibility.

However, only in the unfolding of the history of our lives and its events is the eternal plan of God revealed to each of us. Therefore it is a gradual process; in a certain sense, one that happens day by day.

To be able to discover the actual will of the Lord in our lives always involves the following: a receptive listening to the Word of God and the Church, fervent and constant prayer, recourse to a wise and loving spiritual guide, and a faithful discernment of the gifts and talents given by

God, as well as the different social historic situations in which we live.

From Pope John Paul II's
Vocation and Mission of the Lay Faithful

FORMATION

#60.   The many interrelated aspects of a *totally integrated formation* of the lay faithful are situated within this unity of life.

There is no doubt that *spiritual formation* ought to occupy a privileged place in a person's life. Everyone is called to grow continually in intimate union with Jesus Christ, in conformity to the Father's will, in devotion to others in charity and justice.

The situation today points to an ever-increasing urgency for *a doctrinal formation* of the lay faithful, not simply in a better understanding which is natural to faith's dynamism but also in enabling them to "give a reason for their hoping" in view of the world and its grave and complex problems. Therefore, a systematic approach to *catechesis*, geared to age and the diverse situations of life, is an absolute necessity, as is a more decided Christian promotion of *culture*, in response to the perennial yet always new questions that concern individuals and society today.

This is especially true for the lay faithful who have responsibilities in various fields of society and public life. Above all, it is indispensable that they have *a more exact knowlege* — and this demands a more widespread and precise presentation — of the *Church's social doctrine*, as repeatedly stressed by the Synod Fathers in their presentations. They refer to the participation of the lay faithful in public life, in the following words: "But for the lay faithful to take up actively this noble purpose in political matters, it is not enough to exhort them. They must be offered a proper formation of a social conscience, especially in the Church's social teaching, which contains principles of reflection, criteria for judging and practical directives [cf. Congregation for the Doctrine of the Faith, *Instruction of Christian Freedom and Liberation*, #72], and which must be present in general catechetical instruction and in specialized gatherings, as well as in schools and universities. Nevertheless, this social doctrine of the Church is dynamic; that is, adapted to circumstances of time and place. It is the right and duty of Pastors to propose moral principles even concerning the social order and of all Christians to apply them in defence of human rights.... Nevertheless, active participation in political parties is reserved to the lay faithful."

The *cultivation of human values* finds a place in the context of a totally integrated formation, bearing a particular significance for the missionary and apostolic activities of the lay faithful. In this regard the Council wrote: "[the lay faithful] should also hold in high esteem professional skill, family and civic spirit, and the virtues related to social behaviour, namely, honesty, a spirit of justice, sincerity, courtesy, moral courage; without them there is no true Christian life." [Emphasis added.]

From *Lay Catholics in Schools: Witnesses to Faith*

PERSONAL WITNESS

#32.   Conduct is always much more important than speech; this fact becomes especially important in the formation period of students. The more completely an educator can give concrete witness to the model of the ideal person that is being presented to the students, the more this ideal will be believed and imitated. For it

274

will then be seen as something reasonable and worthy of being lived, something concrete and realizable. It is in this context that the faith witness of the lay teacher becomes especially important. Students should see in their teachers the Christian attitude and behavior that is often so conspicuously absent from the secular atmosphere in which they live. Without this witness, living in such an atmosphere, they may begin to regard Christian behavior as an impossible ideal. It must never be forgotten that, in the crises "which have their greatest effect on the younger generations," the most important element in the educational endeavor is "always the individual person: the person, and the moral dignity of that person which is the result of his or her principles, and the conformity of actions with those principles."

#33.　In this context, what was said above about direct and personal contact between teachers and students becomes especially significant: it is a privileged opportunity for giving witness. A personal relationship is always a dialogue rather than a monologue, and the teacher must be convinced that the enrichment in the relationship is mutual.

* **To hearken to the call to conversion.**

From the Gospel of John, Chapter 15
[*The New Jerusalem Bible*]

THE ONGOING NEED TO BE PRUNED

I am the true vine, and my Father is the vinedresser. Every branch in me that bears no fruit he cuts away, and every branch that does bear fruit he prunes to make it bear even more.

Remain in me, as I in you. As a branch cannot bear fruit all by itself, unless it remains part of the vine, neither can you unless you remain in me.

. . . cut off from me, you can do nothing.

It is to the glory of my Father that you should bear much fruit and be my disciples.

From Pope Paul VI's
On Evangelization in the Modern World

AN INTERIOR CHANGE

#18.   But there is no new humanity if there are not first of all new persons renewed by Baptism and by lives lived according to the Gospel. The purpose of evangelization is therefore this interior change, and if it had to be expressed in one sentence the best way of stating it would be to say that the Church evangelizes when she seeks to convert, solely through the divine power of the message she proclaims, both the personal and collective consciences of people, the activities in which they engage, and the lives and concrete milieu which are theirs.

From Pope John Paul II's
Vocation and Mission of the Lay Faithful

ON OVERCOMING DUALISM

#59.   In discovering and living their proper vocation and mission, the lay faithful must be formed according to the union which exists from their being members of the Church and citizens of human society.

There cannot be two parallel lives in their existence: on the one hand, the so-called "spiritual" life, with its values and demands; and on the other, the so-called "secular" life, that is, life in a family, at work, in social relationships, in the responsibilities of public life and in culture. The branch, engrafted to the vine which is Christ bears its fruit in every sphere of existence and activity. In fact, every area of the lay faithful's lives, as different as they are, enters into the plan of God, who desires that these very areas be the "places in time" where the love of Christ is revealed and realized for both the glory of the Father and service of others. Every activity, every situation, every precise responsibility — as, for example, skill and solidarity in work, love and dedication in the family and the education of children, service to society and public life and the promotion of truth in the area of culture — are the occasions ordained by Providence for a "continuous exercise of faith, hope and charity." [Emphasis added.]

* Appropriating the distinctive vision of the Catholic high school.

1. From the Ontario bishops' *This Moment of Promise*:

Challenge. *We need to develop further and to articulate a Catholic philosophy of education for our times so that our distinctive vision of education will permeate every aspect of our curriculum and all dimensions of the learning process.*

[p. 20]

2. A vision of Catholic education to respond to the hour for re-evangelization. Refer to Chapter 11, 2. EVANGELIZATION IN THE CATHOLIC HIGH SCHOOLS: AN AGENDA FOR THE 1990s (pp. 238 ff.):

- an evangelization faithful to the Catholic tradition;
- an upsetting evangelization;
- an evangelization to brokenness;
- an evangelization into prayer.

3. A vision of Catholic education demanding *a deeper ecclesial consciousness.*

From Pope John Paul II's
Vocation and Mission of the Lay Faithful

#64.   Therefore I make a strong appeal to one and all, Pastors and faithful, never to become tired of maintaining — indeed always taking an active part to fix deeply in one's mind, heart and life — *an ecclesial consciousness,*

277

which is ever mindful of what it means to be members of the Church of Jesus Christ, participants in her mystery of communion and in her dynamism in mission and the apostolate.

The whole Church, Pastors and lay faithful alike, standing on the threshold of the Third Millennium, ought to feel more strongly the Church's responsibility to obey the command of Christ, "Go into the world and preach the gospel to the whole creation" [Mark 16:15] and take up anew the missionary endeavour. A great venture, both challenging and wonderful, is entrusted to the Church — that of a *re-evangelization,* which is so much needed by the present world. The lay faithful ought to regard themselves as an active and responsible part of this venture, called as they are to proclaim and to live the gospel in service to the person and to society while respecting the totality of the values and needs of both. [Emphasis added.]

* **To evangelize in the Catholic high school is to serve.**

The vision of Catholic high school education we elaborate must be grounded in the *theology of service.*

1. Leadership as service.
   "Discipleship has never been a 'career move.'"[7]
   — Refer to the gospel lessons of foot washing, carrying the cross, preferentially loving the poor and the little ones.
   — Refer to the reflections in this chapter on the role of the principal.

2. Teaching as service.
   — Refer again to Chapter 11 and the evangelization agenda for the 1990s.
   — A most urgent service to render to the students of our situation and circumstance is *an integral education* — an education that will allow students to interpret reality and make the fundamental connections from the perspective of the gospel.
   — The model teacher for our complex and sometimes confusing situation and circumstance is Barnabas, the apostle of hope, in the Acts of the Apostles. Barnabas means "son of encouragement." He was likely called Barnabas because of his eloquent and encouraging style of preaching the gospel.

Acts 4:36 [emphasis added]

They sent Bernabas out to Antioch. There he was glad to see for himself that God had given grace and *he urged them all* to remain faithful to the Lord with *heartfelt* devotion; for he was a good man, filled with the Holy Spirit and with faith.

3. Witness as service.

— The urgent need for authentic witness.

From Pope John Paul II's
Vocation and Mission of the Lay Faithful

#3.   A new state of affairs today both in the Church and in social, economic, political and cultural life, calls with a particular urgency for the action of the lay faithful. If lack of commitment is always unacceptable, the present time renders it even more so. *It is not permissible for anyone to remain idle.* [Emphasis added.]

— The urgent need to be witnesses and agents of peace and justice.

From Pope John Paul II's
Concern for the Social Order

#47.   I wish to appeal with simplicity and humility to everyone, to all men and women without exception. I wish to ask them to be convinced of the seriousness of the present moment and of each one's individual responsibility, and to implement — by the way they live as individuals and as families, by the use of their resources, by their civic activity, by contributing to economic and political decisions and by personal commitment to national and international undertakings — the measures inspired by solidarity and love of preference for the poor. This is what is demanded by the present moment....

In this commitment, the sons and daughters of the Church must serve as examples and guides, for they are called upon, in conformity with the programme announced by Jesus himself in the synagogue at Nazareth, to "preach good news to the poor, to proclaim release to the captives and recovering of sight of the blind, to set at liberty those who are oppressed, to proclaim the acceptable year of the Lord." [Luke 4:18-19] It is appropriate to emphasize *the pre-eminent role that belongs to the laity,* both men and women.... It is their task to animate temporal realities with Christian commitment, by which they show that they are witnesses and agents of peace and justice. [Emphasis added.]

* * * * * * * * *

To conclude, I would like to paraphrase the words of Pope John Paul II on the importance of an ecclesial consciousness (*Vocation and Mission of the Lay Faithful*, #64) that we reflected on above, and apply his hopeful theology to the circumstances of the Catholic high school as we make our way through the 1990s:

A great venture, both challenging and wonderful, is entrusted to the Catholic high school — that of *a re-evangelization*, which is so much needed in Catholic education in the 1990s. Teachers ought to regard themselves as active and responsible evangelizers in this venture, called as they are to proclaim and live the gospel in service to their students and to their society.

To brace us, enlighten us, nourish us and direct us on this venture, it is good to make our own the confident words of the Preface of the Holy Spirit that the bishop recently prayed on behalf of the community at my nephew Danny's Confirmation.

Father, you give your gifts of grace for every time and season as you guide the Church in the marvellous ways of your providence.

You give us your Holy Spirit to help us always by his power so that with loving trust we may turn to you in all our troubles and give you thanks in all our joys through Jesus Christ our Lord.

Danny will begin his Catholic high school education this September, 1989. I hope he will experience this agenda for the 1990s, and appreciate its privileged difference.

NOTES
Chapter 12

[1] Ontario Conference of Catholic Bishops, *This Moment of Promise.* A Pastoral Letter on Catholic Education in Ontario (Toronto, 1989), pp. 20-21.

[2] Institute for Catholic Education (ICE), *Empowered by the Spirit,* a brochure prepared as a resource document for *Partners in Catholic Education Symposium II* (Toronto, May 11-13, 1989, sponsored by ICE). (ICE address: 10 St. Mary Street, Suite 604, Toronto, Ontario M4Y 1P9.)

* "Leadership in Catholic Education: Let Our Light Shine" by Mary Malone, St. Jerome's College, Waterloo, Ontario.

An insightful analysis of the Catholic character and its implications for the doing of Catholic education.

* "Catholic Schools Need Leaders with Vision" by Larry Trafford, Catholic Teachers Centre, Metropolitan Separate School Board, Toronto.

An assessment of some contemporary leadership models including a pertinent presentation of leader as visionary.

And a presentation at the symposium:

* "Leadership in Catholic Education" by Guy O'Brien, Director of Education, Lakehead District Roman Catholic Separate School Board.

A general perspective on the Ontario educational context with some concrete application to the workings of a Catholic school board and a challenging, perhaps even prophetic, "Action Plan" for the partners in Catholic education for the 1990s.

[3] Ontario Conference of Catholic Bishops, *op. cit.,* p. 27.

[4] Institute for Catholic Education, *op. cit.*

5 *Ibid.*, p. 25. Refer also to :

* Pope John Paul II, *Vocation and Mission of the Lay Faithful* [*Christifideles Laici*], Chapter V — "That You Bear Much Fruit — The Formation of the Lay Faithful."

* Guy O'Brien — "Leadership in Catholic Education," Institute for Catholic Education, *op. cit.* O'Brien presents a four-point action plan with a very imaginative proposal for an **Institute for Leadership in Catholic Education.**

6 Ontario Conference of Catholic Bishops, *op. cit.*, pp. 26-27.

7 Larry Trafford, "Catholic Schools Need Leaders with Vision," Institute for Catholic Education, *op. cit.*, p. 24.

APPENDIX 1

A GUIDE FOR REFLECTING ON EVANGELIZATION

In *This Moment of Promise*, the Ontario bishops state unequivocally:

> ...the lessening of the financial burden of Catholic education must be seen as freeing us to make *the collective* and *personal* choices and sacrifices necessary to enhance our educational communities of faith.

It is clear that ensuring the Catholic character of the high school is both *a personal* and *a collective* responsibility. I am convinced that *listening* is the appropriate methodology to teach this responsibility. Indeed, as the point of departure, it is the only methodology:

— a reflective listening to, and discerning of, one's own feelings and convictions

— a thoughtful listening to the teaching Church

— an attentive listening to, and reading of, the signs of our times — the social and cultural context of the 1990s

— a sensitive listening and openness to the faith stories of our colleagues in the Catholic high school

— a faithful listening and loving concern for the preoccupations, joys and hopes of our students as they emerge through adolescence during their years with us in the Catholic high school.

This Guide is meant as a listening device — an instrument — to help Catholic educators see to their "personal and collective" responsibility of enhancing our educational communities of faith. The questions, suggestions and ideas presented here are intended to assist the individual teacher and groups of teachers in deepening their experience as evangelizers in the Catholic high school. Questions based on the content of each chapter are offered for personal reflection. Questions elicited from each of the four parts of this book are proposed for *a group sharing experience* — an experience that in itself can become a means of *re-evangelization* for teachers in the Catholic high school. For group sharing I suggest only one rubric : attentive listening and sincere sharing should characterize the experience more than argument and debate.

FOR PERSONAL REFLECTION

Chapter 1   Articulating the Challenge

1. What are some of the accolades and what are some of the criticisms you hear most often about the Catholic high school? Do they have validity?

2. Based on your own experience in the Catholic high school, what is its greatest strength and greatest weakness?

3. Articulate what is most challenging for you teaching in a Catholic high school.

Chapter 2   A Meditation on Evangelization

1. The real conundrum for the Christian is to be part of a society that promotes privilege, power and prestige, a society that offers as many comfort and pleasure zones as possible, and yet to be part of a Church that is rooted in the gospel, that professes **the cross** as the way to salvation and sees power as foot washing and service! It is clear that authentic discipleship must cost! As a teacher in the Catholic high school, how does evangelizing cost you personally? (*E.N.*, #15, pp. 25-26)

2. As an evangelizer in the Catholic high school, in what ways do you see yourself participating in the evangelizing mission of the Church? (*E.N.*, #15, p. 27.)

Chapter 3   A Reflection on Experience — The Practice of Evangelization

1. Reflecting on your own experience as an educator in the Catholic high school, identify some *successes* in evangelization that you have

experienced, participated in or witnessed.

2. And what in the Catholic high school are some *obstacles* to evangelization that you have experienced, participated in or witnessed?

3. What teacher testimony in Chapter 3 speaks most significantly to your experience as an evangelizer in the Catholic high school?

Chapter 4   The Gospel and Culture

1. Let this quote from *Lay Catholics in Schools: Witnesses to Faith*, presented on p. 65, challenge you:

> The vocation of every Catholic educator includes the work of ongoing social development: to form men and women who will be ready to take their place in society, preparing them in such a way that they will make the kind of social commitment which will enable them to work for the improvement of social structures, making these structures more conformed to the principles of the Gospel.

2. An awareness of the local context is essential for evangelization. How aware are you of the context in which your students live: the adolescent culture, the family environment, the political and economic realities of the community? What opportunities have you taken to collaborate with students and colleagues to evaluate the positive and negative aspects of these realities?

Chapter 5   Society — Some Considerations

1. Four ideologies were presented in this chapter as being the sources for several huge obstacles to evangelization in our society. Are there other ideologies or obstacles to evangelization that have not been mentioned? Of the ideologies described, which one do you encounter most often in your vocation as a Catholic educator? How does it affect your work?

2. On p. 74, Bishop Remi DeRoo is quoted:

> So prevalent and integral are violence and competition to our culture that they characterize our educational system, our television entertainment and our sports.

Assess "competition" in your school. Is it healthy? Is it balanced with experiences of co-operation and collaboration?

3. From your own experience, add to the signs of hope presented in Chapter 5.

Chapter 6   A Reflection on Experience — Teachers on the Social Context

1. Based on your experience and *your own* perception of our society, what are the dominant social, economic and psychological forces that make evangelization so difficult?

2. And based on your experience and *your own* perception of our society, identify elements of our social life / fabric that are positive and can be helpful in evangelization?

3. Ponder this question asked on pp. 93-94:

> And as teachers, in our own lives, how much critical distance is there between consumer values and gospel values, and how much creative energy do we spend sharing our ideals and critiquing the dominant ideologies?

Chapter 7   The Church — Some Considerations

1. In what ways does the Church nourish you in your vocation as Catholic educator? In what ways has the Church seemed more a burden to you as Catholic educator?

2. Look at your own faith and approach to life in light of *"the privatization of faith,"* p. 109.

3. A principal is quoted on p. 118:

> I like the idea of a humble Church, a servant Church. The institutional Church has got to see itself as a servant Church. I'm hopeful that this process will continue.

> In reference to your own model of education, are your colleagues and students empowered when they work with you? Are their talents called forth?

Chapter 8   Reflections of the Church on Youth

1. The chapter speaks of the necessity of adapting evangelization to the needs and context of adolescents. What is it in your evangelizing approach — words and actions — that should be adapted?

2. The bishops address students (p. 138), and Pope John Paul II writes to youth (pp. 139-140). In each case the message is the same —

young people are invited to become active participants in the process of Catholic education and evangelization. How do you as Catholic educator communicate this message to students? And how do you facilitate their participation?

3. Let this quote on adolescent emergence (p. 144) speak to you:

> And yet, we want to respect the uniqueness and individuality of each young person. Perhaps the most effective assistance we can provide is an evangelization based on listening and characterized by understanding and encouragement. There is indeed a time to be directive and a time to let go, and that is the real trick, the dynamics of which vary from one young person to the next. The foundational question for us to ask ourselves year in and year out is how to share our "roots" while respecting their freedom.

Chapter 9   Listening to Youth — Reflections on the Catholic High School

1. From pp. 151-152, referring to eavesdropping on the students to get their impressions of Catholic high school education:

> For this eavesdropper, it was a fascinating, enlightening and encouraging experience. Indeed, it was fun — so much so that I found myself wondering: "Why haven't I done this before?" Group reflection of this type, I am now convinced, can be done with students at any grade level or academic level. It is "an integrating" sort of educational experience that gets at the roots, the foundation of a Catholic education.

> Being sure to "de-classroomize" the experience as much as possible, take the time to listen to your students talk about what a Catholic high school education should be.

2. In what ways do the students' testimonies in this chapter surprise you? In what ways do they challenge you?

Chapter 10   A Reflection on Experience — Teachers on Youth

1. This chapter occasions a review of one's philosophy of education and philosophy of Catholic education. Let the "voice and perspec-

tive" of the teaching Church — presented in the passages from *On Evangelization in the Modern World* and *Justice in the World* cited on p. 194 — critique your personal philosophy of Catholic education.

2. What methods of evangelization do you find most effective with young people?

3. How are you evangelized by your students?

Chapter 11   A Catholic High School Education and the Hour for Re-evangelization

1. Ensuring the Catholic character of our school is the agenda for the 1990s. The Ontario bishops maintain that ensuring the Catholic character depends upon the content of our education and the person of the teacher. As a Catholic educator, where are you at in the process of owning and personalizing your faith? What areas in your life right now would you target as needing re-evangelization?

2.   An evangelization faithful to the Catholic tradition... [takes place] in the sharing of one's faith journey — one's experience of Jesus and his forgiveness. This is the type of witness that helps students interpret the gospel and make the connection between faith and culture.

[p. 240]

Look at the possibilities for sharing *your faith story* in what you teach, how you counsel, coach, moderate or administer.

3. Identify elements of understanding or attitudes or values that you would like your students to have made their own on leaving the Catholic high school.

Chapter 12   Evangelizing the Evangelizers — The Challenge of Leadership

1. Let this reflection from pp. 250-251 challenge you:

And how does this [re-evangelization] happen? It happens through self-awareness and prayer, reading and study, a mutual sharing and reflection with my co-workers in the Catholic high school.... My hope is that somehow these pages can be helpful for teachers to look again at our vocation as Catholic educators... [that] these reflections can become an invitation to conversion — to a deepening of one's

288

commitment to the mandate to evangelize in the Catholic high school.

2. For the distinctive vision of the Catholic high school to be realized, *an ecclesial consciousness* is necessary. Reflect on Pope John Paul II's words on *ecclesial consciousness* presented on pp. 277-278.

3. How would you articulate the fundamental leadership challenge in the Catholic high school for the 1990s?

* * * * * * * * *

FOR GROUP SHARING

PART ONE   **THE CHALLENGE OF EVANGELIZATION**

N.B. The questions for personal reflection can also be valuable content for group reflection.

1. Listen to one another's reactions to this description, found on p. 18, of the *down-side* of what we are about in the Catholic high school:

> But there is also the down-side to consider. Why isn't there more of a difference between public high schools and most Catholic high schools? How come our graduates are not significantly different — in the Royackers-Westhues sense? And if we are spending two billion dollars a year with 30,000 teachers [evangelizers!], surely the school environment should be more loving and the bureaucracy less dehumanizing and the approaches to negotiating and administering more cooperative and the teaching more evangelically challenging!

2. Pope Paul VI says: "The Church is an evangelizer but she begins by being evangelized herself" [*E.N.*, #18]. Keeping in mind that the institution of the Catholic high school and the faith community of students and teachers are both very much part of the Church, share reflections on this important dimension of evangelization.

3. What text of *On Evangelization in the Modern World* cited in

Chapter 2 speaks most clearly to you as an evangelizer?

4. Paragraph 19's *(E.N.)* "upsetting notion of evangelization" is the critical challenge for all of us in Catholic education. It articulates the potential for and, indeed, the responsibility of Catholic education to make a transforming difference in our society.... that is what we must be about: to offer a Catholic education that unmasks, questions, critiques and challenges the non-gospel values of our culture and society.

   Share how you understand this dimension of evangelization in the Catholic high school (elaborated on pp. 29-31). Comment on how you find it present and absent in your school.

5. What are the successes in evangelization in your school that you can celebrate as an educational community of faith? And what are the obstacles that pose the greatest challenge to your staff?

6. In a comment quoted on pp. 48-49, Monsignor Dennis Murphy addresses the critical question of Christianizing the institution. In very concrete terms, how does this apply to your school and to your board?

PART TWO THE CONTEXT FOR EVANGELIZATION IN THE CATHOLIC HIGH SCHOOL

1. In *On Evangelization in the Modern World,* Pope Paul VI writes: "The split between the Gospel and culture is without a doubt the drama of our time." How do you interpret this *drama?* How does the drama play out in the Catholic high school?

2. React to the description of the four ideologies presented in Chapter 5. Do you find this description of our present social and cultural context understated, overstated, accurate, inaccurate? What is missing — that should be included — as either an "invitation to grace" or a "barrier to grace"?

3. Identify the dominant cultural pressures affecting the students in your school that make evangelization more difficult. Which of these obstacles to evangelization could you as a staff — or group of concerned Catholic educators — address during the coming months? Sketch a plan of evangelizing action to confront these obstacles.

4. Review the text on pp. 70-71 from Pope John Paul II's encyclical

Concern for the Social Order. Share your own understanding of his references to "blind submission to pure consumerism" and "while deeper aspirations remain unsatisfied... perhaps even stifled."

5. How do you feel we are doing regarding evangelization in the Church? As one who is at the same time a Catholic educator and a member of the Church, evaluate the areas or ways in which the Church is effectively evangelizing. In what ways must the Church herself be evangelized?

6. The themes of interdependence and solidarity are fundamental today in the Church's evangelizing mission. (Refer to pp. 103-104.) Discuss how central these themes are to the total education project of your Catholic high school.

PART THREE   YOUTH – THE BENEFICIARIES OF EVANGELIZATION IN THE CATHOLIC HIGH SCHOOL

1. In *On Evangelization in the Modern World,* #63 (p. 128), Pope Paul VI writes that each local Church has the task of assimilating, transposing and proclaiming the gospel into the social and cultural language of its people. Keeping in mind the way you function as a staff, evaluate how effectively you are proclaiming the gospel message in ways that can be understood by your students. Consider how, from your attitudes and actions, the students could perceive a radical commitment to Jesus.

2. Refer to the Bibby/Posterski quote on p. 134.

   To the extent that religious groups fail to captivate young people, it is not because "the religious market" is not an appreciable one.

   How does this challenge you as the community of evangelizers in your Catholic high school?

3. In a quote on pp. 144-145, Michael Warren describes the evangelizing task of the Catholic high school. Listen to one another's reactions to his description of the task.

4. The students in Chapter 9 were asked to reflect on the following question :

What is it about Jesus and the gospel that speaks most profoundly to you? What part of Jesus' teaching are you fearful of; that is, how does Jesus challenge you and you don't know if you are equal to the challenge — or you are timid in accepting the challenge?

How do you respond to this question?

5. But the testimony was equally loud and clear that despite all the gloom and doom, all is not gloom and doom. The negatives were consistently juxtaposed with irrefutable positives: our students themselves — their intelligence, insight, generosity, searching, tolerance and open-mindedness; a faith which calls us; a Church which teaches us; the reality of the separate school system in our province — we already have a place to do evangelization during a very sacred time in each student's human development, and there are so many teachers in our system who perceive teaching as a vocation at least as much as a profession. Quality Catholic education is happening; students are being touched by it; the potential to do even better is within our grasp.

Focus on "the potential to do even better"! Where is this applicable in your school?

6. React to the discussion on religious literacy in Chapter 10, pp. 203-208, which responded to the question: "How are adolescents today religiously literate, and how are they religiously illiterate?" What would you confirm, debate or add to in the testimony of the teachers?

PART FOUR   EVANGELIZATION — AN AGENDA FOR THE 1990s

1. On pages 230-231, there is a brief discussion on the imperative of integrating faith and the gospel into the total education project of the Catholic school. Refer to the comment of the chairperson, English department: "Really, the leadership at the school has to ask these questions!" Are these questions being asked at your school? What is the response?

2. The bishops write:

Given the increasing fragility of families and the overextension of parishes, it is becoming more obvious that the school, for some, is often the primary place where young people experience the Church as an alternative community which is shaped more by faith, hope and love than by the values of our consumer culture.

[*This Moment of Promise*, p. 16]

The importance of recognizing the new reality of faith, the family, and the Church in Ontario is cited on p. 239. How does the evangelization taking place in your school meet the challenge of this new reality?

3. Keeping in mind the situation in your own school, share your reactions to the two models of Catholic education presented on pp. 241-242: the upsetting model and the accommodating model.

4. Evangelization to brokenness — discussed on pp. 243-245 — is a dimension of evangelization that must be privileged in the Catholic high school. Where is the brokenness in your school among students and staff? What can you do to become more aware of this brokenness? Is there a resource or some in-servicing that would give you more competence and confidence in responding to brokenness?

5. What values and attitudes are most desired for a principal (vice-principal) of a Catholic high school? And what are the least desired aspects of leadership for the principal?

A summary of the teachers' responses to these questions is found on pp. 252-255. What would you confirm, debate or add to in this testimony of the teachers?

6. The focus of Chapter 12 is "The Challenge of Leadership." The questions remain: How are the evangelizers to be evangelized in order to carry out their "sacred privilege and responsibility"? What formation is necessary to complement university and faculty of education training to help a student-teacher, indeed a fully qualified teacher, become a Catholic high school educator in the integral sense elaborated in this book?

7. How should directors of education, superintendents, principals and vice-principals become qualified for their distinctive, most important leadership roles in our communities of faith? Where should we begin? How might we enlist our Catholic teachers associations, Catholic principals associations, Catholic trustees associations, indeed our bishops, to help us meet formation needs?

APPENDIX 2

SELECTED DOCUMENTS;
EXPLANATION OF
ACRONYMS AND TERMS

1. Church Teaching

* On Catholic Education

From the Congregation for Catholic Education:

The Catholic School — March 19, 1977;

Lay Catholics in Schools: Witnesses to Faith — October 15, 1982;

The Religious Dimension of Education in a Catholic School — April 7, 1988.

From the Ontario Conference of Catholic Bishops:

This Moment of Promise — February, 1989.

* On Evangelization

Pope Paul VI:

On Evangelization in the Modern World [Evangelii Nuntiandi] — December 8, 1975.

* On the Laity

Pope John Paul II:

Vocation and Mission of the Lay Faithful [Christifideles Laici] — December, 1988.

* On Society

Pope John Paul II:

Concern for the Social Order [Sollicitudo Rei Socialis] — December, 1987.

Synod of Bishops:
  Justice in the World — November, 1971.

2. Catholic Education in Ontario

1. CEFO   Catholic Education Foundation of Ontario — established to assist in the development of Catholic education in the Province of Ontario.

2. ICE   Institute for Catholic Education — an agency of the Ontario Conference of Catholic Bishops established to work with Catholic educational associations to assure the Catholic dimensions of the schools.

3. OECTA   Ontario English Catholic Teachers' Association — the official professional organization of elementary and secondary school teachers working in English separate schools in Ontario; a constituent body of the Ontario Teachers' Federation.

4. OSSTA   Ontario Separate School Trustees' Association — the provincial association of elected trustees which renders services of co-ordination, communication, research and political lobbying for the Roman Catholic separate school boards throughout Ontario.

3. Education in Ontario

1. OAC/Grade 13 — Ontario Academic Credit; under Ontario's current education policy governing secondary schools, the value of an advanced level course approved by Ontario's universities to qualify for admission. Ontario applicants must earn a minimum of six, which may include specific courses required for admission to particular university programs. The terminology supersedes Grade 13 credits, formerly the requirements for university admission.

2. OISE — The Ontario Institute for Studies in Education, the University of Toronto's faculty for advanced degrees in education.

3. **OS:IS** — Ontario Schools: Intermediate and Senior, the current policy document of Ontario's Ministry of Education governing Grades 7 through 12 in the province's accredited schools.

4. **OSSTF** — Ontario Secondary School Teachers' Federation — the official professional organization of public secondary school teachers in Ontario; the public secondary school counterpart of OECTA; also a constituent body of the Ontario Teachers' Federation.

5. **Separate Schools** — Roman Catholic elementary and secondary schools in Ontario publicly financed but governed by trustees elected by Catholic ratepayers; parellel but distinctive from the public, non-Church-affiliated schools.

4.   Completion of the Separate School System

1. **Bill 30** — Legislation proposed by the Province of Ontario in June, 1984 to integrate Grades 11, 12 and 13 into the publicly-funded separate school system which, until that time, encompassed Junior Kindergarten through Grade 10; thereby finally recognizing the legitimate right of Roman Catholics to a complete publicly-funded elementary and secondary school system.

2. **Full Funding** — the education of students in all grades of Ontario's separate secondary schools is financed with public funds. Consequently, the movement of formerly private schools into the jurisdiction of Ontario's separate school boards. Now almost all Catholic high schools in Ontario are administered by separate school boards.

3. **Private Catholic High Schools** — Until 1984, Separate School Boards did not receive provincial grants for students in the three senior grades: 11, 12 and 13. Consequently, these students, who had to pay tuition, constituted private schools in the same buildings which housed the publicly-financed students in Grades 9 and 10. Additional funding came from the financial contributions of dioceses and religious communities, as well as from extensive fund-raising activities.

Printed in Canada